STRIP CULTURES

STRIP CULTURES

Finding America in Las Vegas

The Project on Vegas: STACY M. JAMESON, KAREN KLUGMAN,
JANE KUENZ & SUSAN WILLIS PHOTOS BY KAREN KLUGMAN

Duke University Press Durham and London 2015

TEXT © 2015 Duke University Press; PHOTOGRAPHS © Karen Klugman
All rights reserved. Printed in the United States of America on acid-free paper ∞
Text designed by Courtney Leigh Baker. Typeset in Helvetica Neue Condensed and
Minion Pro by Tseng Information Systems, Inc.

Library of Congress Cataloging-in-Publication Data
Strip cultures : finding America in Las Vegas / The Project on Vegas (Stacy M. Jameson,
Karen Klugman, Jane Kuenz, and Susan Willis) ; photos by Karen Klugman.
pages cm
Includes bibliographical references and index.
ISBN 978-0-8223-5948-7 (hardcover : alk. paper)
ISBN 978-0-8223-5967-8 (pbk. : alk. paper)
ISBN 978-0-8223-7523-4 (e-book)
1. Las Vegas (Nev.) 2. Strip (Las Vegas, Nev.) I. Project on Vegas.
F849.L35S775 2015
979.3'135—dc23
2015004991

Cover photo by Karen Klugman.

Contents

Riding the Deuce

One late November afternoon, while on our first research trip to Las Vegas, Karen and I decided to take the Deuce.* This is the double-decker bus that plies the Strip from Mandalay Bay to the Stratosphere, then on to the remote Fremont Street area. The Deuce offers the Vegas novice—such as ourselves— a great mobile counterpoint to the paper maps of the Strip that first-time tourists tear out of the free guide and coupon books available at many of the Strip's attractions. Given the particular spatial arrangement of the Las Vegas Strip—a dense urban artery that appears to be wholly divorced from a grid—the Deuce provides end-to-end continuity and articulates the individual megahotel-casinos like a series of spinal vertebrae. Indeed, the Strip is very like a tremendous spinal cord—all neural transmitters bereft of anything that can be considered a brain.

Little did we know on that fateful first day of our research that our project on Vegas would span a decade. We began our intermittent research trips during the boom years just prior to the onset of the Great Recession, and we con-

---

* Susan Willis

tinued to visit the Strip throughout our nation's slow and uncertain crawl to recovery. During this period, the landscape of the Strip fluctuated between its own booms and busts. Hotels like the Desert Inn and Stardust were imploded and not always replaced. The Aladdin went through years of decline until it finally metamorphosed into Planet Hollywood. And the site where City-Center would eventually be built greeted visitors as a great, gaping excavation site for what seemed like an entire year. Had we been prescient, we would have brought a video camera on board the Deuce to begin to document the Strip's transformations. Instead, we were captured by the moment and eager to get the initial overview of the land. Miraculously, there were two empty seats in the front row of the upper deck. Delighted with our good fortune, Karen and I settled in for an unencumbered bird's-eye view.

"It's her first time." A doughy-faced woman leaned between us and ingratiated herself into our prized space. She motioned toward a shy, somewhat embarrassed adolescent girl. Clearly, the woman wanted us to give up our seats for the sake of her daughter's initiation into the wondrous spectacle of Las Vegas that the Deuce delivers casino by casino as the roadway spools out in front of the bus. I guess she figured Karen and I, by dint of being women of a certain age, had already undergone our initiations. We couldn't help but notice the sexual innuendo implicit in the mother's plea.

Observation is the first step in our research. We fashioned ourselves sleuths of the built environment. As such, we ascended the Stratosphere and took in the lay of the land; we sampled the Chippendales; we visited the flamingos in their cement-lined lagoon; we entered the Coke store and tasted colas from around the world; we lingered at the Bellagio fountains; we witnessed the patriotic light show on Fremont Street; and we invariably tried our luck. But all the ingredients of the cultural landscape—no matter how remarkable—are not fully meaningful in themselves. Rather, they become so in the context of what people do with them. Thus, we sharpened our skills as people watchers. In this, Karen had the advantage of her photographer's eye and camera, while Jane, Stacy, and I relied on pen and notepad. It's remarkable that a simple device like a camera or a notepad allowed us to mingle, even chat, with fellow visitors to Las Vegas, while at the same time making us separate and aware of how words and deeds can be read as signs in a system of cultural meanings. Moreover, the mere fact of defining ourselves as observers had the additional effect of causing certain people and situations to stand out as observable from the immensity of milling crowds and saturated spectacle. *Strip Cultures* underscores what caught the eye, the ear, and, in Stacy's case, the olfactory register.

To read these signs critically is to read against cultural expectations, which are most obviously that *Strip Cultures* will necessarily be about stripping. It bears remembering that although Las Vegas as an adult entertainment destination includes strippers and stripping, the Strip actually refers to the four lanes of roadway that slice through its twenty-four-hour, ever-changing spectacle. Consider the Strip a mobile stage where the performance of seeing and being seen folds spectators into spectacle. Money, sex, and booze saturate the Strip and seem to be the obvious descriptors of its culture. But to fully understand culture is to recognize it as a system of practices that we engage in the process of making meanings and defining ourselves. As such, the everyday rather than the exotic offers the best window into the culture. Thus, *Strip Cultures* gleans the everyday to discover what's not obvious about a lot of things we might otherwise take for granted.

To an extent, our method approximates the strategy for radical theater defined and practiced by Bertolt Brecht. Indeed, it's possible to see the entire Las Vegas Strip as an elaborately staged spectacle, dissimilar only in magnitude from the sort of bourgeois theater that Brecht condemned. As he saw it, a conventional stage play seeks to draw its audience into the performance. The success of a play is, thus, proportional to the empathy audiences feel for the actors and the degree to which audiences suspend independent or critical judgment. Similarly, the Strip is apt to absorb its visitors into a bemused or distracted acceptance of the normalcy of all things exaggerated. What Brecht advocated was a theater based on the "alienation effect."[1] He specifically sought out dramatizations that allowed audiences to recognize elements of the performance while perceiving them at the same time as unfamiliar.

The potential of the alienation effect to generate new and critical perceptions caused Brecht to advocate for its practice in everyday life. As he put it, "The A-effect consists in turning the object of which one is to be made aware . . . from something ordinary, familiar, immediately accessible, into something peculiar, striking and unexpected."[2] The mother's comment, "It's her first time," is a stunning example of a statement so commonplace as to be unremarkable, yet so pregnant with the power to alienate as to defamiliarize everything we might take for granted about what Las Vegas means.

"It's her first time." I still hear the woman's voice and feel the shock of recognizing the twofold import of her words—both a desire to introduce her daughter to the wonders of the Strip, and a recognition that "first time" often alludes to sex. First visit, first intercourse—a trip to Las Vegas functions, if only in the imagination, as our culture's rite of passage. This, coupled with many a youngster's first trip to Disney World, grounds the cultural subject

in consumerist constructions of such intangibles as imagination, happiness, desire, and fulfillment.

During the course of our research in Las Vegas, we would encounter many young initiates. There was the awestruck girl of sixteen whose intensely chaperoned birthday vacation included her uncle, aunt, and older cousins. Her initiation wouldn't go beyond a first peek into the wonders of excess. Then there were the slightly older girls who, tipsy, giggling, and clinging desperately to each other, tried to walk down an immobile escalator. "Don't tell me there's stairs! I hate stairs." Theirs was a more immersed rite of passage. So, too, was it for the young man who stood shirtless and grinning, a beer in his hand. He had just opened his hotel room door to a six-foot-tall call girl clad in shorts and a halter. It's worth noting that the escort, as the shaman in this scenario, had already undergone her initiation. What unites these rites of passage is the understanding that in its most fully evolved expression, ours is a culture where sex and consumption are one and the same. Desire can never be extricated from wanting and buying.

For all the initiates, the thrill of the first time may well fold itself into the familiarity of future visits. Many older tourists with whom I chatted spoke fondly of their yearly visits — some proudly claimed a time-share to facilitate more frequent stays. Indeed, as Stacy points out, the Las Vegas time-share industry is inextricable from its wedding industry, thus guaranteeing many happy returns from honeymoon to retirement (chapter 10). In this, Las Vegas seems to mirror popular culture generally. Following Fredric Jameson's reasoning, popular culture is synonymous with repetition.[3] Writing about music, Jameson claims that we never really hear a pop song for the first time. Rather, the song becomes meaningful for us only as we hear it over and over again and begin to recognize ourselves in its refrains. If I apply this reasoning to Las Vegas and think back to my first research trip, I recall feeling utterly overwhelmed, unable even to visualize and name the hotel-casinos in the proper order along the Strip. With subsequent trips, we all became old hands — Karen, the kamikaze of photos; Jane, the detective of surveillance; Stacy, the sleuth of the sensual; and me, the collector of the mundane.

As a footnote to the theme of initiation and repetition, I should clarify that my first research trip to Las Vegas was not my first experience of the city. That trip occurred some time ago — in 1967 when my father escorted me, teenaged and pregnant, and my soon-to-be husband to Las Vegas, a city renowned for providing weddings of convenience. But that's a song that fell off the charts and out of repetition. I mention it here only to suggest that the pleasure we

accrue from familiarity may well derive from the unrepeatability of the first time.

As for our subsequent research trips, we decided to approach the Strip as one might an intricately choreographed ballet. For what is the Strip but a multiplicity of intersecting systems of practice? Where the ethnographer would seek to discover its order, we appreciated its complexity. Our aim was not to reduce the Strip to a logical structure, nor to allocate its denizens — the escorts, whales, and smutters — into discrete categories for study. Rather, we scanned the totality of the Strip's cultures, recognizing that where everyday life is concerned, everything — language, gestures, personal relationships — is part of the same web. To pull at one is to activate the whole.

Our choice of what to study was never randomly determined, although certain fortuitous discoveries like the Jesus cards among the cards for call girls might initiate follow-up investigation. For the most part, each of us focused on those particularities that coincided with our larger intellectual interests. Thus, Karen, whose photography often captures contradictory juxtapositions, was drawn to the problem of reality in Las Vegas and pursued it all the way to greenhouses for artificial plants. Similarly, Stacy's excursions on the Strip were piqued by sensory cues in line with her extensive work on food, media, and the production of affect. Contrariwise, I was drawn to figuring out the class-defined demographics of the Strip. And because the high rollers are hardly representative of everyday life, I knew I'd be spending time on more popular gaming pastimes — the slot machines, and among them, the truly pedestrian penny slots. Finally, Jane, whose larger research interests involve systems of globalized and virtual exchange, concentrated on aspects of the Strip — like surveillance — that the great majority of tourists, myself included, wholly ignore.

Back to the Deuce

One morning in early April, Stacy and I exited our hotel, coffees in hand, to join the sidewalk queue for the Deuce. A couple of sips into the brew, Stacy volunteered, "I had a dream about cows last night. These huge, obnoxious frat boys were herding cows into the ocean. I had to save them."

This isn't your typical Vegas dream. But it makes sense when you consider we had ill timed our Vegas trip for spring break. Indeed, the Strip was packed with broad-shouldered, broad-backed, loud boys walking three or four abreast. The rest of us — tourists of every other stripe — were nothing but a milling herd. Forced to yield the sidewalk, tourists found themselves pressed into buildings or pushed into the street. No one withstood the formidable girth of these linebacker bands of boys.

Most sipped from the straws of their three-foot-long plastic drink containers. These were fastened to straps and worn slung around their necks for hands-free imbibing. Shaped like bongs, the drink vessels seemed to promise that one could mix hash with booze in the same delivery system and still maintain sexual prowess—or am I the only one to see the entire apparatus as a metaphoric strap-on Extenz penis? Stacy would know better than I. After all, she was the target of at least one young man's inebriated ardor: "You're gorgeous," he proclaimed as he spilled his copious drink down her shirt and onto her shoes.

It's rewarding when dreams transcribe reality with such clarity that we fancy ourselves instant Freudians. But not every Vegas experience so graphically encapsulates the condensation and displacement of Freudian dream analysis. For the most part, Las Vegas presents itself as an uninterrupted hodgepodge of sights, sounds, information, and people. How, then, to grasp what's observable, much less capable of crystallizing a dream?

Distance is what's necessary. Stacy's dream was born in anger and gave expression to her unwillingness to identify with either cows or cowboys. The dream bespeaks the dreamer's fundamental sense of estrangement. I don't know if Jane or Karen experienced Vegas-inspired dreams; but I do know that we all sought and benefited from a sense of distance from the field of our research. In this, we take instruction from Zora Neale Hurston, one of our nation's first anthropologists, who wrote extensively on the rural African American folk tradition during the first half of the twentieth century. Hurston emphasized that until she left the South to study at Barnard College, she had no way of seeing the culture of her upbringing as remarkable. The world of tall tales, foodways, herbal curing, religious and secular practices—it was all too close, too familiar to be noticed, much less critically apprehended. Distance— geographic, social, academic—jolted Hurston into seeing and deciphering the world she had left behind.[4]

Our book offers a model for a twofold estrangement. First, there is the impact of arriving in Las Vegas that grounds each of the chapters and jars readers out of the so-called ordinary. One of the challenges we faced as researchers was to maintain the experience of having freshly arrived throughout the sensory onslaught of a four- or five-day stay. It's important to note that all four of us found ways to leave Las Vegas, even while staying there, by taking miniretreats into nature. Here, the proximity of the Grand Canyon, Zion, Red Rock Canyon, and even, as Karen describes it (chapter 8), Springs Preserve,

the city's instructional garden, all provided a necessary antidote to the mind-numbing intensity of the Las Vegas Strip. Indeed, we followed a pattern of research already mapped by Rebecca Solnit, whose book *Wanderlust* includes a chapter on Las Vegas. According to Solnit, walking is a great democratizing activity because it implies and demands public access to space. With the hotel-casinos staking claims to their adjacent sidewalks as extensions of their private property "to give themselves more muscle for prosecuting or removing anyone engaging in First Amendment activities," Solnit was hard pressed to construe her walk on the Strip as subversive, let alone democratizing.[5] She concluded her sojourn in Las Vegas with a day spent hiking in Red Rock. From a high point in the canyon, she looked back to see the city submerged in the brown haze of its smog. Indeed, when seen from the perspective of the surrounding desert, the imposing built environment of Las Vegas withers to a puny aberration upon a landscape long shaped by harsh elements.

The second and even more challenging feature of our research was, then, to turn halfway around and use Las Vegas as a lens for looking back on the world we left behind. This is a tactic Karen developed when we conducted research in Walt Disney World.[6] The halfway turn allows all those daily life pursuits that we think of as ordinary to emerge as the means for seeing what's odd about Las Vegas. Conversely, everything we took as extraordinary about the Strip and its cultures enabled us to reconsider the so-called normalcy of the lives we left behind. The second half of our title, *Finding America in Las Vegas*, instructs readers to be in two places at once. The journey there collides with the journey home again to reveal the exceptionality of what we left and the predictability of what we journeyed to find.

The construction of a critical distance suggests that there must be something of a gap between the observing subject and the field of research. This is the space that theory fills. Here we draw upon our separate and distinct readings in the broad area of cultural studies. Variously, we can claim an understanding of the image, framed and described by writers like Susan Sontag and John Berger.[7] The latter's emphasis on the gaze as an objectifying force is particularly important on the Las Vegas Strip, where the culture of celebrity conditions a generalized sense that we are all somehow being defined by another's gaze. Berger recognized that women are most especially socialized as objects of a societal gaze, which is invariably constructed as masculine. The relevance of gender points to another of our embedded theoretical underpinnings in the burgeoning work done by feminist scholars to imbricate gender and sexuality in the construction of identity. What makes Las Vegas interesting in terms of gender and sexuality is that its ardent espousal of red-hot

heterosexuality—blatantly celebrated in its strip clubs, lap dance parlors, and escort services—floats atop a half-recognized gender-bending subtext that lends itself to the queering of many of its famous acts, including male strippers like the Chippendales who play to women, but for each other.

Also fundamental to our work in Las Vegas is the understanding of culture as a system of signs and symbols that yields itself to interpretation. Here we look to Roland Barthes for his groundbreaking essays on such topics as advertising, photojournalism, toys, cars, sports—the very stuff we use to fashion our "mythologies."[8] Barthes taught us how to unpack the trivial to reveal the culture's bedrock ideologies.

However, Barthes ought to be read not in isolation, but rather in conjunction with other related traditions at the core of cultural studies. Foremost among these is the extensive body of work produced by the Marxist scholars associated with the Frankfurt School whose elaboration of the history of the culture industry underscores the significance of the commodity form as crucial for any understanding of the culture. It goes without saying that on the Strip the commoditized environment achieves supersaturation. Indeed, as Karen points out, even the plants—whether organic or plastic—are commodities (chapter 8). Moreover, as I argue with respect to the slot machines (chapter 2), electronic transactions have redefined exchange, which was once a personal interaction, as an extension of the commodity form.

In fact, it may be that the basic Marxian notions associated with the fetishism of the commodity and the subsequent reification of the subject are now inadequate to understand all that's at stake and on display in Las Vegas. Along these lines, Jane's observations about Facebook and the *Bodies* exhibit seem more in accord with Jean Baudrillard's identification of the simulacrum as the iconic figure for a world where the virtual has eclipsed workaday contingencies and consequences (chapter 9).

Yet one more aspect of cultural studies underpins our work and also dovetails with Barthes. This is the recognition of daily life—the quotidian—as not just worthy of intellectual engagement but absolutely crucial to understanding how we use culture to define ourselves. Michel de Certeau paved the way in defining culture as a body of practices rather than an assortment of objects. As he saw it, a city may be structured by its built environment, but it is defined by the routes through it that are developed by people during the course of their daily pursuits.[9] Where de Certeau applauded the way people carve out routes to disrupt a city's grid, he would be hard pressed to discover utopic pedestrian practices on the Las Vegas Strip, where the rigid contours of sidewalk and roadway leave little possibility for detours. Nevertheless, de

Certeau's identification of agency coincides with some of the newer writing by postmodern geographers who explore how people make sense of the amorphous landscapes that typify postmodern architecture. For these writers, more is at stake than simply getting lost in a postmodern hotel or sprawling casino. Where power—both political and economic—was once imposed in the design of the urban grid, it is now imbricated in the folds and contours of spaces that seem more incomprehensible than imposing. According to theorists of the postmodern such as Fredric Jameson, we engage postmodernism's built environments both physically and mentally. Through a process dubbed "cognitive mapping," we register the inscription of power in spaces where it would otherwise be occluded.[10] Along these lines, Stacy separates our five sensory registers and charts each as a means for mapping Las Vegas (chapter 7). In line with the postmodern geographers, her maps reveal systems of control that bespeak programs and concentrations of power.

In sketching the broad outlines of the theories that underpin cultural studies as a critical practice, we don't want to imply that we go into our research with a toolbox full of trusty implements. Nowadays, common parlance casts everyone who faces a challenge as having a box full of means and measures to be applied as tools. The attribution of a toolbox to people in all walks of life may well function as ressentiment for a bygone era when a considerable portion of the population worked in manual labor and actually had a toolbox. Today, even people in the professional classes can be expected to have tools. Thus, a diplomat facing a tough negotiation will boast of the tools in his toolbox. Or a politician running for reelection will claim a hefty war chest and a reliable toolbox. Such utilitarian reasoning would have us as critics of culture merely reaching for our "Derrida" to deconstruct an object, or grabbing our "Adorno" to get at a tight contradiction. Michel Foucault may be the one to blame for introducing the idea of a toolbox into popular discourse, although his translator called it a "kit," and, unlike its simplification in the hands of the media, Foucault saw the tools as a set of "true propositions" that one would build up over a lifetime of study and thought.[11] Similarly, we see theory as a network of intersecting discourses that can be brought to bear during the processes of viewing, reading, observing, and interpreting. Theory forms a body of knowledge that can't be reduced to selective particular applications. Indeed, theory is so integral to perception as to constitute a way of being in the world. A foundation in critical theory provides a situatedness in an outlook that is always engaged. And it defines the subject as someone who processes the culture instead of merely consuming it.

Back on the Deuce

Not all children on the Deuce are being initiated. Some know the Strip from end to end. Like conductors on a train, they call out the names of the hotels, giving testimony to their frequent visits. Such children often interject themselves into their parents' conversations about the day's lineup of events. And they know when their parents are pawning them off on the free exhibits and when they've sprung for a pricey ticket.

One such savvy child—a bouncy girl of about ten—climbed aboard the Deuce with parents in tow. Unable to stay seated, she cavorted in the aisle and engaged another couple in conversation—presumably friends of her parents. Irrepressible in every way, the chatty child was not in the least put off by a bus full of strangers. Many were silent and possibly listened in on the conversation that the girl avidly broadcast. At one point, apparently out of boredom for the bus's grinding slowness, she announced for all to hear, "We're going to see Barry Manilow." Her dad's properly parental riposte, "If there's any money left," opened the door for the child's memorable quip, "If he's not dead. Isn't he about a thousand years old?"

The child said what adults might fear to say; that is, as one of the Strip's perennial performers, the star could be dead before the performance. As if to echo the child's intuition, the Strip concurrently sported ads for Wayne Newton's *Once before I Go* show. Indeed, Las Vegas seems to reserve a special place in its heart for over-the-hill performers. Witness the building-high images of Donny and Marie Osmond that have long adorned the Flamingo or the digital billboards of Cher. Consider Elvis—the bloated, not the hound dog—and all those Elvis look-alikes who troll the Strip. Peel back the brashness and the glitter and Vegas is apt to emerge as a morgue for Tinseltown has-beens.

Even a lot of the music is dated, like the notions and dry goods that once filled the shelves of a five-and-dime. Would we call the music pop? Or is the Strip a spectacular emporium of adult contemporary, or, worse yet, elevator music? Perhaps the ghost of Frank Sinatra so permeates Las Vegas as to render all contemporary crooners dated, if not dead.

Look around. Does Las Vegas pulse with vitality, or is it embalmed in its reverence for the past—the Rat Pack, Bugsy, Elvis, and the soon-to-join-them? Consider the Legends impersonators, a group of look-alike, sing-alike performers who breathe new life into deceased stars. Doesn't death undergird the spectacle as surely as drought rims the walls of Lake Mead?

Death and celebrity—the conjoined truths of Las Vegas—are nowhere more in evidence than in Madame Tussauds Wax Museum, where stone-cold effigies of currently living stars share scenes with lifelike renditions of the dearly departed. All inhabit walk-in, diorama-like tableaux where tourists mingle with the undead. Marry George Clooney, hop in bed with Hugh and his Bunny. Touch, embrace, even kiss the unyielding smoothness of wax. Follow Stacy's essay on all the dimensions of touch (chapter 7), but consider here the exquisite smoothness of wax.

It has long been recognized that the culture of the commodity is a culture of surfaces, and the more developed that culture, the smoother and more impenetrable those surfaces. Back in the 1980s, the epitome of commodity smoothness was the hard plastic bubble that encased everything from razors to Barbie dolls. Today, the bubble has been incorporated into the skin of the commodity itself. Imagine a smartphone as it glides into palm or pocket. Consider the screen as you slide your fingertips across a host of icons and summon images and texts whose depthless one-dimensionality belies a fetishism more profound than Theodor Adorno dreamed possible when he wrote *Minima Moralia* and mourned the passing of antique levers and door latches whose mechanics put us directly in touch with the actual production of our daily lives.[12] Bereft of moving parts and utterly sealed off from anything that smacks of interiority, the smartphone presents itself as miraculously self-produced. Even if we've heard of Foxconn, said to be as big as a city, where tens of thousands of workers assemble our phones in less than desirable conditions, and even if we know about the rare earth metals that are mined in the blood and war of Congo to make our communication possible, these grim realities leave nary a trace on the marvelously smooth surface of our handheld devices.

Now consider a different enactment of smoothness. Some forty years ago, Donald Barthelme, master of wry modernist short fiction, conjured the tale of a giant balloon that settled over Manhattan and engulfed the city's grid of streets and buildings in its new architecture of amorphous smoothness. Gone were angularities, hard edges, the grist of toil, the detritus of life—in their place only the smoothness of the balloon. Children accepted the balloon and played on its surface. Adults began to map their activities and assignations according to its bulges and bubbles. But the balloon was impermanent. Indeed, the tale ends with the revelation that the narrator inflated the balloon as a prank and will similarly dispose of it, thus allowing the city to resume its grid.[13]

As a city of surfaces, Las Vegas embodies the smoothness of the balloon and smartphone, even though the cacophony of façades that adorn the Strip

have nothing to do with a balloon's rounded surface and instead imitate the shape and angles of a jumble of billboards. The landscape's consummate elaboration of exteriority seems to preclude the possibility of anything that smacks of interior sanctuary or hidden meanings. Nevertheless, we as researchers challenged ourselves to prod, poke, and probe the obdurate surface of Las Vegas, our aim to prize it open and, if possible, turn it inside out.

To that end, I recall that when I visited Madame Tussauds on the Strip, the museum included a video exhibit that demonstrated how the wax statues are made. It showed how the living and breathing real celebrity is photographed from every angle and digitally measured so as to produce a precise body map, which provides the basis for the wax clone. In detailing the production process, the video offered a celebration of technology whose effect was to cancel the impact of the uncanny that shaped my initial apprehension of the statues. In fact, the video demystified the statue as a fetish (something that we perceive to be endowed with a magical reality), even while it affirmed its existence as a commodity (something that is produced for mass consumption). In this, the video, like other seemingly incidental cultural artifacts that the four of us happened upon during the course of our research, would prove to be a lever capable of prizing open not just Madame Tussaud's house of wax, but Las Vegas more generally. Consider that if the Strip is the place where death and celebrity cohabit, so too is it the place where the deeper meaning of celebrity is made tangible as a surface reality. For what is celebrity but the most profound reification of personhood — the transformation of all that's vital into a thing? Does this not spell the death of self as surely as Madame Tussauds is a mausoleum to the entombment of stardom?

Back on the Bus

Given the jammed traffic on the Strip and the delays associated with frequent stops, the Deuce travels at a snail's pace and affords tourists ample time to survey the blockbuster hotels. Being stuck in traffic can deliver compelling views of standout features like the Sphinx, Eiffel Tower, or Statue of Liberty. Indeed, I've overheard more than one tourist proclaim a desire to add a particular site to a vacation's roster of attractions simply because he or she noticed it while stuck on the bus. Such was the case during one midday ride when the two women seated in front of me remarked Caesars Palace and expressed their desire to visit the Forum Shops.

"Is that where they have lions attack someone?" I hadn't noticed the little boy squirming between the legs of one of the women. But who could overlook his comment—especially given his mother's non sequitur reply, "No, it's actually Jerry Seinfeld."

Clearly, the two were speaking at cross-purposes. And of the two, the boy demonstrated a much bigger field of knowledge and references, connecting the Forum to Rome, and these to gladiators and lions, and finally to the Siegfried and Roy mishap, which did involve a lion that tried to eat someone—only at a different hotel. The boy confirmed what I've detected elsewhere in my studies of the culture. Kids, possibly owing to their incomplete acculturation, speak without a filter, and, in so doing, indicate that they grasp the truths that adults have chosen to avoid. Indeed, the mother, pulling herself away from conversation with her friend, merely read the marquee and named the night's performer.

I mention this vignette because the exchange between mother and child maps an important feature of our book that bears on how it can be read. On the one hand, there is the conventional linear front-to-back reading that offers topics and interpretations in a straightforward manner. Such a reading approximates the mother's appeal to facts. In contrast, another reading hopscotches like the little boy across syntagmatic synapses and pulls together a variety of meanings and associations that appear to be disconnected, but are, instead, linked by a deeper rhetorical logic. My choice of the word *hopscotch* is not gratuitous. Indeed, this is the English title of Julio Cortázar's counternovel, published in 1963 under the title *Rayuela*, whose 155 chapters can be read either progressively or, as the author suggests, by hopscotching about. Cortázar was a master of serious play. Needless to say, there are multiple endings.[14]

So too do we invite our readers to assemble our book through a multiplicity of readings. Bear in mind that the sorts of meanings that emerge will vary according to the reader's propensity for hopscotching among the book's varied elements. First there are the photos and the interplay between words and images that ask readers to test literal and nonliteral relationships. Then there are the chapters themselves, whose distinct approaches testify to the different perspectives of the four authors. The common factor throughout is the pedagogy of questions raised but not directly answered. Here we invite readers to puzzle over the implications of what our trips to Las Vegas reveal. And finally, there is the dictum voiced by one Las Vegas resident, "Nothing exists here that doesn't come from elsewhere." Stacy overheard the woman's remark as the plane in which they were both traveling was about to land at McCarran Airport. Stacy was journeying to Las Vegas; the woman, returning home. In transit, the here and the elsewhere came together. Readers who hopscotch from chapter to chapter may find themselves bouncing in and out of Las Vegas. Some may even turn it inside out and end up finding America in Las Vegas.[15]

NOTES

1. *Brecht on Theater: The Development of an Aesthetic*, ed. and trans. John Willett (New York: Hill and Wang, 1992), 192.

2. *Brecht on Theater*, 143.

3. Fredric Jameson, *Signatures of the Visible* (New York: Routledge, Chapman and Hall, 1992), 17–21.

4. Zora Neale Hurston, *Mules and Men* (New York: Harper Perennial, 1990), 8.

5. Rebecca Solnit, *Wanderlust: A History of Walking* (New York: Penguin, 2000), 283.

6. Karen Klugman, "The Alternative Ride," in The Project on Disney, *Inside the Mouse: Work and Play at Disney World* (Durham, NC: Duke University Press, 1995), 166.

7. Susan Sontag, *On Photography* (New York: Farrar, Straus and Giroux, 1977); John Berger, *Ways of Seeing* (New York: Penguin, 1990).

8. Roland Barthes, *Mythologies* (New York: Farrar, Straus and Giroux, 2001).

9. Michel de Certeau, *The Practice of Everyday Life* (Berkeley: University of California Press, 1988).

10. Fredric Jameson, "The Cultural Logic of Late Capitalism," in *Postmodernism* (Durham, NC: Duke University Press, 1991), 9.

11. Michel Foucault, *L'herméneutique du sujet, Cours au Collège de France, 1981–1982* (Paris: Gallimard Seuil, 2001), 341.

12. Theodor Adorno, *Minima Moralia* (London: Verso, 1984), 40.

13. Donald Barthelme, "The Balloon," in *Sixty Stories* (New York: E. P. Dutton, 1982), 53–58.

14. Julio Cortázar, *Rayuela* (New York: Random House, 1966).

15. Those who wish to learn more about the political, social, economic, and cultural histories of Las Vegas and the Strip may wish to consult the following suggested readings: Mike Davis, *City of Quartz: Excavating the Future in Las Vegas* (New York: Vintage, [1990] 2006); Mike Davis, *Ecology of Fear: Los Angeles and the Imagination of Disaster* (New York: Vintage, 1999); Barbara G. Brents, Crystal Jackson, and Kathryn Hausbeck, *The State of Sex: Tourism, Sex, and Sin in the American Heartland* (New York: Routledge, 2010); Marc Cooper, *The Last Honest Place in America: Paradise and Perdition in the New Las Vegas* (New York: Nation, 2004); Sally Denton and Roger Morris, *The Money and the Power: The Making of Las Vegas and Its Hold on America* (New York: Vintage, 2002); John M. Findlay, *Magic Lands: Western Cityscapes and American Culture after 1940* (Berkeley: University of California Press, 1993); Joanne L. Goodwin, *Changing the Game: Women at Work in Las Vegas, 1940–1990* (Las Vegas: University of Las Vegas Press, 2014); Mark Gottdiener, Claudia C. Collins, and David R. Dickens, *Las Vegas: The Social Production of an All-American City* (Oxford: Blackwell, 1999); Barbara Kirshenblatt-Gimblett, *Destination Culture: Tourism, Museums, and Heritage*

(Berkeley: University of California Press, 1998); James P. Kraft, *Vegas at Odds: Labor Conflict in a Leisure Economy, 1960–1985* (Baltimore, MD: Johns Hopkins University Press, 2010); Barbara Land and Myrick Land, *A Short History of Las Vegas* (Reno: University of Nevada Press, 2004); Matthew O'Brian, *Beneath the Neon: Life and Death in the Tunnels of Las Vegas* (Las Vegas: Huntington Press, 2007); Hal Rothman, *Devil's Bargains: Tourism in the Twentieth-Century West* (Lawrence: University Press of Kansas, 2000); Hal Rothman, *Neon Metropolis: How Las Vegas Started the Twenty-First Century* (New York: Routledge, 2003); and Aron Vinegar and Michael J. Golec, eds., *Relearning from Las Vegas* (Minneapolis: University of Minnesota Press, 2009).

ONE

Framing Las Vegas "Reality"

To approach [reality], one has to strip away clichés that keep it hidden from sight. — Michael Ignatieff

On my first day of photographing in Las Vegas, I took a picture of one of the locals, a waitress who was taking a break from her shift at the Harley-Davidson Cafe.* My intent was to make a documentary-style portrait of a particular individual who lives in Vegas and works along the Strip. So I focused my subject in the frame, pushed the button, and said, "Thanks for letting me take your picture, Brenda." Brenda gave me a puzzled look, then glanced down at her bodice, fingered her badge, and replied, "Actually, my name is Angel. I forgot my name tag today, but luckily Brenda left hers in the drawer."

Yes, a waitress anywhere might borrow a name tag, but Angel had so casually slipped into this alternative identity that she seemed to have forgotten about it. Could it be that, in this city where so much is fake, people reinvent themselves as freely as you and I get dressed in the morning? By Angel's reckoning, the recurrent Vegas theme of luck had played a big role in her name that day. However, I suspected that the odds of someone wearing a misleading name tag were greater in Vegas than in other cities.

---

* Karen Klugman

Earlier that morning, as the check-in clerk at Harrah's Las Vegas handed me a book of discount coupons, she said, "Now figure out your game plan. And good luck!" She meant, of course, that I should think about how I was going to optimize my money on gambling, shopping, entertainment, and eating, but my game plan was to take pictures along the Strip in the hopes of uncovering some truths about Vegas. Programmed by the hotel clerk to believe that, no matter how well I strategized, chance would play a role in my day, I indeed felt lucky to have stumbled upon that little white lie of a name tag. But the longer I explored the culture of imagery in Vegas, the more I came to realize that the misleading evidence in my so-called documentary photograph was emblematic of the game of deception that is everywhere in Vegas. The portrait of Angel (a.k.a. Brenda) would resurface in my vision not as a lucky find but as a constant reminder, like the inscriptions on wide-angle mirrors, that in Vegas, nothing is as it appears.

As a teacher of photography, I frequently remind my students that, once a photograph has been taken, what is inside the frame is all that we know. Even though a picture might seem to represent a one-to-one correspondence to the materials of the real world, there is always something missing. A photograph is, after all, a two-dimensional rectangle of visual information that has been removed from its original context in time and place. A photograph is based on the stuff of the real world, and yet it has the potential to deceive. In the picture of the waitress, one might note the woman's expression, her makeup, her hairstyle, her clothing, her gesture with the cigarette, and that little rectangular piece of evidence naming her Brenda. From the information contained within the frame, however, a viewer could not possibly know that outside of her existence in this frame she was known as Angel.

With its reputation for seeming to present evidence and its potential for creating fiction, photography is a perfect medium to play games with notions of reality. In Vegas, renowned for elaborate fabrications, a culture of picture taking has evolved that reinforces the idea that nothing is real. Like every entertainment center, Vegas takes advantage of the hordes of camera-toting visitors to promote an image that supports its main industry. Just as we might primp in front of a mirror before we pose for a picture, Vegas is camera-ready with backdrops, costumed characters, and visual games that tout its reputation for being fake. In other parts of the country, when I ask if I might take someone's picture, the disclaimer "Careful, I might break your camera" is the cliché of choice, conveying both modesty and tacit permission for me to press the shutter button. But in Vegas, the city's motto, "What happens in Vegas stays in Vegas," is recited facetiously as a preamble to picture taking. With

every repetition of this catchy phrase, an imaginary frame forms around the people within earshot to cordon them off from the rest of the world. It's as if they are reciting a mantra to remind one another, just as I remind my students about photographs, that what is inside the frame is all that exists. These days, people are surely aware that any pictures could end up on the Internet, yet the shopworn motto still has the power to invoke temporary amnesia about the present day and conjure up images of Vegas in an era when it might have been possible to control information. When I asked a young man who wore his alcoholic beverage in a plastic guitar strung around his shoulder if I might take his picture, he recited the motto as one might utter a prayer before a risky act, then struck an in-your-face pose as a rock star. A beer-toting man responded to my request for a picture with an abbreviated, "Okay, baby, but remember . . ." as he swelled out his chest for me to read the Vegas motto printed on his T-shirt. I overheard the phrase recited by two young couples who took turns posing with their hands on the brass frieze of female buttocks—a favorite photo spot in the hallway of the Riviera Casino Hotel. A middle-aged man who was imitating a "smutter" (Las Vegas lingo for a distributor of "calling cards") by flicking his own collection of porno cards and pretending to offer them to passersby, paused to pose for his wife's camera and then (because he noticed me watching?) recited the magic protective words.

A hodgepodge of costumed characters located throughout Vegas helps to create this "anything goes" atmosphere that encourages people to momentarily suspend the notion of reality. Costumed actors within the resorts, such as groups of gladiators in the shopping area of Caesars Palace and the dwarf in a leprechaun suit advertising cheap beer outside O'Sheas Casino fit the theme of their territory. But on the sidewalks of the Strip, the cast of costumed characters resists classification. There are the characters paid to advertise for events and resorts—rows of Rollerbladers in sleek silver outfits bearing flags to advertise the Russian Ice Capades, scantily clad women with feather headdresses handing out coupons for bars and restaurants, men draped in sandwich boards depicting helicopter rides over the Grand Canyon, and of course Liberace. The everyday street party includes a rotating crew of costumed visitors—pairs of brides and grooms, groups of guys wearing fraternity letters, and squadrons of bikers clad in silver-studded black leather. Amid this cast of regular characters, individuals parade the streets wearing T-shirts with messages that normally wouldn't be seen outside a bar, such as "My Mother Wanted Me to Be Something, So I Became an Asshole" or "I ♥ to Fart." On St. Patrick's Day, women stroll the sidewalks wearing skirts with sewn-in nude butts on the back. Within this Felliniesque setting, even the Catholic priest who silently holds a donation basket outside the Excalibur Resort seems to be just another character playing a temporary role.

In an area of the Strip lined with cheap souvenir shops and rent-me convertibles, one of the costumed regulars, an Elvis impersonator, implores tourists to pose with him for a picture. But, unlike Mickey Mouse, whose simultaneous appearances in several places in the Magic Kingdom are carefully choreographed to make it seem as if there is only one Mickey, two Elvises often work as a team. A visitor can pose with Elvis or, for the same price, pose with two Elvises. In exposing the Elvises as actors, Vegas works like the MGM Studios portion of Disney World, where everything is acknowledged to be fake. Over and over again, by posing together, the two Elvises invite visitors to share the joke that they are only pretending to be Elvis. Their mirror-image poses frame the take-home photos (suggested price of $5) as a true Las Vegas souvenir that flaunts the idea that everything is artificial.

The idea that no particular Elvis is authentic is also promoted by wedding businesses that encourage prospective marriage couples to select the Elvis of their choice. Clients are encouraged to read the actors' bios, learn their real-life names, and view pictures of them in costume in order to select the style and age of Elvis that suits their tastes. Not only will a particular business offer multiple Elvis packages (options to ride in the convertible, have Elvis sing and officiate the ceremony, or even ride in a helicopter with him), but many of the packages include multiple Elvises. In one of the Vegas wedding videos posted online, a bride was accompanied by four Elvis impersonators—the wedding minister, the Cadillac driver, an escort, and the groom. I couldn't help but wonder if the Elvis-themed package included the husband as part of the deal.

The two sidewalk Elvises often work alongside a woman who looks as if she stepped out of the Folies Bergère in a long, tight, sequined skirt, a bra-like top, and a feathered headdress. Like the Elvises, she works the Strip posing for pictures. She has a huge smile for everyone's camera and adds sexual innuendo to her pose with men, who often recite the Vegas motto to acknowledge their embarrassment as their wives snap the photo. After each picture, the Folies Bergère woman discreetly pulls down the waistband of her skirt from her bare midriff and adds a bill to her growing wad. One day I watched her pose with a family that included two young boys, one of whom attempted to pull down her bra top as she held the toddler in her arms. She and the family laughed at the boy's indiscretion, but no one seemed to feel that posing a child with this sexual charmer was out of the ordinary. It was simply what was done here, as if the woman herself were merely another backdrop indicating that one had been to Vegas.

I took several pictures of the Folies Bergère woman posing with various men before her smile turned downward and she suddenly asked if I personally knew the man around whose body she currently had her leg curled. "What kind of creepy person are you, anyway?" she yelled. "Taking pictures of another woman's husband! What are you going to do with the picture? Put it under your pillow?" At this point, the wife of the posing man became alarmed, and suddenly everyone in the vicinity imagined that I was a pornographer. Even the Elvises broke character and glared at me. Here I was in Las Vegas, accustomed to a public persona as a nearly invisible older woman in a society that worships youth and beauty, and, simply by breaking an unspoken code about photography, I had achieved the status of sexual deviant in Sin City. I might as well have been wearing a badge naming me "sexual predator." Like Angel, I wanted to explain that there had been a misunderstanding—that I would never put the photo under my pillow. But it seemed way too complicated to explain that I might put it in a book.

I had a similar experience of stealing attention from a Vegas attraction when I tried to take a picture of two Chippendales (again, like the Elvises, this Vegas species occurs in pairs) in the very public plaza of the Fremont Street Experience north of the Strip. When the bare-chested Chippendales pose for pictures with women, they select from a menu of choreographed poses as predictable as the order in which they remove their clothing in their performances at the Rio. They pull their signature black sleeveless vests off their shoulders and, depending on the woman's age and probable agility, they either hold the woman's leg against their bodies or place her hand on their nipples or flat against their six-packs. On this particular day, they were each holding a young girl, one perhaps eight years old and the other a little younger, whose mother had volunteered them for a picture. When the Chippendales opened their vests and arranged the girls to reveal more skin and breast for the mother's camera, I was truly shocked—shocked by their suggestive pose with the girls, shocked that the mother was delighted, and shocked that no one else in the crowd appeared to be shocked. Had the Chips realized that they had crossed a line when they spotted my camera in the midst of a crowd and yelled, "Stop! No picture taking"? Or did they just want to be paid?

Observing strangers in the act of fantasy play seemed to be perfectly acceptable and even encouraged. The Elvises, the Folies Bergère actress, and the Chippendales attracted crowds of people who watched groups of friends or families mug for the camera. Even though these performances occurred in public places, where free speech laws include the right to take pictures, there seemed to be some prohibition on picture taking in Vegas that overrode the

First Amendment. Was the rule a variation on the Vegas motto allowing for what happens in Vegas to leave Vegas so long as it stays in the family, as the Folies Bergère poser had implied? Or did these performers claim to be immune from free-speech laws simply because they too wanted to be paid?

The unspoken rules of photography in Vegas were confusing. Costumed street workers hired by businesses—those employed to hand out monorail discounts, restaurant advertisements, and theater specials—happily posed for pictures for free. Selling a commodity other than their appearance in photographs, they were paid either by the hour or by the number of tickets that would be cashed in. None of them seemed to mind or even notice that I took pictures of multiple people posing with them. The problem is that it is hard to distinguish the posers whose reproductions were the commodity being sold and those whose images helped to sell another product. For example, when I snapped a picture of two women in green sequins and feathers who were dressed almost exactly like a woman who had been posing near Bally's for free, the pair yelled at me indignantly, saying that they "only allow pictures for money." Was I supposed to recognize that because they, like the Elvises and the Chippendales, were already identical reproductions of one another, they had some the authority to charge people for making yet another reproduction of them?

On the same day that I was publicly humiliated in front of the Elvis–Folies Bergère crowd, I was called a whore by a smutter wearing a Santa Claus hat. Again, my transgression was trying to take a picture of a public act in a public place. Smutters are men and women usually wearing brightly colored T-shirts advertising "Girls Direct to You," who hand out small cards with phone numbers and pictures of nude women flaunting large breasts, often in spread-eagle or bare-butt poses with tiny stars in crucial spots. In keeping with other duplicates in Vegas, some of the cards advertise two women, such as the Barbie twins or the Asian schoolgirls. One card offered a special for $65 or two for $99. Like many other street workers in Vegas, smutters also work in groups. They stand in a row, offering cards to males of a certain age (I don't know how they assess the lower limit, but there is definitely no upper age limit for the men they target). The solicitors all flick their stack of cards in the same manner, which produces a regular clicking noise as if they are using sound to reinforce an addiction. Their hands operate quickly, so that it is very difficult to get a picture of one of these cards actually being handed off to a potential customer. I had various experiences trying to photograph them. A few distributors reluctantly let me take their pictures while they hid their deck of cards from the camera as if they were concealing a poker hand.

A few smiled for the camera and splayed the cards at crotch level. But most scattered like pigeons when I raised the camera and settled back into formation after I passed. On this particular day in December, Salvation Army workers were huddled around collection baskets and ringing bells, forming a second battalion behind the line of smutters. I especially loved the image of the smutter with the Santa Claus hat passing out escort cards near a Salvation Army person collecting money from a family. And so I raised my camera to take the picture. And that's when the smutter swore at me. "Whore!" he yelled. My mind shuffled through a rapid sequence of possible responses, such as, "Why am I surprised that you detest the product you are selling?" and "Another first for me!" Instead, I essentially put myself in the same category as a smutter. "Hey, I'm just doing my job," I retorted. "You work the streets and I work the streets."

No guidebook tells people that smutters are as opposed to having their pictures taken as the Amish in Pennsylvania. Yet everyone seemed to understand that this quintessential Vegas phenomenon needed to stay in Las Vegas. The smutters were real people, mostly Latinos, and photographing social reality was not part of the Vegas game plan. Not only did people not take pictures of them, most dared not even look their way. For a man, looking at a smutter would be an invitation to have the escort card flashed in his face for a longer period. The smutter might even walk a few paces beside a man who did not keep his eyes averted.

True, there are exceptions to the prohibition on looking at smutters or showing interest in the porno handouts. Some men flaunt their collections of cards and flip through their pile like boys admiring baseball heroes. Other men accept every card offered to them, take a quick peek, and then throw them away. Perhaps they are trying to get a complete collection and they already have Joanie or Cheryl. Or perhaps they are window shoppers "just looking." Some men, presumably on their first visit to Vegas, accept the handout thinking it is a discount coupon for dinner or a show, then react as if they've been handed a hot potato and drop it onto the sidewalk. For one reason or another, therefore, sidewalks, streets, artificial ponds, and cactus planters are littered with rejected escort cards.

Most people train their eyes ahead and consciously avoid looking at the hundreds of cards strewn on the walkways or the dozens of porno cards strung at eye level on utility poles at major intersections. But there is a notable exception to this collective taboo against looking at discarded escort cards. Boys between the ages of eight and fourteen often hang back from their families to steal glances at the sidewalk. I trailed two women in fur coats, hoping

to learn why they allowed the two young boys with them to make a game of dodging pedestrians in order to pick up every porno card within reach. The four of them paused for a long time at the Buddhist temple that had been commissioned by a Thai businessman as an expression of his good luck at the Caesars Palace slots. The fur-clad women held an animated conversation in Russian while the boys tallied their take of X-rated images, and the golden Buddha presided over all. It was a Vegas moment, a congruence of conflicting themes that once again seemed to convey the message that everything that happened was just pretend.

On the northern end of the Strip near the Stratosphere, another confluence of religion and sex is played out on the streets with the picture cards. There, utility poles and gutters contain the usual potpourri of pornographic images of women, but there is a startling addition—cards produced by the Church of Jesus Christ of Latter-Day Saints. Unlike the rejected porno cards, depicting an ethnic cross section of nude women filling the frames with inventive poses and inscribed with their first names, these promo cards depict a bearded man with beckoning arms standing in a flowing white robe overlaid with neat diagonal script in green ink proclaiming, "I love you!" These Jesus multiples are so abundant that one has to wonder if they too were rejects or if they were purposely thrown on the sidewalks as advertisements.

In spite of the opportunities in Vegas to wear outrageous costumes, to get drunk and perform outrageous acts, to strike sexy poses, and to look at pornographic images, the majority of Vegas visitors appear to be a regular Saturday crowd at the mall—except that most of them are taking pictures. They take home souvenir pictures of themselves with the costumed figures or of friends and relatives posing in front of "foreign monuments." Some act out their sexual fantasies for the camera with the many nude statues on the sites. But for visitors to Las Vegas who might be too shy to act out their fantasies on the streets, Photoshop opens up whole new possibilities.

Located in many of the mall areas of the casino resorts, Cashman's Photo Magic invites shoppers, "Be whoever you want to be." Mall-goers browse catalogs containing hundreds of such images in which models have white ovals in place of heads where a customer is invited, "[put] your face here" or even "use your own hair." While the slogans suggest a freedom to take on new roles, including gender-bending, the depictions of the genders are limited to those one might find in magazines. At Cashman's, people who identify as women can "be whoever [they] want," provided that they want to clone their faces onto a young, slim body with supersized breasts. A female might take on the identity of a bikini-clad Harley-Davidson rider or choose from three scantily

clad females enacting various plays in touch football. Male images include young muscular torsos often clothed in outfits signifying male authority. Just as in the Chippendale productions, the buff torsos pose in multiples clothed as firemen, policemen, businessmen, or construction workers. The templates for guy groups suggest that if the professionals were to remove their clothing piece by piece as the Chips do in their performances, they would reveal that underneath their uniforms, they all look alike. In the context of Vegas, where one is so conditioned to reading sexual connotations that advertisements for hotdogs seem pornographic, even the few templates that in other circumstances might seem family friendly are loaded with sexual innuendo. The template of a woman posing with Bill Clinton is an obvious example, but posing with George W. Bush . . . well, let's face it, we are not in the Hall of Presidents.

I watched three men, who looked to be in their mid-sixties and were of various shapes and sizes, partake in the Cashman Magic. They posed in succession for a digital camera in front of a green backdrop, known as the green screen in photography lingo. Each man was instructed to tilt his head to match the angle of the oval-shaped opening on an image that was superimposed on the figure. The composite image was projected on an overhead monitor screen while passersby gathered to watch the process. As the camera operator aligned the body that each man had selected from the Cashman album with an image of the man's actual head, the crowd sometimes called out to the sitter, "Hold it!" Then everyone quieted as the computer operator used software to erase bits of cheek and cloned more hair so that men's faces were seamlessly attached to the young muscular bodies they had chosen to take home to their wives. It was another of those shared group photographic fantasies, much like men posing with the Folies Bergère model. But here at the private enterprise of Cashman's, big signs made it clear that No Photography by camera-toting visitors was allowed.

In an outdoor booth near Harrah's casino resort, another version of the virtual experience records groups of friends or families on an overhead video screen. As paying customers gyrate to commands from an enthusiastic coach, their moving bodies are projected against a backdrop that makes them seem as if they are riding a motorcycle through busy city streets or sailing on a flying carpet. Like the voyeurs of Cashman's photographic magic, crowds of people assemble in this very public arena to enjoy the fantasy, but overhead signs warn, No Pictures Are Allowed. But this is a public place, right? Wrong. It is a section of sidewalk owned by Harrah's and thus rules of free speech do not necessary apply.

In some of the malls, one can purchase another version of a photo souve-

nir—a holographic self-portrait that appears as a three-dimensional image embedded in a geometric piece of glass. As I was studying these handheld miniature reproductions, I had the same visceral reaction that I have to taxidermy. I felt sick to my stomach. "Who buys these?" I asked the young salesman in his twenties, expecting that he would share my view that the little three-dimensional people in glass mausoleums were creepy. Without a hint of irony, he responded that he had sent one of himself to his mother and when she called to thank him, she cried on the phone, saying it was the most touching gift she had ever received. I had to admit that my mother might also like a paperweight version of me, but I made it clear that I wasn't interested. But the persistent salesman assured me that, after seeing myself in three dimensions, I would change my mind. So I sat on a high director's chair and held as still as possible while a swiveling camera took a series of pictures that were then stitched together by a software program. The camera technician was as ecstatic as a dental hygienist after successful X-rays, because I had apparently done an excellent job of holding still and the resulting picture was full of rich detail. As he rotated the image that was projected on a two-dimensional monitor screen, I could see lines on my face and folds of skin on my neck that I never knew were there. "Maybe another time," I said, thinking that I should consider a face-lift after all or at least settle for cloning a frontal view of my face onto one of the bodies in Cashman's Magic.

Along a hallway in the Mandalay Bay, I saw what appeared at a distance to be an exhibit of empty picture frames, but as I approached and viewed them straight on, they turned out to be holographic portraits. The three-dimensional images of people inside each frame were bathed in yellow light, but otherwise they looked disturbingly realistic. I took a picture of one of the three-dimensional illusions and was surprised to see that, on the viewing screen of my digital camera, the image looked like a regular photographic portrait. Of course, this collapsing of the third dimension is exactly what happens anytime one takes a picture of a real person. I don't feel shocked each time I take a picture of a person and see the person recorded as a two-dimensional reproduction. So why had it surprised me that I was unable to capture the illusion of tangible beings in the holograms?

In general, a picture of a picture—a picture of a poster, an advertisement, or another photograph—has the potential to make a viewer of the resulting photograph believe that the photographer had taken a picture of the original subject. For example, a student of mine made a print of a bear foraging in a field, which caused his classmates to ooh and aah over his fantastic post-vacation image until I pointed out that the print had a slight texture to it and

he confessed that he had photographed a picture of a bear on a calendar. By objectively transforming everything into two dimensions, the camera has the power to breathe more life into inanimate objects. In the case of the holograms that amaze because they appear to be three-dimensional, photography can flatten them into two dimensions and kill the illusion.

The fact that photography collapses one whole dimension of our experience is usually fodder for creating fantasies, not destroying them. It's possible that there would be no difference between a picture of a person taken at the Grand Canyon (which is a three-dimensional hole in the ground) and a picture of that person taken in front of a large poster of the Grand Canyon (the poster being a two-dimensional piece of paper). This layering of photographic images is the trick that is used at many of the ticketed exhibits in Vegas to provide visitors with souvenir moments that never happened. At the entrance to exhibits such as the Shark Reef and the Stratosphere, visitors hand over their admission ticket and are then invited to pose for a picture in front of a plain backdrop. Just before the exit, monitor screens display images of people in which the plain backdrop has been replaced by a scenic picture. At the Shark Reef, for example, visitors can choose to purchase a photograph in which their likeness appears before the shark tank at a decisive moment when a shark is swimming with its jaw agape, or in front of a skyline of Vegas, or beside the ever-popular sign on Route 5 that officially says, "Welcome to fabulous Las Vegas Nevada."

The Venetian Resort offers several games that play with the notion that, within a photograph, living people and realistic representations of people share the same level of verisimilitude. Casually located near the escalators on the veranda, celebrities such as Whoopi Goldberg and Nicolas Cage first startle passersby who believe they have spotted a famous person and then amaze them because they realize that these stationary forms are really statues from Madame Tussauds Wax Museum. Visitors line up for pictures because they instinctively understand that when the statues appear in a photograph side by side with a live person whose action is frozen at 1/125th of a second, they come to life. Even in the moment before a picture is taken, when a real person holds a pose alongside the wax model and a crowd of onlookers anticipates the click of the shutter button, the statue appears to be momentarily holding its breath. Over and over again, the magic of the photographic moment is repeated as people take turns mugging with wax.

Inside Madame Tussauds, it feels as if all life-sized bodies are intermingling at a big cocktail party. People mistake other real people for statues and confuse the statues with real people. I overheard a woman apologize when she

accidentally backed into Lawrence Welk. All around me, visitors enjoyed role-altering experiences as they responded to the inviting gestures of the statues and posed for pictures, often reciting the protective Vegas mantra. Women snuggled (bunny ears provided) with an aging Hugh Hefner who permanently lounges on a bed in his silk bathrobe. Young people rapped with a life-like Tupac Shakur, who had been killed in a drive-by shooting in Vegas years ago, although he appears in tours as a holographic performer. Men fondled porn star Jenna Jameson. Frozen in a kneeling pose with her legs spread and with her elbows conveniently covering her nipples, Jenna is portable, so the men actually picked her up to arrange her as they pleased. When visitors asked who Jenna Jameson is, the guard delivered a tongue-in-cheek response with a well-practiced eye roll: "She's a librarian."

Quintessential Vegas humor, the practiced response of the guard at the wax museum suggested that even the most staid among us could have a wild, alternative persona. It was a joke that encouraged us to act out our fantasies among strangers and to support others in their crazy antics. Maybe the woman choosing to kiss George Clooney as she posed for a friend's camera is in fact a librarian in her life beyond the bounds of Vegas.

Within the setting of a pretend Venice, the Living Statue entices people to join in another mind-bending game. Played by a rotating crew of male or female white-faced mimes in flowing robes, the Living Statue attempts to look and behave like a marble cast—that is, he or she does nothing. As with the wax models, people take pictures of friends posing with the immobile figures, but afterward they acknowledge that the statue is alive, for they usually leave a tip, which the mime acknowledges with a slow blink. It seemed odd to me that the Living Statue, being a featured attraction that fit with the theme of Venice, is not isolated against a photogenic backdrop as a performer in Disney World might be. Instead of fitting with the Italian Renaissance theme, the context surrounding the statue's pedestal reflects the contradictions that people either love or hate about Las Vegas, for the Living Statue is framed with a backdrop of designer shops such as Gandini or Ann Taylor and a foreground that features a pile of dollar bills.

Wherever I took pictures of iconic Vegas attractions, I found this same lack of concern for whether surrounding details fit the theme of the attraction. In fact, there seemed to be no attempt to make the context of any fantasy completely realistic. I had fully expected that the themed resorts would have thoroughly vetted design features to encourage picture taking that would maintain the illusion of being in a foreign land. I had imagined stage sets complete with props just waiting to be photographed—St. Mark's Square in Venice,

the Eiffel Tower in Paris, and a New York skyline. I expected that the Egyptian statues would be set against a context that would make it seem as if they were actually located in the ancient city of Luxor, Egypt. What I discovered is that the themed architectural attractions of Vegas are often side by side with competing attractions and advertisements that spoil the illusion. It is indeed possible to frame a picture of an Egyptian statue at the Luxor nestled amid overhanging palm tree fronds, but if the lens is zoomed out at all, the picture might include a billboard featuring a row of women covering their breasts with their hands advertising the "best topless show in Vegas."

Designers of the Venetian Resort went to great lengths to make the entrance to the Doge's Palace true to the Venice original with details such as inlay tiles and figurines custom-made with the patina of age, but the façade is perennially draped with a huge banner advertising the latest in-house entertainment extravaganza. One can take a picture of a portion of the Doge's Palace by aiming the camera to the left, but don't go too far or you will take in the multistory advertisement for the Tao Nightclub promising a religious experience with a "happy ending," a euphemism for getting laid that is visually illustrated by graphics that lead the eye down the torso of a woman wearing a backless dress. If there is not a planned intention to break the illusion that one might really be in a foreign land, there is certainly little effort in Vegas to maintain it.

It was in the Venetian that I became entranced by my first Vegas experience with a faux sky—the clouds that appeared to be receding into the cerulean backdrop and the soft evening light were very realistic. Just below the skyline, the illusion continued downward seamlessly to include murals of the second stories of buildings in ornate Venetian architectural styles. Walkways flanked either side of the flowing canal with occasional bridge crossings just as they do in Venice. But between the canal and the second story, the fantasy was broken by shops—some Italian-based specialty stores, but also souvenir shops, advertisements, American-based coffee shops, and miscellaneous Vegas offerings such as oxygen bars and massage parlors. I wanted to frame a picture of the Grand Canal inside the Venetian Resort to eliminate the surrounding context of shops and signage that referred to Las Vegas. I felt that I should hurry because it seemed that at any moment the sun was about to set. As I followed the labyrinthine canal to St. Mark's Square, I looked for a vantage point where I could take a picture that could fool someone into thinking that I had actually been to Venice. But this was not Disney's Epcot, where a stage manager had worked out the authenticating details and set up a Picture Spot sign that told me where to stand. I settled for a place on one of the bridges where I could compose a shot so that a pillar obscured the signage on the shops. I steadied my camera on the handrail of the bridge because the lighting, although lovely for an evening stroll, was too dim to take a handheld picture. I waited for a moment when the gondolier slowed his boat so that its movement wouldn't blur during my relatively long shutter time. The resulting image was very convincing unless you have actually visited Venice and know that its canal water is not the color of the Caribbean seas.

Some of the advertising for Vegas does suggest that one can experience an internally consistent themed getaway. But when you visit these spots in person and try to take the picture that was in the advertisement, it becomes a lesson in selective framing. The website for the Island Wedding Chapel at the Tropicana states that it is "nestled amid lush tropical foliage and cool tumbling waterfalls," and the ad includes a lovely photographic illustration. What I found when I actually visited the chapel was that both text and image omit the fact that a high-rise hotel flanks the little chapel on one side. Even if you frame the picture to eliminate the skyscraper, it is still possible that your picture will show the wedding chapel nestled amid lush tropical foliage with an orange neon sign atop Hooters in the distance, inviting by association the buxom young girls in tight tank tops and shorts to invade the wedding fantasy.

Similarly misleading, in the website for the Paris Las Vegas hotel, a picture of the Eiffel Tower as one looks upward from one of its legs is accompanied by text that touts its authenticity: "A signature of the Las Vegas skyline, the replica Eiffel Tower at Paris Las Vegas is a half-scale exact reproduction of one of Europe's most famous landmarks." In Vegas, you see tourists lying on the sidewalk trying to frame a similar shot. If they took a picture straight on, it would reveal that the other legs of the Eiffel Tower plunge through the ceiling of the hotel. Why are there so many more people trying to frame fantasies that they are in Paris when it's those legs of the Eiffel Tower on the casino floor that are the real Vegas memory?

Not only is a picture a piece cut out of a larger space, but it represents a sliver of time that acknowledges no history and anticipates no future, not even what happened moments before or after the shutter button is pressed. It is a portrait of newlyweds holding hands at the Trevi Fountain moments after the bride has snuffed her cigarette and moments before both make calls on their cell phones. Or, if the photographer chooses, it is a shot grabbed during the instant when they are walking down the sidewalk, staring vacantly in

opposite directions as they engage in separate phone conversations. Is either one of these moments more truthful than the other? What are the forces that might steer us to choose one of these instances of time to preserve a memory?

How often do we smile as a picture is taken, even if, moments before the shutter button is pressed, we are sad, angry, or exhausted? The resulting snapshots that show smiling individuals, smiling couples, smiling families will later be used as memory prompts. They are selective slices of history and, since memory is malleable, the images can distort or even reconfigure our idea of who we are or who we were.

The constant breach of authenticity in Vegas is no accident. The hodgepodge mix of themed attractions and advertising has evolved as a style that promotes the notion that everything is a game and therefore not serious. Our take-home Vegas memories present us in a world of make-believe.

One of the most popular tourist destinations of the world, Vegas attracts camera-toting visitors in droves. These travel photographers choose what subjects to photograph, when to press the button, how to frame an image, and how they compose elements within the frame. But do they really choose? An entertainment capital such as Vegas influences or even controls any or all of these creative decisions — what is allowed to be photographed, what is encouraged to be photographed, when the photographer should take the picture, how the picture is framed, and how the elements within the frame are composed. In Las Vegas, photography has evolved to serve the city's overriding goal, which is to encourage people to spend money by making them constantly aware that nothing is real in this town. Instead of encouraging photography that reinforces the carefully crafted illusions, Las Vegas promotes photography that reveals that everything is fake. For all of the advertised authenticity of the exotically themed resorts, the images that people take home and post on the web share the same punch line — "Ha, ha, we're really in Las Vegas."

What is being photographed along the Strip is a tongue-in-cheek version of reality — in other words, "reality." It's really hard to get your head around the concept of reality when it appears in quotation marks. For example, what in the world is a "real margarita" as advertised in a Mexican restaurant in Planet Hollywood? Can one get drunk on such a metaphysical concept? I decided to try it out. Sitting in the Mexican-themed restaurant with a supersized "real" margarita, a presumably real chicken fajita, and a book by John McPhee, I honestly cannot say whether the margarita — real or not — had anything to do with my lightheadedness. Although every tangible object in my immediate vicinity reinforced the theme of Mexico, Elvis Presley's "You Ain't

Nothin' but a Hound Dog" was blared over the surround-sound speakers. Unable to concentrate on my book, I wrote a postcard. The image on the card was a fairly realistic view of the Arc de Triomphe, but the diagonal script on the front was the reason I bought the card. A succinct expression of the confounded identity, it offered a simple greeting from "Paris, Las Vegas."

NOTE

Epigraph: Michael Ignatieff, introduction to *Magnum Degrees* (Hong Kong: Phaidon, 2000).

TWO

Playing the Penny Slots

Penny slots—what could be more egalitarian? There, tucked in the rows of quarter machines and the truly pricey dollar machines, was a cluster of penny slots. And they were popular; almost every machine was taken. I had no idea you could come to Las Vegas and gamble for pennies.*

Discovering the penny slots was a bit like stumbling into the Penny Arcade on Disneyland's Main Street, where for an actual penny a pop, visitors can watch silent movie vignettes in the kinetoscopes or activate the fortune-telling machines whose gypsy automatons read the future. As an oasis of the past, the Penny Arcade offers quaintly simple amusements as antitheses and respite from Main Street's other shops, so overstuffed with Disney merchandise. Most kids today know that pennies are worthless. They won't buy you candy as they did during the Depression, nor moving picture amusements as Disney imagines they did around 1910. What's curious (and possibly contradictory) about Disney's Penny Arcade is its grasp of America on the cusp of becoming the mass entertainment capital of the world. In that bygone world,

---

* Susan Willis

a penny may have really mattered, and not just for its value prior to inflation, but because it actually functioned as an instrument of exchange. Thus, a penny, dropped in the kinetoscope's slot, activates the machine and renders the exchange between moving images and the consumer's gratification.

Steeped in recollections of the Penny Arcade, I made my way through densely packed rows of machines to better inspect the penny slots. Clearly, the Disney Imagineers had not worked their magic on the casino floor. The penny slots were in no way distinguishable from the other machines but for the 1¢ sign suspended over them. They were merely thrust in between quarter and dollar machines, like a Dollar General store interjected into a suburban shopping mall, its tacky storefront next to a Sears and just steps away from Macy's. With a Dollar General store, no one need leave the mall empty handed. Air freshener, hair accessories, cat toys, and scores of useful but unnecessary items—the Dollar General offers something for everyone and makes anyone a consumer.

Similarly, the penny slots offer every visitor to Las Vegas a piece of the action. Slide a dollar bill into the machine's maw and get a hundred plays. Sadly, the penny slots don't have a penny slot. The booming economy of the 1990s and the soft money of the early 2000s made the dollar the new penny. But even at a dollar per hundred plays, the penny slot offers a much bigger bang for a buck than all those other mechanical maws on vending and change-making machines that eat our dollars in exchange for Snickers bars and quarters for the Laundromat.

Today, it can cost $3.50 or more to run a load of wash at a Laundromat—and $4.50 for the bigger machines. Add the dryers, and the price of one load of washed and dried clothes comes to at least $5.00. Imagine how long you can play a penny slot for $5.00. If you drag the play out, watch the little icons roll into place and avoid maximizing your bet with nonlinear and diagonal combinations that cost 5–10¢ a play, you can spend two or three hours on a machine, especially if you win "free" additional plays.

At the penny slots, players are spending time, not money—and for good reason. The weather in Las Vegas is more often harsh than hospitable. A biting wind and daytime temperatures in the forties greeted me in early December. And I'm sure summer is even more exacting. Against the desert's raw reality, the casinos offer climate-controlled refuge. The Harrah's where I stayed vacuums visitors in through widely gaping entrances that curiously can't be found when you want to leave (an effect of a sunken playing floor that puts the exit above eye level). I finally learned how to chart my way out by memorizing a path past a row of potted plants, then alongside the gaming tables. When the line of people queueing up for the buffet came into view, I knew the exit would be near.

If spending time in the casino is a consequence of an architecture designed to get you in and keep you there, then it's time spent in postmodern limbo. A huge but entirely closed world compressed under low ceilings and bathed in subdued artificial light, the casino wholly erases the temporal and spatial markers that otherwise define a visitor's life at home or work. In their place, a thousand electronic ringtone-like bleeps and bells—the sound of the ceaseless slots—replace clock time and the shift from diurnal to nocturnal life with an unremitting temporality of the ever present. As for space, it's both fragmented and highly Taylorized, with slots separate from playing tables, and playing tables set apart from the sports betting area. The casino replicates the particularization of function once commonly associated with the industrial workplace, here retooled for the work of spending.

Writing on postmodern hyperspace, Fredric Jameson cites the Bonaventure Hotel in Los Angeles as one of the earliest examples of the bewildering interior design that has come to typify this aesthetic.[1] At the Bonaventure, the symmetry of the hotel's four conjoined towers makes it impossible for a visitor to use the lobby as a compass. At particular disadvantage are the shopkeepers tucked into the hotel's upper balconies. Only luck or advanced GPS can guide a prospective customer to a particular shop. The hotel's belated solution was the addition of color-coded signs and arrows to demarcate red, blue, green, and yellow areas and elevators.

What Jameson proposes in lieu of colored markers as a means for comprehending and negotiating the spatial ambiguities of postmodern architecture is cognitive mapping.[2] As Jameson sees it, cognitive mapping positions the individual not only in space as a paper or digital map would do, but also with regard to our knowledge of history and economics. Defining where we are when we are in the Bonaventure Hotel means knowing what was there before the city razed previously existing blocks, businesses, and residences. It also means plotting the self with respect to the globalized system of capital investment that erases its signature even while it presents itself in the form of a world-class hotel.

What makes cognitive mapping particularly important as a strategy for negotiating Las Vegas is the history of dramatic redevelopment that has made the Strip the site of continual implosions, excavation, and construction. The difficulty we encounter when we attempt to find our way around a massive gaming floor designed to keep us indoors and in play is a minor inconvenience when we compare it to the bewildering prospects of charting our rela-

tionship as consumers to the vast leisure and gaming industry, whose hyperspace is a machine for the extraction of wealth, increment by increment and venue by venue. The symptomatic expression of not knowing the complex interlocking contractual and proprietary relations that define the Strip is the experience of not knowing where we are when, engulfed in a casino, we desperately search for an exit.

But what if you want to spend your time on pursuits other than gambling? Sorry, no such luck. All walkways and transportation options on the Strip are designed to take you nowhere but into another casino—or shopping mall—or mall/casino. Everything parallels the Strip, the roadway where cars and vans outfitted with billboards cruise up and down in a continual display that might lead you to believe that the Strip folds back on itself, in Möbius fashion. From Mandalay Bay to Circus Circus, sidewalks extend top to bottom, their Strip-hugging trajectories broken only by four elaborate pedestrian bridges, designed to protect visitors from the hazards of bumper-to-bumper traffic and ever-gawking drivers. For speedy but expensive transport, a monorail plies the Strip, moving footsore vacationers from one casino to the next. The entire built environment is intended to keep visitors in line and on their game.

What's more, there is no place where the weary tourist can sit that doesn't involve spending money. Because the hotels exist solely to funnel visitors to the gaming floor, all obstructions have been removed. There are no lobby chairs or couches—indeed, there's no lobby, just a counter for checking in. And outside, there's only the flow of the Strip—not a single grassy knoll, park bench, or boxed planter—nowhere to rest or recline. Hence, visitors who want to catch the Bellagio's fountain display are forced to stand and wait. Tired, they grip the parapets that surround the hotel's rendition of Lake Cuomo. To sit would require a graceful leap to the top of the parapet and then a balancing act on its rounded surface. In Las Vegas, being on your feet and moving has more to do with recycling visitors back into the casinos, where, with the only chairs in town allocated to the buffet, bars, restaurants, gaming tables, sports betting lounge, and slot machines, the penny slots offer the exhausted tourist a bit of rest at a bargain price.

Many of the players on the penny slots appeared to be killing time, especially the ones I encountered at 4:00 AM as I walked bleary-eyed through the animated and brightly lit casino on my way to the airport for a crack-of-dawn departure. Struck by the number of predawn players, I wondered if they had played all night. Were they somehow captivated by the machine's action and unable to tear themselves away for fear of missing that one play that would score a jackpot? Or maybe they, like me, have a neighbor back home who re-

turned from his Las Vegas vacation glowing with tales of hitting $2,000 on the penny slots—and not once, but twice! As he described it, the tedium of his late-night play was suddenly broken by bells, whistles, and a staff person who magically emerged to bestow $2,000—both times. Of course, he was maximizing his pennies, spending $1.50 per play. As he put it, "The wins canceled my losses."

Enough observation. The time had come to give the penny slots a whirl. As a neophyte, I eschewed the advice of a more experienced gambling friend who told me to always choose a machine at the end of a row and on an aisle. Apparently, casinos want their customers to see and get excited by the wins, so the machines closest to pedestrian traffic are more often set to win. Putting aside all thoughts of tactics, I let myself be guided by the graphics. At first, I gravitated toward the old-style iconography—the cherries, grapes, limes, and lucky number 7s that I associated with the one-armed bandits of the 1950s. Seeing them on one of the penny slots, I instantly recalled one of my family's long summer road trips. It must have been in the late 1950s. On our way from Southern California to Utah's natural wonders, we were somewhere in Nevada's endlessly barren and hot landscape, where the only point of attraction was the occasional overheated car, its hood raised and spewing steam out of the radiator. At one point, we pulled off the highway and into a gas station. Escaping the car and endless hours of confinement, I followed my dad into the station. There, perched on stools, two leather-skinned cowboys played the slots. Stunned to see real cowboys and old enough to consider gambling illegal, I couldn't help but stare. My dad broke my trance with something of a fatherly gesture. He reached into his pocket for some quarters and showed me how to work the machine—insert the coin, pull the lever, then watch the fruits spin until they fall fatally into place.

On the verge of reliving the past and as I started toward the machine with old-style graphics, my eyes were sidetracked by the amazing visuals on many of the adjacent machines. They had themes! My favorite—the one I finally fed $20.00 over three days of sporadic play—offered a pre-Columbian lost world. Rather than limes and cherries, golden masks, turquoise necklaces, and feathered headdresses cycled through the machine's visuals. The wild card was a Mayan temple. Four temples anywhere and a big version of the temple immediately filled the screen, while a deep and mysterious voice announced that I—the lucky player—would now be able to enter the temple for some free plays. By succeeding in opening the temple for some off-penny play, I had essentially won free time—time not computed in dollars and cents. Given that so much of our free time (vacations, sick days, discretionary time, comp time) is really factored into and tabulated with our work time, the penny slot's interlude of free plays allows the player the thrill of getting something for nothing.

But my victory was brief and quickly absorbed back into the longer duration of play. Once inside the temple, I made a wrong choice. The temple disappeared and the slot machine put me back into the real time of pennies yet to be spent.

During my three-day sojourn in and around the slot machines, I did encounter some actual winners—people who attested to wins of $500 or more. But watching the majority of players engrossed in their play, I realized that the real point of the penny slot is not to hit the jackpot but to keep the game going. It's an aim inherited from video games, where the fun ends when you "die" and have to start all over again back at level one. In the case of the penny slots, overcoming death requires the infusion of additional money. Although I never won any money back from the machine, I did succeed in cheating time with numerous excursions into the temple.

Hence, some of the time I killed was my own "free" time.

My experience as a player piqued my interest in others who play the penny slots. Most seemed ill disposed to talk, intent as they were on the business of playing. What's more, the machine itself is built to cocoon the player within the narrow confines of seat, screen, and play button, making conversation between players unlikely. Even the waitress circling about with free drinks can be a bothersome distraction. Nevertheless, one day while sampling the machines at New York–New York, I struck up a conversation with a woman who chose the machine next to mine. She had arrived on a scooter, and during the time she required to hoist herself off the scooter and onto the machine's chair, I dropped a greeting. She proved to be loquacious, immediately explaining that she had just arrived from Massachusetts. I put her age at just over seventy. Indeed, early December (the slow and cheaper season) brought many seniors to Las Vegas and with them a number of scooters and wheelchairs. I continued to pepper my slot mate with small talk and learned she was a real devotee of the casinos. She confessed to frequent trips to Foxwoods, a casino near her home, where she consistently plays the slots. Seeing me for a novice, she asked if I had a computer and explained that I could buy gambling games at Walmart. I began to wonder why this woman, who had so many gambling options—both at home and at her local casino—bothered to come to Las Vegas. Travel, what with the scooter, would be awkward at best. When I put the question to her, she explained that she owned a Las Vegas time-share with her husband. It was then that I noticed an elderly man skulking about. "My

husband." She pointed with her thumb. "He's already lost his daily limit at the tables." It was barely 2:00 in the afternoon. Clearly, my slot mate was going to be able to kill a lot more of the day than her husband, particularly as I'd just seen her slide a $20 bill into the machine.

Seeing the man who had already shot his wad while his wife prepared to play and play, I began to wonder if playing the penny slots is comparable to a minimum wage job. Was the woman devalued as a player, even though she would be able to play much longer than her high-stakes professional husband? The wage laborer might make a hundred dollars in a day, whereas the professional can make that amount in an hour. But in terms of sex, a trope that haunts my analogy, the woman's prolonged play might be prized over the man's briefer play. As I pondered the comparison, it occurred to me that players on the penny slots have a better chance of breaking even when they lose, if you consider the number of free drinks that can be consumed during the time it takes to kill a $20 bill.

My conversation with the woman from Massachusetts made me curious about the other devotees of the penny slots. Those on cell phones chatting with players in other casinos while avidly punching their own play buttons were definitely unapproachable. Casting about, I spied a man sitting idly at a machine as if he were taking a break. When he smiled in my direction, I took the opportunity to join him. On closer inspection, I realized he was not alone. There on the chair next to him was his eighty-plus-year-old dad. The son confessed to being in his sixties, and went on to explain that he makes the trip from London, Ontario, to Las Vegas a couple of times a year—sometimes with his wife (who likes the shows) and other times with his dad (who whiles away his time at the penny slots). The dad's health seemed iffy; and, indeed, the next day he stayed in his room. My two conversations with older visitors to Las Vegas alerted me to the numbers of elderly parents being escorted by only slightly less elderly sons and daughters. Glancing about and seeing hunched backs, canes, even mobile oxygen tanks, I suddenly saw the casino as a geriatric final fling where vacationers could spend their pre-postmortems. Perhaps sensing my morbid thoughts, the Canadian mouthed an oft-heard refrain: "We want to spend our money. After all, you can't take it with you."

A true baby boomer, the sixty-year-old had dragooned his dad—and his dad's possible Depression-era inclination toward saving—into a junket devoted to eliminating the family inheritance. Unlike the pharaohs, who really thought they could take their possessions with them and thus filled their tombs with their wives and cats, boomers aim to reap the rewards of accumulated wealth in the here and now. Forget passing it along to future generations or making a donation to a worthy cause. Sadly, the Canadian won $1,000 at the penny slots, thus encumbering himself with a whole lot more to get rid of. In a macabre turn, I wondered if his dad had enough time left to kill.

In contrast to my bleak mood, the slot machines are the liveliest part of the casino floor. Their blinking lights and bells lure children who hover about on the margins of play, yearning desperately to test the machines, but warned away by security guards and signs that declare the gaming areas off-limits to children. I caught myself imagining that toddlers would get a real hoot out of the slot machines—boost the fun of a Fisher-Price busy box to the next level! But instead of kids, I saw only zombies, like the man right there in front of me who appeared to be plugged into his machine as if on life support. The man's face was ghastly under the casino's fluorescent lights. His eyes stared vacantly into the slot machine's screen. Only his hand moved in minimal, repetitive cadence on the play button.

The scene captured the ironic pointlessness that Jean Baudrillard found so attractive in his journeys across America. A jogger running catatonically, en-livened only by the music in his earbuds; a Santa Barbara housewife watering her mortuary houseplants; the dilapidated Porterville Hotel, illuminated by the TVs playing to empty rooms—these are the images that Baudrillard pro-jected back to us as evidence of the "tragedy of a utopian dream made reality."[3] And what could be more utopian than a man playing his way to fortune?

Fascinated, I studied the cord looped around the man's neck and then plugged into the machine. Was it some sort of assisted breathing device? Un-able to tear my eyes away and imagining that he might keel over at any minute, I scrutinized the point where his cord entered the machine. Just then, the man, preparing to stand, yanked the cord and pulled a plastic card out of the machine. Was this his credit lifeline? And would the moment of maxing out his card be analogous to heart attack?

No. The plastic card was a Harrah's Rewards card—an accoutrement given to all hotel guests that I had for some reason not yet received. As soon as I spotted this particular card, I began to see scores of players with similar re-wards cards, most of them dangling from cords about their necks, in the same way that workers at hospitals and factories wear their security clearances. So the man with the ghastly face was not hovering close to death, but actively working to accumulate reward points with every play. His card inserted into a card reader, the machine converted every penny spent into fractions of points that added up in a system of recycled rewards.

Wow! Suddenly I was in a whole new ball game. All of my assumptions about playing the penny slots fell by the wayside. Here I had been plotting the benefits of killing time against costs calculated on a sliding scale that ran from the low-stakes penny slots to the high-end gaming tables. Embedded in an old-style calculus where value is pegged to labor, and labor to alienated time on the job, I had construed access to free time as a win. But the system of rewards overturns the logic of productivity just as surely as it does away with free time. Accruing rewards bundles all expenditures of time and money into additional consumptions. Thus, time is never free but always employed in a process of earning points. Even my free time spent in the Mayan temple contributed to my accumulation of points. Rewards recycle consumptions into future consumptions and position the consumer as always already entered into the next consumption.

Immediately, I understood Guy Debord's dictum forty-two: "The spectacle is the moment when the commodity has attained the total occupation of social life."[4] Writing on the penetration of image culture into every sector of life and thought, Debord characterized late capitalism as the "society of the spectacle." It's not hard to see the Las Vegas Strip as a fully elaborated spectacle, but Debord's words point to something more profound. Because the image is synonymous with the commodity form, its insinuation into zones of experience that might be considered free speaks to the reification of all social interactions and suggests the appropriation of our dreams and desires as well.

Sadly, my five-day Las Vegas stay yielded very little free play and I netted only a measly thirty-eight reward points. Granted, I spent little more than $20 on various penny machines, and it took me a while to understand the system of interlocking casino ownerships that work either for or against earning points. With my Harrah's Rewards card, I could play and gain points at the Rio and Bally's. But New York–New York figured in a different ownership package. Any points that I might have earned during my play there fell into the void of rewards that would never be tabulated. On the whole, I gained a tremendous appreciation for those visitors whose points earned them a free meal at the buffet. Allowed to line up in a special queue, they glowed with the patina of big spenders. After all, you need 400 points to enter the breakfast buffet free of charge, and 900 for the dinner buffet. Put that in the context of 4,000 points for a dinner at the Steakhouse, or 50,000 points for free airfare for a return visit (coach, booked thirty days in advance). Reflecting on my own efforts to accumulate flier miles on Southwest and US Airways, I found myself wondering if the ratio of expenditure to reward that the airlines use is comparable to the system at Harrah's. No wonder I've achieved so few free trips.

Luckily, everything in life has its reward. The frequent buyer program at my local animal feed store tabulates my purchases of wild-bird seed toward the reward of a free sack of sunflower seeds. Twelve forty-pound sacks earn a free one. How many winters will it take the birds in my backyard to go through twelve sacks? Then there's the rewards program attached to my credit cards. One converts every thousand dollars spent at L. L. Bean into a $10 coupon good for more L. L. Bean purchases. Another transforms charged purchases into flier miles. The circularity of purchases and rewards recycles every purchase into future expenditures. Rewards offer the elusive promise of getting something for nothing, aside from also shackling the consumer to a particular retailer (or casino franchise), thus ensuring customer loyalty and brand recognition. As the advertisement for the Harrah's Rewards card puts it, "Get more out of life. Save credits up for special occasions or use them to make every visit memorable." Erased are the losses and high interest payments against which all rewards are mortgaged.

Given the fast-paced environment of wins versus losses, my biggest letdown in Las Vegas was the absence of cash. I had expected to see greenbacks on the tables and cascades of coins pouring out of the slot machines. Prior to my trip, I had primed myself with Las Vegas movies. One in particular, *Casino*, with Robert De Niro, takes the viewer into a casino counting room. Here, money is processed on an assembly line where deft-fingered employees bundle and package the loot that the machines have sorted according to denomination. The movie's voice-over narration mentions that many a counting room employee develops a dangerous case of sticky fingers. The comment triggered my memory of Harry the Hat, a drifter who lived in his van and used the gym where I worked out for his daily shower. A quirky humanitarian, Harry claimed to run something of an underground railroad for the homeless, transporting them from towns where they were persecuted to places he deemed more hospitable. Harry also rescued stray cats. At the time I knew him, he shared his van and the truck-stop food he favored with six cats. Harry was talkative, but never very coherent. I sensed he had been a grifter who spent his heyday in Las Vegas. One traumatic tale kept cycling through Harry's reminiscences. Piecing together the bits, I gathered that Harry and a team of his cohorts had worked out a system to skim off the casino's take. They made themselves rich—had more money than they could spend. Of course, they flashed it, bought clothes and jewelry. Eventually, they were caught. Harry, as ringleader, was taken before the casino's owner, who roughed him up in his office. Then, in true movie fashion, he ordered his henchmen to take Harry into the desert. There they beat him and left him for dead. Did I believe Harry? Even if I doubted the particulars of his tale, I couldn't doubt that Harry was a broken man. Nor could I disregard the invective that peppered his comments about the casino owner (a man still alive today—a prominent and respected businessman, whose casinos are only a portion of his larger financial empire). Then, too, there was De Niro, who slid in and out of Harry's rote condemnations. According to Harry, the actor was in cahoots with his erstwhile boss. So, what's real? Is Harry's tale a blend of fantasy and paranoia? Had he seen too many mob-inspired movies, or was his story the reality behind the movies?

Much of the romance—and infamy—of Las Vegas is rooted in the dream of winning fistfuls of cash. But what if there is no cash in Las Vegas? What if, instead of coins gushing into a trough, the slot machine issues a crummy cash register receipt? What if, instead of the clatter of loot falling out of the trough and onto the floor, we have to take our crummy receipts to the Rewards counter, there to redeem them? And for what—the breakfast buffet? I wonder how many visitors just don't bother to redeem a chit for $5 or $10. Do some fear being taken for penny-pinchers when they line up to redeem a paltry winning? How many chits go unredeemed? Are the casinos allied with the retailers who double their profits on the thousands of Christmas gift certificates that each year go unredeemed? The chit we tear up, the gift certificate we lose in a drawer—think of all the pennies that return to corporate winners.

Dismayed at seeing Las Vegas as a cashless desert, I recalled that as a child, in the 1950s, I regarded money with absolute wonderment. Neither I nor anyone I knew received an allowance. Except for the dimes we banked with our in-school passbook accounts, real money came into our hands only with a birthday card from a distant, barely remembered, but presumably wealthy relative. Imagine, then, how exciting it was to behold the rolls of quarters that my aunt and uncle carted home from the bank and packed in their suitcase in preparation for their annual Las Vegas vacation. Imagine, too, the silver dollars that my dad brought home after a business trip to Las Vegas—two each for my brother and me. Apparently, the hotel had given him a whole roll of silver dollars to warm up his play on the machines. My eyes were probably as big around as the dollars themselves, not realizing that at that time I could take any silver certificate to the bank and demand the silver dollar for which it stood.

Mulling over my reaction to the dearth of silver on the Strip, I sought out a colleague who spent his childhood on the Nevada side of Lake Tahoe. Growing up in a culture of legalized gambling, he said he considered slot machines a fact of life—ubiquitous and unremarkable. When I told him about the paper chits that I won in Las Vegas, his eyes blazed with a sudden remembrance. "Really?" he said. "When I was a kid, people walked from casino to casino carrying buckets of coins. I remember seeing them bent over to exaggerate the weight or clanking them to show they were either big winners or prepared to play all day."

The image of people so burdened by their cash that it might be considered a trophy is absolutely contrary to today's razor-thin and ultralight aesthetic. Only in the carnival environment of a state fair are we apt to equate success with encumbrance. Recall those preposterously huge stuffed animals that the lucky winners at the shooting gallery or penny pitch are condemned to tote about for the duration of their day. By comparison to giant teddy bears and buckets of cash, rewards points accrued in Las Vegas are discreet, like all our other financial transactions. A phantom electronic currency, the system of rewards gained, tabulated, and redeemed mimics our society's all but total transition from a world where there were once concrete and verifiable forms of money, like silver certificates, to a world where all that matters is virtual. Now that we have direct deposit and online banking, we need never go to the bank, much less carry cash. Consider the scant instances when only cash will suffice: the panhandler who asks, "Can you spare a dollar?"; the carpenter who gives a good rate for payment under the table; the man pushing a mower from block to block who will cut the grass for payment on the spot. Even McDonalds's and Starbucks are working to wean customers off cash with their prepaid cards (which can be bought with the swipe of a credit card). Cash has become the currency of the marginal, the casual, the informal and illegal. It's the medium of exchange for children too young to appropriate a parent's credit card and the Al Qaeda financier who transports loot by camel back. These are the mythic last enclaves of a cash economy. Even the cards for call girls that litter the Strip proclaim "all credit cards accepted."

Why has currency become obsolete? By all accounts, cash is just plain expensive. It costs more to print or mint many denominations of our bills and coins than the value they purport to represent. The production cost of a penny is certainly more than the 1¢ stamped on its backside. Then there's the cost of transfers and transport. Think of those gas-guzzling Brinks trucks required to haul our money around, not to mention all those employees needed to accept payments and make change. Why pay people when a machine can scan the bar codes on our purchases, tabulate the total, and conclude the transaction by reading our debit card? Poof! The payment moves from one computerized system to another, and we, the happy shoppers, go home with a car full of groceries.

Yes, electronic transfers keep the economic system well greased—goods and people choreographed in a transaction ballet where filthy lucre never changes hands. How odd that my supermarket now provides its shoppers with antibiotic hand wipes. With everything so clean and efficient, we appear to inhabit the world depicted in the Visa Check Card commercial that aired on TV. Here, life's a big fast-food restaurant. Burgers slide effortlessly off the grills and onto customers' trays. Drinks stream out of machines and into waiting plastic cups. Workers and customers move about effortlessly, transcribing patterns that recall the wheels of a precisely functioning Swiss watch—until some loser arrives at the register and fumbles in his wallet for cash. All hell breaks loose as burgers, drinks, and people come to a jarring and messy halt. Cash is just not old fashioned; it's a hindrance to orderly, efficient exchange. Only a Luddite disrupts the flow with cash.

And who would want to be a Luddite, when electronic transactions are so effortless? Indeed, they seem to make every purchase a gift—a gift that we give to ourselves. The magical moment of sliding our debit card seems to erase the fact of spending, just as all traces of ever having been made are erased from the commodities that we buy. The Barbie dolls appear in their plastic bubble packages on the toy store shelf, as do the skinless, boneless, plastic-wrapped chickens in the refrigerated section of the supermarket. No one, it seems, has plucked the chicken or dressed Barbie to hide her cyborg hips. No—they're all magical gifts. What connects commodity fetishism to the fetishizing of the transaction is distance and separation. Our perception of the commodity as a magically produced object corresponds with the removal of the work of production—first from our cities, as factories were displaced to anonymous suburban districts, then out of the heavily populated northern states to the more rural south; and now, with globalization, to the far corners of the world (where only the rumor of sweatshop labor need ever challenge the commodity's pristine appearance). So, too, has the transaction been removed from our daily routines. Not too long ago, the work of consuming required monthly, if not weekly, trips to the bank, and payments for utilities and telephone service were made in person at the company's bills payable counter. Now the fetishism that we once attributed solely to the commodity has permeated all the instances when we pay or receive money. The transaction, which was once a social act, has been displaced into the virtual space of pay and debit points.

Once upon a time and shrouded in the lore of traditional anthropology, Marcel Mauss wrote a treatise on gifts and societies whose social economies were based solely on the giving, receiving, and regifting of gifts.[5] The model gift givers were the Trobriand Islanders, who annually traveled from island to island to exchange their treasured objects—the sorts of things like headdresses and necklaces that so captured my fancy in the Mayan temple. Because wealth circulated, no one individual could accumulate great power. Absent money, the gifts bound individuals to each other. What's more, each gift stood as a pledge of a future gift, thus preserving the past in an unbroken process of exchange.

Rewards are our society's shabby gifts. Rather than binding us to each other in a community of exchange, rewards block our relationships with others and bind us, instead, to the corporate entity that tabulates our points and bestows our rewards. Unlike the Trobriand Islanders, whose wealth was held collectively, we know that real wealth is held—indeed hoarded—elsewhere, and then meagerly doled out to us according to a ratio of expenditures. Rather than gift givers, we resemble anxious cargo cultists trapped in the suspended animation of our next anticipated reward.

I've long known the anticipation of a reward, because storing up points is nothing new. As a child, I collected my mother's s&h Green Stamps. It was my job to affix them in booklets, moistening their gluey backs with my tongue and pressing them—either singly or in sheets—to the page. One stamp per dollar spent, Green Stamps were the silver certificates of the redemption economy, as each one was the concrete and actual embodiment of money spent. So we saved our booklets for the hallowed day when we might take them to the redemption center—a veritable treasure trove of glistening home appliances: toasters, blenders, electric skillets. Like some bastard, godforsaken Trobriand Islanders, we would exchange our painstakingly saved booklets of stamps for an item—something my thrifty mother would never buy, but something she truly coveted. We would take it home packed in its box—a three-speed Mixmaster. What a gift!

Thus, every spender is a saver; every loser, a winner.

Back at the penny slots, I settled into a machine deep in the casino's forgotten recesses. I wanted a vantage point from which to gaze out and embrace as much of the playing floor as possible. I was alone—but for the woman mumbling into her cell phone from a position even more remote than my own. Surprised that she had service in this most bunkered enclave of the casino, I caught myself listening to snatches of her conversation:

Did Bud tell you I won?
Yeah.
On the penny slots.

At this point I was all ears and strained to overhear the full story of another happy winner. Curiously, though, the winner seemed totally blasé. Unwilling to emit a single ecstatic whoop, she merely mouthed the facts.

Yeah—$500.
I thought Bud told you.
Yeah, on the penny slots.
So, where do you want to eat?

Apparently, winning is just another trivial detail in the day's events. When a system of rewards buffers the grim reality of losing, it also cheats the win of its exceptionality. And playing the penny slots becomes no different from shopping—we spend to accumulate.

NOTES

1. Fredric Jameson, "The Cultural Logic of Late Capitalism," in *Postmodernism* (Durham, NC: Duke University Press, 1991), 38–54.
2. Jameson, "The Cultural Logic of Late Capitalism," 51–54.
3. Jean Baudrillard, *America* (London: Verso, 1989), 30.
4. Guy Debord, *Society of the Spectacle* (Detroit: Red and Black, 1977).
5. Marcel Mauss, *The Gift* (New York: Norton, 1967).

THREE

S.I.N. City

In Las Vegas's McCarran Airport, posters from the Transportation Security Administration line the walls for the edification of travelers crawling through security.* Each poster profiles a different uniformed TSA officer, the whole collection consisting of extremely everyday-looking folks identified by first name only, as though we are all already acquainted, if not friends in a Facebook world where one can claim hundreds of them. In one poster, "Tony" looks directly at us, hands folded in front of him, in that awkward and uncomfortable pose most of us know from the experience of being photographed head-on when we would have preferred the candid shot—that is, the way we look when we don't know we're being photographed, which is another way of saying the way we look through the surveillance camera, or, more to the point, the way Tony looks at us. If his posture and half smile betray his nerves, they are also intended to reassure us that, "like every other Transportation Security Officer," Tony is "proactive, not reactive," which means he doesn't wait

---

* Jane Kuenz

for trouble to come to him, but goes out and finds it among the millions who pass through McCarran security every year.

Put in place after 9/11, the posters are an indication of how the attacks marked, not the introduction of security in everyday life, but its normalization. Now, the daily experience of covert surveillance as routine is complemented by the self-conscious staging of it in public settings—not just Tony and his TSA kin on the walls, but the armed guards patrolling airports and "high-threat urban areas" in the flesh, outfitted in camouflage and gear that, rather than hide the wearers, call attention instead to the sheer theatricality of their presence. Elsewhere, the stage is the point, as public safety and surveillance take the form of urban planning and new styles of architecture. In the Las Vegas federal courthouse, security is not hidden within the design but is the design itself, with broad neoclassical steps and a raised entry plaza that together serve the political function of connecting the building to the street, suggesting government's doors open to all, and the need to keep the place out of reach of car bombs. The effect is to make the building more fortified while seeming less so.

The TSA posters are a fitting introduction to a city whose popular slogan promises visitors that "what happens in Vegas stays in Vegas," as though Tony were there to make sure of it. Unfortunately, "what happens in Vegas" is pretty much what happens everywhere else. Not a metaphor, but a model, Las Vegas is ground zero for the "security aesthetics" of contemporary culture and the consequent habituation to total visibility that will soon be required for participation in it. The stew of leisure, entertainment, consumption, and work that is the Strip is less an alternative to daily life back home than an intensification of it. Today, less than half of the revenue collected on the Strip will come from gambling; the rest will come from food, shopping, and shows, all taking place under the watchful "eye in the sky" and in the midst of computer networks capable of finding, within minutes, "nonobvious" but potentially sinister relationships among gamblers, dealers, tourists, and shoppers, saints and sinners alike.

This is Sin City after all, though rather than lap dances, S.I.N. now stands for Surveillance Information Network, a web of databases maintained in Las Vegas that links personal and surveillance information on the consumption, gaming, and work habits of the employees, professional gamblers, and tourists who work and play in the more than 160 casinos (so far) across the United States and Caribbean that subscribe to the service. It is because of integrated databases and monitoring systems like S.I.N. that federal agencies turned to

Las Vegas after the 9/11 attacks, hoping that a city already famous for the ubiquitous and constant surveillance in its resorts would share its secrets for identifying cheats, counters, and other "advantage players." And it is Vegas that served as the testing ground for the technologies in biometrics and data mining that are used to identify and track "terrorists" across the nation. The same technologies also drive social networking sites and the online economy, which rely on the same data gathering and monitoring software and the same rhetoric of security, freedom, and individual choice to justify the use of devices formerly reserved for prisons and tactics otherwise devoted to controlling labor and maximizing consumption.

I have borrowed the term *security aesthetics* from Christian Parenti's *The Soft Cage*, a history of surveillance in the United States. He means especially the ubiquity of surveillance cameras in public and private spaces, such as when we see ourselves coming in the video monitors at Best Buy and Sears, the cameras simultaneously advertising the products and warning us that we'll be seen if we try to shoplift. Having internalized permanent observation, we no longer need the panopticon; the cameras are hidden in plain sight. Or, as in Vegas, they are integrated into vast neural systems embedded in the architectural structure of entire cities, where they influence entertainment and culture, if they do not, in fact, constitute them. They line the glass ceiling of the atrium in the Bellagio—at first glance, they look like birds complementing the flora below—while multiple black bubble eyes rotate 360 degrees above every blackjack, roulette, poker, and craps table in every casino. Compared to the kind of technology available to modern casinos, the security guys dressed like Italian Carabinieri in shorts on bikes outside the Venetian seem a quaint throwback, needed more to restrain the occasional drunk falling into the water from a gondola ride than for the real work of casino policing and surveillance. There are so many cameras that the only places visitors are not filmed are their hotel rooms or the public bathrooms (sometimes), though cameras will record when we enter and exit. Cameras watch us in taxis and when we step out of the taxi at the hotel. They record us in the elevators, halls, and garages, and along the privately owned and maintained sidewalks that link resorts.

Within the gaming area proper, the surveillance is more inventive. Poker chips embedded with radio frequency identification devices (RFIDs) allow the house to track how much is waged on any one roulette number or baccarat spot and know instantly how much a player has won or lost. Blackjack tables, such as Bally Technology's iTable, are outfitted with infrared scanners, encoded cards, and tiny cameras at table level able to read every card played and, from that, collect data on a particular player's strategies. This information can then be used to grade and evaluate players based on their activity so the casino can decide how to pitch them and even whether to let them play at all.[1] The iTable also cheats, counting cards the same way a person would and noting any difference in the size of a player's bet so as to alert supervisors to a possible counter. At the high-stakes tables, cameras are aimed at both players and dealers, who periodically flip or "wash" their hands to show the overhead eye that no chips are being hidden. The cameras are so high powered that surveillance personnel secreted away in the building can read serial numbers on a dollar bill or the date on a coin. Slot machines are wired and networked to provide thermographic readouts of the entire casino floor, showing who's where when as well as data on the popularity of individual machines or kinds of machines, which ones are played and which avoided.

Outside on the Strip, the feeling of constantly being watched is subtler and more nuanced, an effect of the layout and architecture. As many photographers have learned, there is no obvious place to stand to see Las Vegas, no clear point of view, at least not the point of view of an actual human person rather than that of multiple cameras aimed in different directions. The buildings seem to crop up and out of each other, oblivious to the thematic integrity and coherence that distinguishes traditional theme parks such as Walt Disney World. Here, Egyptian pyramids, medieval castles, and the Empire State Building all compete for attention in the same Photoshopped picture. Like Keanu Reeves's face, everything on the Strip looks like it's already been digitized.[2] This is exemplified by MGM's new CityCenter, whose towers climb alongside each other, but in opposite directions, while other buildings jut out over the street in ways that seem to defy perspective, if not gravity. The lesson of the streetscape is that you have to look everywhere at once; also, that you can be seen at once from any direction, like the four sides of the Luxor pyramid, both gazing out and reflecting, though the best angle may be from above, where Google Earth's satellite, available to anyone with an Internet connection, can capture even more: the *Hairspray* advertisement on one side of the hotel, the make of the cars parked beside it, the people sitting inside them.[3]

Whether on the street or inside the resorts, the kinds of "entertainment experiences" touted in Vegas epitomize the militarization of perception characterized by both the presumption of total surveillance and the advertisement of it in the form of simultaneous images coming from multiple, juxtaposed screens or perspectives, such as the mix of ads and broadcast images running continuously inside and outside the Miracle Mile Shops at Planet Hollywood or the banks of LCDs above the video screens of the slot and poker machines

inside the casinos. It's the aesthetic of Mission Control, of the White House Situation Room, reproduced on the Internet, in the media, and by corporate shills, where screens line the walls, projecting data or images from different places around the world, side by side, simultaneously, in a look we've come to equate with safety, expertise, and authority.[4] And it's the look of 9/11: In *United 93*, the 2006 film about the hijacked United flight that crashed in Shanksville, Pennsylvania, we see the action from the point of view of the air traffic controllers in New York as they see it through the dozens of computer screens and overhead monitors on the desks and walls around them, each offering a different view of the same sequence of events. When the second plane hits the south tower, it appears in double: through the window and on the TV monitor next to it where CNN is broadcasting live. The proximity of window and video screen reinforces the conviction that everything can be seen at once even though what is seen is always mediated and produced, even the view of "the real world." *The Real World*, of course, is a reality TV show on MTV, one of the first to stage Big Brother–style surveillance as entertainment and fun, especially for the young and well heeled. This is what Las Vegas is now: the real world of total visibility experienced as the good life.[5]

That world is now familiar to us as ever-broader swaths of daily life adapt the surveillance technologies that have long been a feature of Las Vegas: homes, offices, and cars have now joined the usual suspects—malls, airports, and factories—in featuring "security" as part of the decor and ambience, especially in the form of cameras and the largely unquestioned acceptance of them. They watch us in stores and schools, on city streets, in all airports, all malls, and from almost every cell phone. Academics old enough to have had concerns about students tape recording lectures are now faced with the prospect that everyone in the room has come outfitted with multiple recording devices, while the classrooms themselves are equipped with wireless technology that enables anyone inside to share or post their images and recordings immediately online. Homes are miniature command centers with motion sensors and nanny cams, either themed or muted, depending on the age or taste of the room's primary occupants.[6] Kids are recorded on buses as they ride to schools where they are recorded in the classroom, the halls, the playground, even from their own school-issued laptops, and not just the urban public schools of *The Wire*, but tony suburban schools outside Philadelphia and Seattle.[7] Cookies trail us across the Internet, while digital signs equipped with the same facial recognition technology used in casinos, airports, and urban CCTV networks capture pictures of us as we walk by. Facebook, of course, now uses the same technology to invite account holders to identify themselves in pictures they didn't post and may not have known even existed. Text and instant messages can be traced and followed. Metro cards, E-ZPasses, passports, and frequent flyer numbers stalk us through subways, tollbooths, and airports, though following ATM withdrawals and debit or credit purchases is more efficient and thorough. Most use the same RFID tags that are embedded in casino chips and which may soon be a feature of clothes. Now the State Department, alert to the tenor of the times, issues Border Crossing Cards, with its cute pun on "guards," specifically for Mexican visa applicants, so that those who need to know can monitor the person's movements even before he or she gets to the border.[8] We carry smartphones linked to satellites capable of pinpointing us by longitude and latitude as we move from place to place. Our cars come equipped with cameras in the back and GPS systems up front, some of them advertised specifically as devices to monitor the speed and destinations of teenage drivers. Younger kids are just tagged outright with GPS devices or cell phones that monitor their doings, while private day care centers reassure anxious parents with real-time webcam feeds of their tots at play or sleep.

At work, the situation is no better, since those parents are probably watching their sleeping angels from offices on computers that, like the phones, are connected to networks that make the company aware of their arrival and departure and what they do in between. If necessary, an enterprising IT person can enter their PCs and command them from a remote location. If they're really harassed, passive software programs on the network deploy algorithms to discern patterns in online use to detect fraud or insider trading or simply to block access to websites deemed a distraction from their work, while the office itself may be decorated with LCD screens posting their and their colleague's minute-by-minute productivity scores: how many calls each makes, how many successful calls. Truckers and those who make deliveries move around in vehicles tagged with tracking devices that monitor not just where they are and whether or not they're following a predesigned and approved route, but also what they're carrying in vehicles equipped with biometric fingerprint pads that can identify the person behind the wheel. Nurses wear ID badges that transmit signals so that, like children, their whereabouts can always be known. Sometimes these are linked to bedside call stations so that their rounds can be timed and evaluated. Restaurant servers use computerized ordering pads that double as devices for detecting or deterring theft while providing a reliable accounting of the server's activities during the shift.[9]

The usual justification for these devices is safety and convenience, such as the "smart rooms" or other "interactive video environments" that wake you and start the coffee, or the bathroom mirrors that examine your skin for melanoma while you shower or shave. Eventually, however, the effect is to limit flexibility and, in the case of workers, increase productivity. The babysitter never assaulted the baby, but she is also now not nibbling on leftovers out of the fridge or talking on the phone; the trucker no longer has independence on the road—surely the only real attraction of the job—so the occasional personal detour is a thing of the past; the server can no longer adjust a tab off the record for the possibility of a bigger tip; the nurse visits all the patients but spends less time with any one of them; and gone is the World Wide Web as playground. Harnessed to work and consumption, the Internet becomes the new time clock and security camera all rolled into one. In other words, living something approaching a typical life in the United States today requires acclimating to constant surveillance, such that being at home, at work, or merely walking down a public street consists of moving in and out of different camera shots, virtual and real.

But we don't just accept total visibility as a fact of everyday life; we demand it as evidence of the protection we need from global terror and then convince ourselves that this is normal, even fun, and that we already are or should be potential Tonys, on the lookout ourselves, patrolling our communities in neighborhood watches and scouting Facebook profiles and status updates for information about possible criminal activity or suspicious photos of other people's kids to turn over to the FBI. On the bureau's own Facebook site, feel-good public relations stories ("No Safe Haven for Human Rights Violators" or "What New Agents Learn from the Holocaust") compete for attention with solicitations for help from citizen spies straight out of *America's Most Wanted*. For example, besides taking a quiz "to determine what kind of FBI career best suits you," friends can download or embed a widget for the bureau's Ten Most Wanted or provide feedback to posted surveillance footage of lesser villains like the Granddad Bandit, who looks, as one commenter puts it, like "a very common guy we meet everyday. You just never know."[10] What you just never know is who among the innocuous-looking people around you at any given moment is the one to watch. Best to watch them all.

The possibility that we all might be, as another TSA poster puts it, "empowered to detect, deter, and report potential or actual security threats" tempts the patrons of two of Las Vegas's popular attractions: MGM's CSI: *The Experience*, where visitors pretend to identify and investigate criminals, and The Gun Store down on Tropicana, where they can fantasize about actually shooting them. Of the two, the appeal of The Gun Store is the most direct: beginning in the airport and continuing throughout town, signs lure visitors with the opportunity to "Shoot a Real Machine Gun," versus watching some-

one else shoot one on TV or shooting only virtually in video games. "If you're not ready to gamble, drink, and objectify showgirls," the ad says, tongue in cheek, but clearly aware of the target audience, "then it's time to fire deadly assault weapons." Another features a woman posing with an MP5 submachine gun inviting travelers to "Try Me."

The place was crowded with people when I went, 99 percent of them tourists, at least according to Jocelyn, the young woman working outside. Locals come to the store itself (a Nevada license is required to purchase a weapon). All kinds of people come to shoot, she said, though, when pressed, Jocelyn admitted it was primarily men between twenty-five and forty, generally in groups, often from abroad—"Canada and Australia"—because "they have strict gun control laws and don't get the opportunity to fire guns like these," unlike the United States, where practically anyone can.

As if on cue, two Brits immediately step out of a car in the parking lot and come forward, followed soon after by a carload of their compatriots, all required to sign the same release swearing that they are not drunk, insane, or felons, else the management will be entitled to shoot them. I study the various deals offering gun adventures tailored to patrons' individualist fantasies: the World War II package for $99.95, the Coalition Package (Iraq Paq) for the same. Shooting zombies is more expensive: $149.94 for twenty rounds with an FS2000, fifty rounds with an Uzi, and another twenty with an unspecified handgun. Premium and VIP packages range from $500 to almost $800. There's even a Kid's Package for children under twelve. Jocelyn advises me to buy the Ladies Package (a bargain at three guns for $50). Afterward, my attendant, Adam, noting with newfound respect that most of my shots are to the head and groin, hands me my bullet-ridden target as a souvenir.

As it turns out, this matters because at The Gun Store we get to choose whom we shoot, the aforementioned zombies, for example, or miscellaneous bad guys in assorted poses and variously identified by gender, race, and ethnicity in a kind of multicultural smorgasbord of villains: a black guy, cap on backward, pointing a gun; a white guy in a ski mask, pointing a gun; a blonde woman in camo on one knee behind a desk, pointing a gun; Arab men in kaffiyehs with guns; and, of course, Osama Bin Laden himself, not a surrogate, the only identifiable celebrity among the mix, unarmed, as in most images of him in the West. What's interesting about this list is that, except for Bin Laden, all of the targets are clearly and immediately threatening, pointing guns either at the shooter or at someone else pictured in the target, always a white woman, as though even at a place advertising simply the thrill of the hands-on experience, we have to justify the fantasy under the heading of protection or defense in a culture of fear.

This conceit is taken a bit further at CSI: *The Experience*. In fact, the two attractions exemplify the split in casino policing between security, usually involving armed manpower on the ground—ads for casino security jobs often highlight the need for physical strength, presumably to remove disruptive patrons—and surveillance: "spooks" in "spook rooms" within the resorts who rely on technology, data, and expertise. Based on the CSI: *Crime Scene Investigation* TV series, the interactive exhibit at MGM assuages any anxieties we might have about living in a panopticon prison with the prospect of being a guard in it. As in those reality TV shows like *Survivor* and *American Idol* where audiences decide who stays and who goes, thereby enforcing normative behavior or aesthetics, MGM's "immersive, interactive forensic science exhibit" enlists participants to play a part in the repressive state apparatus by "becom[ing] a part of the CSI team," specifically by using surveillance and information technologies such as national databases and cameras to track and investigate hypothetical crimes. Depending on which of the three cases they choose, visitors might study footprints and other pieces of physical evidence, learn how to hack e-mails and access cell phone records, or otherwise play with "cutting edge technology straight from the crime lab."

This "cutting edge technology" relies on "real science" and "real science" equipment, ranging from lab standards like the microscope to "cell phone seizure kits," "DNA instrument systems," and "ballistics identification systems and bullet traps." In my own "experience," I studied a crime scene and pieces of physical evidence (bloody fingerprints on a beer bottle, the arrangement of a body in a car wreck) before retreating to several of the "state of the art crime labs" where I was made—literally: the MGM staff didn't want me to leave the exhibit without going through the motions—to analyze my data and finally report my findings by entering them in a computer, essentially by checking off options as though taking an online quiz. At one point, participants even stand in front of a camera and relate their conclusions to it, like inhabitants of a reality TV show speaking directly to viewers out of earshot of the rest of the clan; only in this case we speak to "Gil Grissom," "the enigmatic CSI head investigator" from the TV show. Grissom promptly appears on the monitor to thank me for my hard work and invite me to the gift shop, where, besides the usual coffee cups and T-shirts ("People Lie. Evidence Doesn't"), one can stock up on all sorts of surveillance and forensic souvenirs: syringe pens, CSI caution tape, CSI flip-flops with green toe prints, or a black CSI vest with a badge

and multiple pockets and pouches for keeping all of your crime scene gear within arm's reach. It all has the feel of The King's Ransom, the Elvis Presley museum at the Imperial Palace, where, among other things, we get a sense of Elvis's fascination with police paraphernalia: besides the guns (a .380 caliber Walter PPK semiautomatic pistol and an "EIG 38 special two-shot Derringer"), the collection includes the flashing blue light from a cruiser and Elvis's own personal Kel-Lite police-issued flashlight.

The emphasis on "realness," expertise, and science throughout the exhibit is calculated to convince schoolteachers trolling for possible field trips that CSI: The Experience is more educational than merely watching a TV episode. In fact, the promotional material makes this claim explicit, saying, "More brain processes are involved as you employ inductive reasoning, deductive logic, and trial and error to solve the mysteries and crack the case." We even get a diploma at the end. The exhibit makes a game of investigating crime, using surveillance to discover "the truth." As with The Gun Store, part of the attraction is actually doing something, rather than watching, in this case going through the motions of police work, though its connection to the TV show and the frequent references to it highlight the way the real is now experienced in relation to media or as an effect of it. Throughout CSI, video screens periodically flip on to reveal a clip from the show in which a character explains the forensic process; elsewhere, as with Grissom, actors address us directly in character. Because some of the videos are "never-before-seen footage of [our] favorite CSI characters" while others come "from real-life crime scene investigators and forensic analysts," the effect again is to blur the distinction between the two, though eventually one gets the feeling that the main point is to test our knowledge of the TV series, that, as the exhibit's website says, "what matters is that the exhibit stay true to the show." In fact, the "inductive reasoning and deductive logic" required to solve the cases at CSI: The Experience are so simple that it's difficult to believe that anyone ever fails. Perhaps this is the point: playing cop or believing that all your TV watching is good for something is offered as compensation for what we've lost at the slots or tables and to soothe our more general powerlessness and loss in the culture overall, especially at a time when those bodies formerly charged with protection and the public good subcontract these functions to private industry more interested in profit.

This lesson is general in Las Vegas, where the state's libertarian bent and the city's historic willingness to cede control for cash illustrate the effects of abandoning the social contract, while the Strip highlights the kinds of pleasures available to offset them. Nevada spends less per student in the pub-

lic schools than Mississippi and hovers perennially near the bottom of state rankings for health services. It has a high rate of unimmunized children and a low rate of Medicaid spending.[11] Its tax structure is regressive—heavy on sales, light on income—and Las Vegas collects no gambling or property taxes from the Strip. The homeless in town live in the storm drains under the casinos, and, off the Strip, flyers announce weekly foreclosure workshops for all those who moved to Vegas during the boom years of casino growth, attracted by the middle-class life made possible by good union jobs, and now find themselves cut back or out of work in "Foreclosure City."[12] More aid for the homeless comes from Washington than from state and local government, and the unions make up the rest: after 9/11 and the consequent decline in air travel and tourism to the region, Culinary Workers Local 226 set up a makeshift employment agency and food center in a tent outside the Stratosphere for laid-off casino workers.

Those not taken care of by the union may end up in the tank in a place where the prison population has grown faster than the population of the state as a whole. Nevada incarcerates its citizens at above-average rates—an astonishing 1,287 percent increase in prison occupancy between 1969 and 1999—while spending less than average to maintain them. Once inside, though, inmates have the opportunity to cultivate their skills through the state's partnership with private companies like Prison Industries, which "provides productive, compensated work" for them, such as in its mattress factory and bookbindery or its factory for producing "high performance sports car components for sale" or the "paint, body, and upholstery operation for the restoration of classic and historic autos," like the ones that end up on display in the Auto Collections in the Imperial Palace for perusal and possibly purchase by Vegas tourists. A lucky few prisoners may get to work on the Department of Corrections Ranch near the Carson River, where they will engage in milk, livestock, and hay production, though this may not involve ever actually leaving the prison since "a portion of this property also became the site of the Northern Nevada Correctional Center."[13] Perhaps eventually the Nevada Department of Corrections will figure out how to farm out prisoners to private firms as labor to monitor security cameras on the Strip.

Like the state overall, Las Vegas is a model of neoliberal government at the local level, happy to turn over public responsibilities to private enterprise: it recently closed its own public art museum, no longer able to support it or willing to compete with the Bellagio's Gallery of Fine Art or Steve Wynn's private collections. More famously, it accepted the resorts' proposal to build sidewalks and pedestrian bridges on their own dime, sacrificing in the process any claims to them as public property. The results were predictable: while convenient for avoiding car traffic on the Strip, the overhead walkways direct pedestrians from one casino to another so that they never encounter the actual street or the people on it, most obviously the rows of immigrant men handing out the calling cards of local prostitutes. In fact, simply crossing Las Vegas Boulevard can be time-consuming and difficult since it may require being routed through buildings or walking out of the way just to get to a place where you can access the walkways.

Once on the street, the distinction between public and private is muted. Signs for city bus stops, for example, are posted among the foliage in the private landscape installation. One night I walked from Paris all the way to Treasure Island not because I had misjudged the distance, as the visual cues famously encourage, but because I could not find the bus stop signs along the street. It was dark, but I still had to ask directions in the morning to make sure I could get out of the casino and to a stop close by so I wouldn't miss it again. Eventually, the guy on the street handing out girly cards let me know where to stand and then signaled when the bus was coming.

Within the casinos, a similar confusion of public and private is cultivated. As with malls, where the seemingly public street or sidewalk is marked by benches, fountains, skylights, and greenery, an illusory difference between public thoroughfares and the private property of the casino is maintained by differently patterned carpeted paths that wind among the slots and card tables so that parents with kids can get through the casino to the buffet, monorail, or shops. Slots are arranged as much as possible to create seemingly private nooks where patrons can curl up with a good machine, out of view of others, except, of course, for the cameras overhead. The impression of distinct public and private property is easier to maintain in a massive complex like the MGM Grand, simply by virtue of its size and apparent variety, though staying there will eventually begin to feel like being stuck for days in a permanent, endless airport, always between flights, with multiple hotels and condos, pools, shops, restaurants, nightclubs, and gaming rooms joined by a maze of moving sidewalks, escalators, elevators, skywalks, and monorails. Here differences between spaces are articulated as differences between consumer products or leisure purchases; it's the feeling of difference, variety, and choice rather than the fact of them in areas otherwise so devoid of organic or local features that anthropologists refer to them helpfully as "non-places."

I grant that some people like this, and many, including me, may like it in

small doses. As we take the moving sidewalks from our hotel to MGM's main area, passing through a boardwalk of shops that could have been in any better mall or airport, lights flashing and music blaring, my older daughter, Chloe, says, "It's exciting," but her sister is less sure: at six, Lily is more interested in the flora and fauna. While Chloe explored at great length our suite's various amenities, including a TV that rises out of a desk like something in a James Bond film, Lily wants only to play outside on the small balcony that looks out at McCarren Airport and the distant mountains. After she catches a moth that has found its way in, she carries it throughout the whole of MGM hoping to find a way outside so she can let it go. It dies before she can.

Indeed, finding the outside is not encouraged; I didn't walk on an actual city street other than the Strip until the third day of my first visit, when I left MGM early and headed out on foot to find a grocery store. It was a hike. I took a bus back—not the Deuce, which caters almost exclusively to tourists, but a real city bus that dropped me off at the corner of Tropicana and Las Vegas Boulevard along with a lot of uniformed people heading into MGM for work. Many of them glanced at my grocery bags with clear disapproval that I had gone out for breakfast supplies rather than bringing those kids down to the buffet for their $11 Rice Krispies and orange juice, sans tax and tip. Similarly, I promised the girls a trip to the amusement rides at Circus Circus for the last day, but the monorail took us only as far as the Las Vegas Hilton, so we had to walk the final half mile outside, past the noise and dust of workmen making street repairs. This is how you can tell the low-rent casinos or those that have fallen out of favor: to get to them, you have to cross the divide between the phony public space and the real thing, that is, by walking on an actual city street in the heat where you can see people working at something other than cards, food, sex, or booze.

It's more pleasant to stay inside, though eventually one may be forced to realize that as goes true public space, so go the rights exercised therein. This lesson was learned the hard way by casino employees when the Culinary Workers Union struck at MGM in 1993, and picketing workers were quickly escorted off the walkways close to the casino and directed down to the street below, effectively away from contact with anyone actually entering or leaving. Homeless activists marching on Fremont Street under the 1,500-foot LED canopy—the largest in the world, where the Fremont Street Experience plays nightly—were also told they were on private property even though the canopy tops a public street. The union and the activists eventually won in court, but the fact that free speech rights continue to be fought for underscores how tenuous they are. In 2010, the city, following the example first set by former president George W. Bush, proposed an ordinance establishing two twelve-by-one-hundred-foot "free expression zones" on the Third Street promenade, adjacent to the Fremont Street Mall.[14] While signs outside the casinos announce that the sidewalks are private property "upon which an easement has been granted to facilitate pedestrian movement," in fact "anyone found loitering or otherwise impeding pedestrian movement is subject to arrest for trespass."[15] In this, they echo the trend of recent law in redefining public space as essentially moving zones of privacy in which individuals have the right not to hear certain kinds of speech, rather than the right to express it.[16]

Most visitors in Vegas probably never notice or articulate concern about how their environment is controlled, just as they don't notice the disappearance of public spaces until they're shown the door or the absorption of civic functions into the private sphere until they actually need them. While the city simply wants to save the expense of erecting and maintaining public walkways, the casinos' rationale for privatizing ostensibly public space is convenience and safety, which are secured and maintained by creating spaces that are self-contained and constantly monitored. Eventually, visitors come to expect this kind of control, if not to demand it in the name of protection and security.

The effect, however, of the collapse of public space into private property and the colonization of the private by surveillance cameras is to make every place a potential csi crime scene and everyone in it a presumptive criminal. At this point, wanting to keep one's face out of the picture is by definition a threat to the safety of others. Moreover, while figured as an instrument of safety when used for surveillance, cameras are, at the same time, increasingly seen as a kind of weapon if put in the wrong hands, such as the hands of ordinary people on a public street. As police have become more comfortable drawing Tasers on citizens, states have enacted laws against photographing or videotaping on-duty police officers, while professional photographers and even tourists are now questioned by police or private security for taking pictures of prominent public buildings or sites because, like nail files on airplanes, the pictures might be used in a terrorist attack. One recent tsa poster features a man in a blue hoodie—the new signifier of danger—taking a picture at an airport; underneath him, the caption warns, "Don't let our planes get into the wrong hands."[17]

Both csi: The Experience and The Gun Store exploit our fear of crime and terrorism and the growing sense that, as the state reduces social services like the police or aid to the indigent or simply outsources these responsibilities to private companies for profit, we will have to defend ourselves. The csi ex-

hibit, however, captures more closely the fascination with technologies that conceive of security in terms of access to and control of information in a world where personal identity itself is increasingly seen as simply the accumulation of data encoded in systems where it can be measured, compared, and aggregated: the face displaced by the fingerprint, itself meaningful only in relation to the millions of other fingerprints on record, and even it now ceding authority to retinal scans, genetic markers, and other biometrics. This fascination is on display at the Elvis museum, where we can see Elvis's favorite "mermaid" costume still marked with blood from the B_{12} injections to his hip, meaning its significance is not that Elvis really liked dressing like a mermaid, or even that Elvis took B_{12} injections at all, but that the costume "holds the unique DNA of the greatest entertainer the world has ever known." There's also an X-ray showing a "rare detailed view of the most famous lungs to ever belt out a song in the history of music." The rare view shows that in the summer of 1973, Elvis had borderline pneumonia. Whatever else we might think of it, here the body is first evidence. As the CSI exhibit makes clear, all of that newfangled technology for examining fingerprints is useful only if the database has a large enough pool of prints against which to compare them. Throughout the exhibit, signs cite the famous observation of Edmond Locard, "the Sherlock Holmes of France," that "every contact leaves a trace." Though intended as a reminder to be thorough, it increasingly comes off as a threat, as though any inadvertent or unconscious gesture on our part simply adds to the store of data that eventually will be used against us.

This was also the case with TSA agent Tony, who can be "proactive" precisely because, as the poster says, he "has been armed with intelligence information" that gives him "situational awareness." Figuring intelligence as a weapon with which it arms its officers, the TSA signals the cultural shift away from guns to data and information as the key to security. Indeed, one TSA promotional video comforts fliers with the news that the appearance of their name on the Terrorist Watchlist will not constitute a problem since the TSA has enough data on all of us to filter out anyone unlikely to cause the kind of situation that gets Tony's attention. While the TSA posters have sometimes been objects of ridicule in the general public, perhaps especially among those whose names do not get filtered out of the Terrorist Watchlist, the accumulation and coordination of data about us is now routine, increasingly inseparable from our participation in everyday life, both public and private.

The most obvious instance of this accumulation of data is probably online browsing and shopping, where every click of the mouse adds to a database of consumer preferences, either my own or those of people like me in one way or another, as determined by the aggregating capabilities of the particular software. Thus, Amazon is able to suggest purchases for me based not only on my prior clicks but also on those of other women my age, with a comparable level of education or income, living in the same region of the country. While shopping at Amazon, I can also field a pitch from the pop-up ad for two nights at the Bellagio, which is being made to me "personally" ("Hello, Jane") because one day last November I spent an afternoon online booking hotel and airline reservations for a research trip to Las Vegas. If I read a newspaper article online, some software program at the *New York Times* immediately canvasses my past reading and lists other articles it has decided are "recommended" for me. Every item in my Netflix queue and every show I TiVo or DVR adds to the mother lode of data about me circulating online that can be collected, packaged and repackaged, sold and resold to other companies hoping to anticipate and customize products just for me. Similarly, pharmaceutical companies collect data on prescriptions made by physicians in order to target advertisements to specific doctors who are relying more heavily on competing drugs. Political parties employ microtargeting, gathering and analyzing data from multiple sources—consumer preferences, level of income and education, voting habits—to pinpoint who should be asked for contributions or driven to the polls and who should be left alone.

Meanwhile, all those "smart signs" that record and file away pictures of passersby are used by advertisers to tailor ads according to gender, age, and ethnicity by quickly examining the contours of individual faces and cross-referencing that information with data it has already collected about the consumer preferences of that demographic. This is similar to retail loyalty cards embedded with RFID chips that allow the store to enumerate purchases and, in turn, target ads or coupons to the holder, except that a smart ad gauges our reactions to whatever it shows us—how long we look, the expressions we make—collecting and storing that data so as to display a more effective ad for us next time.[18] In other words, as the catchy slogan of one digital signage company makes clear, Every Face Counts, whether you want it to or not.

Being targeted by digital signs is rather like gathering cookies all across the Internet simply by walking down the street with the significant difference that the person casually looking at an ad on a smart sign hasn't volunteered, even unwittingly, to participate. Indeed, not volunteering is one of the attractions of this stealth technology for companies like TruMedia offering Audience Measurement Solutions because the very lack of conscious viewer cooperation is more likely to produce accurate and unbiased information.[19] Perhaps this is why digital signage companies are reluctant to reveal the location of

smart signs, though avoiding a possible backlash or boycott is also possible. Boycotters will likely be a small and early minority, however, since most of us have already acclimated to public displays of surveillance and eventually will also get used to digital advertisements that adapt to us, no longer noticing when we're being watched, only registering at some level that we could be watched at any time.

Like signs that spy on us, web browsing, interacting on social media sites, and online shopping provide the market research someone else used to be paid to do and often the work as well. As Mark Andrejevik has argued persuasively, while the surveillance and data mining technologies justify themselves in terms of consumer safety and the promise of individuality and uniqueness, their purpose is the same as any other exploitation in the workplace: to maximize profit by promoting purchases by a consumer, who often doubles here as worker by adding even more value in the form of data to a product sold by and for someone else.[20] If my dress size, reading material, grocery list, and other data and preferences have no real value to me as commodities, that's only because I do not own or control the machinery or software necessary to make that data profitable. With a fast enough computer and access to other people's data, I might be able to profit from it too. This is an old story.

In Las Vegas, the new game in town is also data, millions of pieces of information gathered in multiple databases capable of searching and cross-referencing all of it. What is significant about Vegas security now is not the number of technologies spying on us, but the number of technologies that work together. As with the online economy, the data gathered in casinos is used to rationalize gambling and create new opportunities for selling more to players. Casinos need all that data on slots, for example, in order to meet but not exceed the 75 percent minimum return rate required by Nevada law. Digital networks connect the slot machines not just within one casino or even within Las Vegas, but across the country. Slots are programmed to the decimal point in order to achieve predetermined rates of return, and the same machine can be set to produce different payouts according to what the house needs to meet the rate. The house already knows how much it will make off each machine annually, which is probably why the primary manufacturer of slot machines, International Game Technology, prefers to give the casino a cut of the annual profits rather than sell the devices outright. When someone wins big anywhere, it is International Game Technology's people, possibly hundreds of miles away, who know first how much was won, in which state, in which casino, and on what machine. They maintain the machines and they pay the winners.[21] Because the slots are networked and progressive, it is possible to offer larger payouts than a coin slot ever could; the odds are also correspondingly worse. Bigger prizes are available because so many people across the country participate, and the bigger the payout, the more players will risk to win while playing at what still looks and sounds like an old-fashioned machine with spinning reels. Because the three or four spinning reels on the old machines suggested to players a lower number of possible combinations and better odds of winning than is actually the case, digital slots try to recreate the effect of a spinning reel when no such reel is actually needed in the new technology.

As in online shopping, however, the most valuable commodity is information about visitors themselves. The town's motto should be that what happens in Vegas stays in Vegas a really long time. Casinos collect information they don't yet have a use for, confident that eventually they will find a way to make money off it. Harrah's sets the standard for this; as one miscellaneous vice president put it, "At Harrah's, we love numbers a lot."[22] Player's cards double as daily journals of a player's movements, documenting every move like a debit card or E-ZPass. Data banking and analysis systems produce individual profiles based on personal data such as name, birthday, and address, which are then linked to records from hotel and restaurant purchases and casino losses and winnings. All those free meals and discounted rates, after all, are calculated by the house using data collected electronically and according to a prediction of how much it will eventually take in from a player's "wins," by which it means the house's wins and the player's losses. The goal is not just to concentrate gambling in one place, but to collect enough data on enough people in order to modify comps and other offers to the people most likely to drop money, a fact that helps clarify why so many of the people who design and manage these rewards programs were hired away from the credit card industry.

As with microtargeted ads, comps are based mainly on "predictive behavior," where information on what you've bought is used to try to direct future purchases. While reservations clerks at Disney World were allowed to discuss only three possible resort hotels for inquiring guests, with the goal of speeding up calls and maximizing efficiency, new technology allows the reservations desk at casino resorts to pull up customer data that will provide a "unique answer" to each request for rates and availability. At Harrah's, for example, that answer would be based on twenty years of information collected on the 44 million people in Harrah's database. Similarly, rewards cards decrease the need for traditional marketing and, like tailored and pop-up ads, the impersonality of the slot and video poker games is offset by the "uniqueness" of the treatment one receives, the personal attention to a particular player's individual needs or desires—Oh look, the floor manager brought me a drink! How did he know it's my birthday? And they provide a rationale for all those cameras, which exist, we are told, to protect not just the casino's assets but the guests' as well, though in fact, as we know from CSI: The Experience, cameras can't protect someone, only record and provide evidence after the fact.

To high rollers, rewards cards can be extremely valuable, so much so that some casinos are now attaching pictures and fingerprints to them, but one senses that, in the same way that people apply for a new credit card without entirely realizing how it will affect their credit rating or fill out online surveys without realizing they've doomed themselves to endless spam, others sign up for player's cards for the simplest of reasons, unaware of how even their breakfast choice contributes to the network. As we ride the Deuce in the morning, a retired Canadian couple, in town for twelve weeks every winter, debates where to eat. He wants ham steak at the Riviera, but she says no, they don't have a player's card there, as though unwilling to dine anywhere that didn't add to their total count. In other words, she treated the player's cards like store coupons or any other gimmick that brings us into the store or makes us feel special, as though buying something we don't particularly want or need is somehow a bargain.

Finally, all of the transactions recorded on rewards cards become a permanent feature in the city's digital infrastructure when it is sent to labs at places like Systems Research and Development Inc., which is funded by the CIA and already has on file other extensive data about casino employees and vendors. Systems Research and Development uses a system called NORA (Non-obvious Relationship Awareness) to identify "nonobvious" relations, such as shared phone numbers, credit card numbers, addresses, or emergency contacts that suggest possible collusion between dealers or other casino employees and players. This information can then be cross-referenced with the databases containing information on known suspicious types collected in the Surveillance Information Network. It's not accidental that these combined systems link tourist and employee data with the criminal histories of known cheats. In the same way that Homeland Security's data mining in phone and banking records requires treating everyone as possible terrorists in order to identify those who actually are, casino surveillance in the service of either profit or crime prevention works only if all casino guests and employees are considered potential thieves. In fact, a sure way to get your mug into the S.I.N. system is to win big or win often.

While limiting theft and maximizing profit are stated goals of those sur-veillance technology and data mining systems companies that cater to both Las Vegas casinos and the various federal security and intelligence agencies, including Homeland Security, these outfits also make explicit pitches for their products in terms of controlling labor. Biometrica's Visual Casino, for ex-ample, is a suite of integrated surveillance technologies that includes face recognition, membership in s.i.n. and other local and industry-wide data-bases, and digital recording equipment capable of inputting images into the databases from any camera on the premises. A chief selling point for Visual Casino, prominently featured in its promotional material, is that with it casi-nos are now capable of "turning surveillance into a profit center." It does this not just by avoiding losses through identifying card counters, but by reducing the number of people required to do the work of surveillance and the amount of time required to do it. Processes that were once "entirely manual," requiring hours of staff time, now take seconds, and the remaining work that still re-quires an actual human person has been regularized by Visual Casino's "inci-dent reporting software" and "daily log modules," designed to "organize and standardize all of your surveillance incident reporting."[23]

Similarly, SmartConnect, a "video-centric business intelligence service," assures clients, "transforming your surveillance department into a profit cen-ter is relatively simple and easy," and will "enhance surveillance profitability." It is more profitable because the new digital DVR system will allow casinos to eliminate the tapes it has to buy, change, review, and maintain, and thus reduce or reassign the people hired to do these tasks. Moreover, as casinos transition from analog to digital recording and storage, cameras will increas-ingly do the work of employees, who, instead of watching a suspicious bag or person, can simply highlight something on the screen and ask the software to report when it moves. In general, the next generation of technology will be more automated, such as cameras with built-in facial recognition software that work unattended, unlike actual workers, if positioned in places where people are likely to be looking one way while standing relatively still, such as at the bottom or top of escalators.

For new table game systems that track player bets, the goal is also less a matter of catching card counters than of reducing labor costs, pit bosses spe-cifically, who are among the highest-paid employees on the floor. As pro-motional materials for MindPlay helpfully point out, "The challenge was to bring factory-like automation and control to the action on a casino floor." In the same way that player's cards supplanted the pit boss's traditional role of granting comps, machines that gather and track players' data as they are playing will also do the work of floor and surveillance personnel, counting the chips and money, verifying correct payouts, warning the cage when the chip tray needs to be refilled, even calling upstairs to the surveillance department if a player's bets seem suspicious. Shuffle Master lists "Operating Savings" as a "Key Feature," second only to "Security." The savings are labor costs specifically: less pit supervision required; less dealer training required; fewer pit clerks required. One casino executive asks, "How many bosses do you see in the slot department? All you see are change girls and an occasional security guard," none of whom make as much money as a pit boss.[24] As with player's cards, wired game tables will be presented to players in terms of convenience and safety: as devices for guaranteeing against dealer error or house deceit as well as a way to ensure that they get all the comps they deserve without having to depend on the largess or whim of the pit bosses. Pit bosses, meanwhile, will be told that it will help them identify cheats when in fact it will identify cheats on its own faster and more efficiently, without the added burden of needing health care and retirement benefits.

Devices like SmartConnect have other uses, however, since eliminating casino personnel alone "does not make a surveillance department into a profit center." What does make it profitable is extending surveillance technology to the "many other department heads [within the resort] that traditionally don't receive the benefits of surveillance data," at which point "problem employees can be identified and documented thoroughly and efficiently." In the best Taylorist fashion, SmartConnect works by defining "'normal,' quantifiable operating procedures," which means, among other things, determining "how long . . . a cash register drawer [should] be open during a cash transaction," deciding "the acceptable number of voids per employee per shift," or knowing "that a discount or comp that is run up is actually given to the intended person," that is, the employee intended for the employee discount and not the "cashier's brother." The system will know whether any server in any restaurant receives an unusually large tip; in fact, it can retrieve data on all tips to search among them for anomalies. It can verify that bartenders are serving bottled beer but ringing up only bottled water. It knows whether the cashier gave the patron change for $10 when the patron gave her a $20.

Even more helpful, SmartConnect stores digital images from throughout the casino and integrates them with data from cash registers, thereby allowing casino owners "to index and save video clips with supporting documentation for risk management issues, internal boards of review, union grievances, and gaming enforcement agencies."[25] Those employees who do ever manage to get out of view of the cameras still carry ID cards with chips that can be read by monitors in the door frames, so that someone will always know when they take a break and for how long. Slot machines, of course, don't join unions.

The technology used by SmartConnect, Shuffle Master, and Visual Casino is the same as that used by online retailers, who adapted it from the military, which got it from Las Vegas, a place where the people in charge of casino promotions used to deal credit cards and where security chiefs are recruited from the FBI. Indeed, Biometrica Systems, the developer of Visual Casino, is owned by L-1 Identity Solutions, a company that develops surveillance and data software systems for federal, state, and commercial clients, as well as anyone else who wants to "ensure information superiority over our enemy." For prospective clients, the L-1 website provides a helpful list of the federal agencies from which it recruits its employees and consultants: these include the CIA, the NGA (also known as the NIMA), the FBI, the USSSS, the AFOSI, the INS, the ATF, and the DOS. L-1 Identity Solutions never explains these acronyms; apparently, anyone likely to be hired by L-1 or to hire them is already in the system. The system, meanwhile, is now so large that not even the secretary of defense can say how many agencies are involved in national security and intelligence, much less how many people, whom they report to or what they do, the information they gather, or the scope of their mission.[26]

Not to worry. As Bentham understood, the beauty of the panopticon is its efficiency: all the prisoners double as guards. On the Deuce, the couple in front of me remark to each other about the new building construction visible along the route from the Strip to Fremont Street. I point out, half to them, half to myself, that many of the sites are actually abandoned, probably because loans funding the construction had dried up. Now, half-built structures gape silently at the street, pavilions for prostitutes or anyone else abandoned by the neoliberal state. They are only one of the many visible signs in Las Vegas of how hard the city has been hit by globalization and the recession. In 2004, MGM shocked residents by selling the Golden Nugget and effectively signaling to everyone who lives and works downtown that the big Strip resorts were abandoning them for better gaming and hotel markets out of state. CityCenter, MGM's latest local project, almost died on the vine when funding collapsed in 2009, and Dubai World, its partner in this joint venture, sued for breach of contract. In its current troubles, the city again mirrors and models the financial collapse of the rest of the country. First built on Teamsters' pension funds, Las Vegas was then rebuilt on bad assets and suspicious financial "products"—the Mirage appropriately financed by junk bonds from Michael Milken—and its modern success is also fundamentally dependent on credit and financial technologies like the ATM machines that dot the casino floor

(in California they accept welfare cards) or the computer networks that allow me to charge food in one café to any of eight different hotels or to buy tickets for *Bodies . . . the Exhibition* at the Luxor or for Cirque du Soleil at Treasure Island from the concierge at the MGM Grand. The cashless economy of the casino extends to the Strip where, as in the larger world of global capital, one can move in and out of one or another hotel without ever leaving the boundaries of MGM Resorts International.

There's no exile in a unified world, as Debord says, and in Vegas it often feels that there really is no outside.[27] The resorts seem not to compete with each other anymore or to do so only jokingly. They all sell the same thing. As we watch the Siren show at Treasure Island, a sign overhead and across the street says that when we're tired of pirates we should come over to the Palazzo. While eating outside by The Cloud at Fashion Show Mall, we're surrounded by Jumbotrons for the Wynn. Still, the easy cash and credit are harder to come by now, and the contrast between glitz and reality can be jarring. In the enclosed pedestrian mall between Paris and Bally's, a sign invites us to Bally's adult show, *Jubilee*, where one can see "100,000s of rhinestones covering practically nothing," while nearby, the storefront at L'Art de Paris hawks jewelry at 80 percent off. Back on the Deuce to Fremont, the couple in front of me registers the implicit criticism in my remark about stalled construction on the Strip. Turning to look at me, the man points to the DriveCam at the front of the bus. "Be careful," he says, smiling. "They got you on the camera. They'll put you in jail."

Coda

There are drawbacks to thinking too much about surveillance: every day brings more news of it, so much, in fact, that eventually you don't know when to stop reading. Plus and, obviously, therefore, you become paranoid, which, as the old saw goes, doesn't mean they aren't really after you.

On the last night of my second research trip to Las Vegas, I lost my pink notebook, the one containing all of my pithy observations and trenchant analysis from four days on the Strip. I lost it in the Luxor, at some point between seeing *Bodies . . . the Exhibition* and getting a coffee in the food court. Since I hadn't even left the area when I realized it was gone, I retraced my steps in search of it, recruiting whoever I could as I went, until several Luxor employees were poking through trash cans and under booths for my benefit. We found nothing. I filed a report at the security desk downstairs in the casino but didn't get much encouragement. It was, after all, just a small spiral-bound flip pad of the kind that can be bought anywhere for 89 cents. No one really understood why it was valuable to me, only that I was desperate to get it back. I was crushed. Even the prospect of attending the Composers Showcase at the Liberace Museum later that night could not offset the loss of a week's worth of work I could never re-create.

Later, still hoping for a miracle, I called the Luxor and identified myself to the front desk as the person who had been looking for a little pink notebook in the trash. I was immediately put through to the Luxor's security manager. He was very interested in me. Was the notebook mine, he asked? Had anyone else read it? Who was with me? Was I still in Las Vegas and could I come back to the Luxor, preferably right now? I was so thrilled at the prospect of recovering my notebook that I didn't register that he never offered to return it.

At the Luxor, I went straight to security by the cage, and there he was, in his nondescript security-style suit, clearly waiting for me. He was nice, but deliberate. I still had no idea what was going on. I thought I was just picking up my research notes. As two women in thongs danced on a raised platform behind us, he queried me again about who I was and what I was doing in Las Vegas. Again he asked, was I alone and was the notebook mine? He made me describe its contents. Then, looking me over once more, apparently satisfied, he flipped the notebook open and began going through it. It wasn't the first time, for, as he skipped through the pages, I could see where he had dog-eared some and highlighted others in yellow: my observations on the number of casino personnel working the craps tables in Paris; descriptions of the placement of cameras in the Bellagio; information about Nevada prisons; the URL for L-1 Identity Solutions; cryptic notes on the Surveillance Information Network and *Washington Post* stories about Homeland Security; and, most ominously, the phone number and address of The Gun Store. "That one really got my attention," he told me. Indeed, it must have.

I pointed out the more innocuous stuff in my notes and appealed to his sense of humor. We discussed irony. I referenced my everyday, harmless appearance and tried to sound professorial. I told him Susan was writing about buffets. Finally, I said how great it was to meet someone in Las Vegas actually working in surveillance and could I interview him? Cameras clicked all around us. The meeting was over. Outside in the brisk January night, searching for a cab to get to the now-defunct Liberace Museum, I praised my good luck, clutching my own book of secrets close in the dark.

1. This is, in fact, how the machines are pitched in sales materials. The iTable, for example, boasts "an intuitive electronic betting interface" (to complement the actual living dealer) that enables the "integrated card and bet recognition functionality" to "instantaneously record a variety of crucial table game data points including actual win/loss and handle per player while providing accurate player ratings and skill analysis." "Shuffle Master, Inc. to Exhibit at the Global Gaming Expo (g2e), November 18–20, 2008," Business Wire, November 11, 2008, http://www.businesswire.com/news/home/20081111006450/en/Shuffle-Master-Exhibit-Global-Gaming-Expo-G2E. The iTable is produced by Bally Technologies and described on their website at https://www.ballytech.com/Table-Products/Electronic-Tables/i-Table (accessed January 5, 2015).

2. Joshua Clover makes this observation about Reeves as the ideal actor for Neo in *The Matrix* (London: BFI, 2004), 19–23.

3. "Google Releases Very High Resolution Imagery for Las Vegas," Google Earth Blog, March 31, 2006, http://www.gearthblog.com/blog/archives/2006/03/google_re leases.html.

4. Sometimes, this can backfire, such as when BP attempted to convince the country of its competence in fixing the Deep Water Horizon rig by releasing a picture of its Houston command center. In it, company engineers stand watch before a panel of six screens, each running continuous feeds of various views of the disaster, as though watching oil gush into the Gulf from several discrete angles constituted actually doing something about it. Later it was revealed that at least two of the six screens had been blank in the original photo and were doctored in the released image in order to avoid the suggestion that, at least some of the time, the BP guys were staring into space. See also Beatriz Colomina's discussion of Charles and Ray Eames's multiscreen presentation *Glimpses of the USA*, at the Moscow World's Fair in 1959, "Enclosed by Images: Architecture in the Post-Sputnik Age," in *CTRL[SPACE]: Rhetorics of Surveillance from Bentham to 9/11*, ed. Thomas Y. Levin, Ursula Frohne, and Peter Weibel (Cambridge, MA: MIT Press, 2002), 323–37.

5. David Banash reports that *Survivor*, an early reality TV show, had its highest ratings in households with incomes over $80,000 and lowest with those under $30,000. Perhaps those at the lower end of the spectrum never saw the fun in a "corporatist allegory of ruthless competition in the face of total surveillance" disguised as a contest designed to reward the person best able to "survive" by getting along with the group "without giving in to pesky emotions or critical judgments about the company's overall means or ends." David Banash, "Selling Surveillance, Anonymity and VTV," *Postmodern Culture* 11, no. 1 (2000): n.p.

6. Alison Clarke, "Sweet Dreams™ Security: Aesthetics for the Paranoid Home," *Home Cultures* 3, no. 2 (2006): 191–93.

7. Gregg Keizer, "Pennsylvania Schools Spying on Students Using Laptop Webcams, Claims Lawsuit," *Computer World*, February 18, 2010, http://www.computerworld.com /s/article/9158818.

8. "Border Crossing Cards," U.S. Visas, U.S. Department of State, Bureau of Con-

sular Affairs, http://travel.state.gov/content/visas/english/visit/border-crossing-card
.html (accessed January 3, 2015).

9. Workplace examples are taken from Chris Parenti, *The Soft Cage: Surveillance in America from Slavery to the War on Terror* (New York: Basic Books, 2003), 131–47.

10. Daniel Nasaw, "FBI Using Facebook in Fight against Crime," *Guardian*, March 16, 2010, http://www.guardian.co.uk/world/2010/mar/16/fbi-facebook-crime-study; http://www.facebook.com/FBI.

11. The numbers are for 2012. America's Health Rankings, http://www.americas healthrankings.org (accessed May 24, 2013).

12. See Matthew O'Brian, *Beneath the Neon: Life and Death in the Tunnels of Las Vegas* (Las Vegas: Huntington Press, 2007), for an exploration of Las Vegas's homeless living underground.

13. The growth in Nevada's incarceration rate is even faster than the national figures, which show only a 500 percent increase over the past thirty years. Quotations are taken from State of Nevada, Department of Corrections, http://www.doc.nv.gov (accessed May 21, 2013). Statistics are gathered from there, the National Institute of Corrections, http://nicic.gov (accessed May 21, 2013), and the Sentencing Project, http://www .sentencingproject.org (accessed May 21, 2013).

14. Alan Choate, "Fremont Street 'Free Expression Zones' on Hold," *Las Vegas Review-Journal*, July 17, 2010, http://www.reviewjournal.com/news/fremont-street-free -expression-zones-hold.

15. Quoted in Rebecca Solnit, *Wanderlust: A History of Walking* (New York: Viking, 2000), 284.

16. Don Mitchell, "The SUV Model of Citizenship: Floating Bubbles, Buffer Zones, and the Rise of the 'Purely Atomic' Individual," *Political Geography* 24 (2005): 78–79.

17. David W. Dunlap, "'Step Away from the Camera!,'" *New York Times*, July 28, 2010, http://lens.blogs.nytimes.com/2010/07/28/behind-47/?hp&_r=0. Carlos Miller, "TSA Publishes New Posters Depicting Photographers as Terrorists," *PINAC*, September 7, 2010, http://photographyisnotacrime.com/2010/09/tsa-publishes-new-posters -depicting-photographers-as-terrorists/.

18. "Ads Will Be Able to Watch Consumer," CNN, July 17, 2010, http://www.cnn.com /video/data/2.0/video/tech/2010/07/17/pkg.lah.ads.eyes.cnn.html.

19. TruMedia, http://www.tru-media.com/ (accessed May 28, 2013).

20. See Mark Andrejevic, *Reality TV: The Work of Being Watched* (Lanham, MD: Rowman and Littlefield, 2003), especially chapter 2, "The Promise of the Digital Revolution," 23–60.

21. Marc Cooper, *The Last Honest Place in America: Paradise and Perdition in the New Las Vegas* (New York: Avalon, 2004), 116–17.

22. Quoted in Cooper, *The Last Honest Place in America*, 130.

23. Quoted passages are taken from product brochures for L-1 Identity Systems' Biometrica Gaming Solutions, "Enhancing Casino Intelligence" and "Biometrica Visual Casino Helps the Stratosphere Hotel and Casino Protect Assets," http://www.biomet rica.com (accessed May 29, 2013).

24. Arnold Snyder, "Bye Bye Pit Boss: Here Comes Mindplay," *Blackjack Forum* 23, no. 1 (2003), http://www.blackjackforumonline.com/content/Mindplay.htm.

25. Quoted passages about SmartConnect are taken from Claudia Winkler and Nancy Ziolkowski, "Put Profit under (and into) Surveillance," *Casino Enterprise Management*, November 2004. This article is no longer archived on the trade journal's website. In 2013, SmartConnect filed for Chapter 7 bankruptcy and subsequently reemerged as eConnect, offering "Loss Prevention through Video Business Intelligence" not just to casinos, bars, and restaurants, but now also to hotels, airports, retail stores and malls, and stadiums and other amusement sites. https://www.econnectglobal.com (accessed December 2014).

26. A three-part story in the *Washington Post* describes "an alternative geography of the United States" that is home to the 845,000 people holding top-secret security clearances working on national security, surveillance, and intelligence for one of the hundreds of private corporations who've been contracted by the federal government and whose operations are now indistinguishable from it. Of those 845,000 people, 265,000 work in 1,931 private companies contracted by the federal government. According to the *Post*, "Private firms have become so thoroughly entwined with the government's most sensitive activities that without them important military and intelligence missions would have to cease or would be jeopardized." Three articles by Dana Priest and William M. Arkin appearing in the *Washington Post*: "A Hidden World, Growing beyond Control," July 19, 2010; "National Security, Inc.," July 20, 2010; and "The Secrets Next Door," July 21, 2010.

27. Guy Debord, *Panegeric*, vol. 1, trans. James Brook (London: Verso, 1991), 47.

FOUR

sH$_2$Ow

"Water: one dollar! Water: one dollar! Water!" calls a man on the overpass connecting Caesars Palace to the Bellagio.* His voice is matched by those of other men and women selling bottled water. They catch the tourists as they ascend the escalators or pass through the rotating doors from the retail complex of the hotel-casino. The often Latino water sellers with their red and blue ice coolers are a habitual feature of the obscured bridges, corners, and turns of the Las Vegas Strip. I've encountered as many as six sellers at a time lining a single archway. On one day during a visit to the city, on which temperatures on the Strip reached 113 degrees and tourists complained about the soles of their shoes melting in contact with the hot pavement, the water sellers provided an essential service. The cheap necessity physically enables tourism in the dry hot environment, allowing visitors to see more and keep going. Like the elemental goods they sell, these laborers are at the most basic level of the workforce. As they wave a bottle of water in one hand and hold a folded wad

---

* Stacy M. Jameson

of one dollar bills in the other—like the stripper or the waitress—the sellers' livelihood is piecemeal. Yet, at the same time, their assets are liquid.

Occasionally, these sellers are flanked by vendors hawking knockoffs of designer watches or sunglasses—street goods typical of other urban pedestrian zones. But in this town the water vendors and their product are unique. Their goods remain elemental; not once have I seen sellers of sports drinks, sodas, or the alcoholic fare typically sold in the bars and restaurants of the Strip. Instead, Vegas, with its distinct geographic, political, and social structure, engenders the black-market sale specifically of water. Here, in this urban entertainment metropolis in the desert where water equals power and privilege, the illicit street product is Aquafina and Arrowhead.

I watch one day as a younger Latino man wheels a dolly along the courtyard of Caesars Palace, taking the elevator up to the overpass. On the dolly is a package of water bottles bought in bulk and wrapped like contraband in a black plastic garbage bag. His cautious looks over his shoulder and the fast pace of his determined walk stand out amid the typical demeanor of carefree vacationing pedestrians. Are these workers illegals, or merely rendered such by the context? They move outside of the legal and economic structures of the city, trading in the taboo. At the same time, however, the vendors I have seen are not completely without agency, as this restocking service attests. The young man delivers the water to more than one of the seemingly individual sellers on the same overpass. They appear to operate as a cohesive organized unit and subvert the regulatory structures in place. This more hidden and illegal organization of trade in water is indicative of meanings enacted around the resource across every stratum of Vegas society. Water is both "liquid gold" and at the same time a basic necessity—a complexity that has the effect of making status and privilege appear natural.

Water dominates Las Vegas politics and the popular mythology of the resort destination in addition to being a central component of the built environment: the city's pools with swim-up poker and bars, the fountains and waterfalls that decorate most hotel-casinos, and the entertainments with dancing wet bodies both human and animal. Water plays a role in every level of Vegas life, from that marvel of civil engineering, the Hoover Dam, which makes the city viable, to the aquatic theaters that stun audiences with performances of diving, acrobatics, and synchronized swimming. These two elements—water infrastructure and entertainment practice—are often oversimplified and condensed into a wholly environmental debate. Indeed, the logics of a prominent city built in the country's driest state—incidentally a fundamental compo-

nent of the city's oasis mystique—is certainly troubling from the perspective of the sustainability of natural resources and ought to be discussed as such. And yet, the story of water that I *see* as a visitor to Las Vegas is always more than the environmental politics. Indeed, the very questions of sustainability and environmental politics are structurally obscured for the visiting tourist in favor of a carnival-like water exhibition.

"Sin City encourages irresponsible behavior about everything from sex to water," argues Robert Glennon, author of *Unquenchable: America's Water Crisis and What to Do about It*. Las Vegas, defined by its opulence and extravagance, seems to be an extreme case rather than one reflecting America's own future. Yet, as Glennon suggests, the city reflects many of the ecological concerns becoming evident across the country while further modeling some expensive and controversial solutions to water resource depletion.[1] However, the water story has another aspect, one for which Las Vegas is also the harbinger: the high-tech liquid display.

This fundamental and elemental substance is vacated of its use value in Las Vegas culture (for this touches too closely upon those pesky resource problems), and instead water becomes glorified for its sign value. Examples of water in the gaming city—the fountains, the drinks, the hotel baths, and the swimming pools—mark moments of transformation when biological necessity becomes its opposite: a sign of leisure, entertainment, and luxury. Indeed, it is a new channel of mass media, technologically enhanced and controlled for maximum visual appeal. What do we make of an everyday need in a context so keen on diverting our attention from the quotidian? H_2O is a complex component of both social and cultural spheres that defines itself through a series of tensions, first between water as the stuff of both mundane need and consumerist spectacle, and then between the ways in which this basic elemental substance marks a difference between leisure and employment, hotel-casino and resident, and a social stratification of workers.

Despite the advent of designer water and vitamin water, which marks a commodification and privatization of water on one level, the basic substance for the most part lacks the status in American consumer culture associated with, for example, wine or even soda. Water is a workout drink, a necessity. It is praised when it is clear and tasteless, in contrast to drinks we explore for aroma, mouthfeel, and flavors in tasting, or those we treat ourselves to as an indulgence. Imagine visitors to the Las Vegas Coca-Cola Store paying for a chance to sample water from around the world, instead of the international sodas featured in the Coke tasting parlor. Such a thought instead invokes troubling security, health, and often racist anxieties over cleanliness and purity. Or imagine diners at the upscale restaurant Aureole—with its prominent forty-two-foot glass-enclosed wine tower serviced by "wine angels" dangling from rappelling ropes—instead swooshing and swirling glasses of *agua*. Would a buffet be a buffet if the abundance and variety of drinks on offer were differing brands of water? No, water is the consummate ingredient rather than a product in its own right. It is the base substance behind the scenes. And yet, in western drought culture, water has a unique and contentious status as "liquid gold"—a label, we shall see, that is reserved for particular water purposes, where drinking is not included.

In Las Vegas and the desert environs, tourists are reminded in restaurants that a drink of water must be requested. Even a virtual teetotaler like me hesitates to ask for something as simple as a glass of water when those casino barmaids pass among the slot machines with their calls of "Drinks?" Though fountains outside put on a show of water dripping, spilling, spraying, I am at times hard pressed to locate a water fountain intended for actual consumption. Rather, water is an exhibition. "Water, water, everywhere / Nor any drop to drink," I recall one day while walking alongside the dancing Bellagio fountain. This phrase from the poem "The Rime of the Ancient Mariner" by Samuel Taylor Coleridge is so easily refashioned in this capitalist context. On that July day in Vegas with temperatures reaching well into triple digits, the driver of the Deuce, the tourist bus that plies the Strip, offered passengers a safety tip that highlights the common paradox between mundane and indulgence, accessibility and privilege invoked by the drink: "I know those drinks at the casino are free," she says, but with temperatures expected to hit 113 degrees by 1:30, "avoid heat stroke by drinking lots of water." In a town where alcohol consumption is continuously promoted, indulged in, and flaunted—tourists walking the streets sporting their colorful oversized souvenir drink cups with their abundant alcohol filler—water is conversely the drink that is regulated.

The elemental substance is refracted through Sin City activities as consummate entertainment commodity. It is separated from the history and politics of its production, and its essential function as physical necessity is obscured. In this way visitors are actively insulated from the costs of their leisure. In the traditions of the city's many magic shows, engineering, politics, and design produce a sleight of hand for the tourist who is invested only in the immediate moment.

When I asked the Bellagio concierge about the source and the history of the casino pool and fountain display, this hotel service provider was at a loss to find me information beyond entertainment value and show times. The water spectacle appears without origin, and its value is disconnected from a sense of cost. Indeed, the Fountains of Bellagio top most lists of "free" shows and attractions in the city. Referred to by Steven Spielberg as the greatest piece of public entertainment on earth,[2] the fountains wave, rocket, and dance for all accompanied by patriotic, classical, and Broadway tunes. The reoccurring, free public display in which water shoots forth and falls back into the abundant pool perpetuates an image seemingly without labor or expense. Throughout Las Vegas, water features, landscapes, and shows like the Bellagio fountains are supported by an invisible infrastructure—digital, mechanical, physical, environmental, and political—all of it paradoxically erased by the clear liquid that we perceive as pure spectacle. It is the very unseen nature of the infrastructure and expense that generates a citywide illusion of aqua bounty.[3]

Hundreds of years ago, natural springs are what made the valley in which the city now rests a popular way station, first for native peoples and later white scouts, travelers, and settlers. Indeed, the name itself, Las Vegas, is Spanish for "the meadows," drawing attention to the area as an oasis of life in contrast to the harsh desert surroundings. In both history and popular mythology the locale is touted as a refuge, watering hole, and sanctuary from the dry and inhospitable environs. Fast-forward to the Las Vegas of today, where this narrative is turned on its head in at least one prominent respect. The palm trees and pools and landscapes outside many casinos reflect the imagery of a cartoon haven in the desert—typically a mirage on the horizon too good to be true when seen from the perspective of the inhospitable, stark desert context. However, it is the desert itself that the city projects (for the visitor at least) as a mirage.

The dry heat and sun are the only evidences of the actual desert landscape, which is barely visible from the Strip, and even these are made distant for the tourist by climate control (you cannot open the hotel windows even if you would like to). By contrast, the open doors of bars, shops, and casinos leak mechanically generated cool air out of the buildings and onto pedestrians walking the Strip. Misting fans set up by the outdoor shops at the entrance to Harrah's perpetuate the illusion of another climate zone. Taking a trip up to the viewing area of the Stratosphere, I see the desert visibly stretching in each direction, but behind glass, "over there," accessible only via coin-operated binoculars. The dry, desolate landscape becomes a view, not a destination; a tableau, not a reality. Similarly, the water politics of the city are distanced; a concern for political pundits rather than the material concern for visiting tourists, who are offered instead the image of water abundance without consequence. That past image of refuge from the desert seems to run counter to

the tourist destination's image as a break from necessity, a place of luxury and excess, not survival.

The landscape of the city interior is managed to appear rich and bountiful in contrast to the surrounding environment. The themes of the hotel-casinos are not the only thing brought into Vegas. The Strip perpetuates a culture of what ecologists term "imported landscapes." Rather than an arid or marginally fertile landscape, the desert becomes instead a sort of blank canvas onto which the copied, "better" environments are constructed. You would be hard pressed to find the drought-resistant foliage and rock gardens encouraged in Las Vegas neighborhoods within the city center. Instead, the image of water abundance is central to the architecture and display fashioned by the more luxurious of resort hotel-casinos and shopping centers. Bellagio's pool and courtyard plantings—featuring Italian cypress and olive trees—construct a Mediterranean villa, not the American Southwest. While local residents are encouraged to go "indigenous" with low-water-use zeroscaping, the Vegas Strip instead cultivates a more lush, upscale, resort atmosphere.[4]

Traversing the walkway along the edge of the Bellagio Lake, a man remarks to a woman I assume to be his wife, "See? That's the kind of water I expected them to have at Treasure Island." Water is central to both the conceptualization and the actualization of the illusion of place created by the major casinos. Like the real-life resort locations of which the casinos are made representative—Italy's lakeside Bellagio, the canals of Venice, Indonesian seaside Mandalay Bay—the hotels are based on themes that are predominantly water related. When choosing a place to visit, the tourist can opt for a range of watery getaways including the ocean islands of the Caribbean, the desert oasis of the Mirage, or the beach paradise of the Flamingo. Each of these spaces is marked by its distinction from the local Nevada scenery constructed via watery grottos, falls, and pools.

As Las Vegas evolves with new and renovated casinos with new owners, the arid desert is increasingly banished from the Strip. Consider the closing of the Sahara resort in May 2011. A popular hot spot for celebrities when it opened in the 1950s, this Moroccan-themed "jewel of the desert," as the original owner proclaimed it, was at odds with the prominent contemporary Las Vegas aura.[5] A few years before its closing, another desert-themed hotel-casino underwent its own transformation, following similar claims that the desert-themed resort was not economically viable. The historic Aladdin that played host to the wedding of Elvis and Priscilla became the new Planet Hollywood Resort and Casino in 2007, thus shedding its Arabian Nights theme in favor of so-called LA sophistication. Central to the makeover was the conversion of the now

Miracle Mile Shops. Once called Desert Passage, invoking the Middle Eastern theme of the former resort, the upscale mall has undergone a face-lift after sluggish sales following the 9/11 attacks caused the developers to sell the property. Instead the shopping center now has a high-tech, new media exterior of LED signage and electronic billboards that gives the feel of New York City's Times Square. Yet another signal of the death of its desert identity is found in its interior: a multimillion-dollar water feature that constructs an indoor rainstorm. This indoor fountain entertains with color-changing fog, fifty-foot water spires, and light and music accompaniment. In light of such closures and makeovers, it is clear that the desert (particularly when associated with the Middle East) is not such a trendy place to visit, stay, or shop.

When the city imports its water and its landscapes, the process is never just about aesthetics, design, or style, but has real, lasting physical consequences—often greater in other places and for other people invisible to the urban tourist. The most recent effort to keep up with water demand in the gaming capital is a proposal adamantly supported by the Southern Nevada Water Authority for a pipeline that would draw groundwater from the water-rich ranching and agricultural lands of the Snake and Spring valleys, over two hundred miles north of the city. Indeed, millions of dollars have already been spent buying up ranches and water rights in these areas, with the hopes of transporting over 90,000 acre-feet of water back to Las Vegas through the proposed $2 billion pipeline. The local environmental impact of such a process is much debated, but antagonists to the plan turn to examples such as the Owens River valley in California: a lush landscape until the aquifer was used to provide water to the city of Los Angeles, leaving behind an arid desert. Along with the transfer of ecological and agricultural vigor from one location to another, the Owens valley further draws attention to the scaffolding of power and wealth behind the water diversion, where city insiders made millions on newly purchased and newly watered San Fernando Valley real estate.[6] Thus, pulling water from regional aquifers does not just relocate the liquid resource but can drastically alter the remaining flora and fauna and impact the structures of local businesses and everyday life in regional communities.[7] Consider, then, the reality behind the notion of banishing the desert to someplace else. The Southern Nevada Water Authority and Las Vegas gaming businesses argue that excessive water use on the Strip is a misconception—that features and facilities are quite water efficient (a valid though by no means innocent claim I address later). And yet the illusion of the city, as it is constructed through its fountains and pools, departs from the long-standing material reality of water scarcity and depends upon increasingly aggressive future proposals for resource relocation, including one to draw water from the Mississippi River to be transported across several states. Behind the fun of a visit to Las Vegas, then, is a politics of thirst that stretches back decades.

The damming of water and its reallocation to growing U.S. urban centers, swimming pools, and golf courses is tied to questions of nationalism, class, and ethnicity. The allocation of water from the Colorado River to the region including Las Vegas has not technically changed since 1922, when then commerce secretary Herbert Hoover met with representatives from seven states to apportion river water to states along the river's path. With its small population of around 4,000 residents, the state of Nevada was allocated 300,000 acre-feet, or about 2 percent of the Colorado's resources.[8] This and later allocations of water perpetuate a literal trickle-down economic and social structure that leaves little for those at the end of the stream. The pleasures of the gaming city are tied to the structures and people at the other end of the river, where the water resources controlled by government officials and power companies enact not only a geographic but a social structure of partiality. The twenty-first-century international issue of water scarcity is producing what journalist Steven Solomon refers to as the "freshwater fault line" between the water haves and have-nots.[9] Certainly, water resources are impacted by other things—drought conditions and climate change can both affect the runoff from the mountain glaciers that feed the Colorado River—and not just by increased demand of western desert cities. However, there is a clear process of cultural and social differentiation in the allocation to, and use of water by, western cities and tourist entertainment centers rather than, and to the detriment of, our southern neighbor Mexico or peoples such as the Cocopah Indians, who have survived and built their cultural and religious traditions around the Colorado River for centuries.[10] The relocation and allocation of elemental resources to Vegas is in part a process of culture partiality that privileges tourism, gaming, and entertainment over other ways of life. As former Arizona water official Rita Maguire puts it, "They have more money than water . . . and they're using the money to bring more water."[11]

Other peoples and places downriver, on the other side of a proposed pipeline, or even in the residential neighborhood out of walking distance from the Strip, are out of both the sight and the mind of the Las Vegas tourist, who is stimulated by extensive and varied water spectacles at each hotel-casino. A range of water features line the Strip, forming the contexts and focus of leisure in Vegas. The manufactured Fountains of Bellagio are like the Yellowstone geyser Old Faithful, reliable in their adherence to a schedule. The lake begins to spray and dance to music every half hour during the day and every fifteen minutes in the evening, presenting its choreographed five-to-seven-minute display to passersby on the Strip who crowd along the railing of the lake to watch. The water performs in sync with the tolls of the Bellagio belltower and in step with the chosen music. Though the water spectacles vary with the music, their arrangement and calculability make water something to count on — a reliable substance that does not disappoint.

On my last visit, over the busy winter holiday break, I watched the fountains dance to Michael Jackson's "Billie Jean." Is it just me, or does the watery spray look like the pop idol? Each showing is choreographed to be unique; in this case the "shooters" seem to reproduce the singer's characteristic dancing posture and moonwalk. The spray enacts its own popping dance motion, appearing to lift up on its "toes" till the stream cuts off and seems to freeze or hang for a second in midair before resuming its Jacksonesque dance. The water feature is anthropomorphic, appearing to exhibit the qualities of human bodies, in this case reifying the seemingly inimitable now-departed performer. Such an association is not neutral, as Jane Desmond teaches us in *Staging Tourism*. The display and performance of bodies is a mainstay of tourist industries (both cultural and animal tourism). According to Desmond, spectacles of corporality in these contexts structure categories of identity; displays of bodies, from hula dancers in Hawaii to Shamu at SeaWorld, stage the "them" and by contradistinction stage the "us."[12] In this case the question is about seeing our relationships to nature versus culture. On one hand, we have a reassurance of human supremacy in the knowledge that even a fluid body of water can be tamed and trained to perform. The natural attributes are managed and manufactured, represented every day on schedule. Moreover, this is not merely the action and gimmicks of a seal at an aquarium, clapping or spinning in the water; the watery bodies in the Bellagio fountain at times quite literally become ballerinas, aestheticizing nature through the construction of symmetrical designs, graceful movement, and geometrical patterns.[13] The bodies at the end of the dance return to the Bellagio Lake, which is apparently unchanged by the show. This formula adheres to the necessity of ecotourism, which demands the boundaries between nature and culture must ultimately be reinstated, suggesting our own tourist "bodily presence as absence, our unobtrusive intrusion."[14] When the liquid facsimile of Jackson returns to the lake, we are offered assurance both of nature's consistency and of our ultimate control over it.

The Bellagio fountain is a watery example of mechanical reproduction. As Walter Benjamin describes the change with respect to art in the era of photography and film, consider here the refashioning of the seemingly fluid,

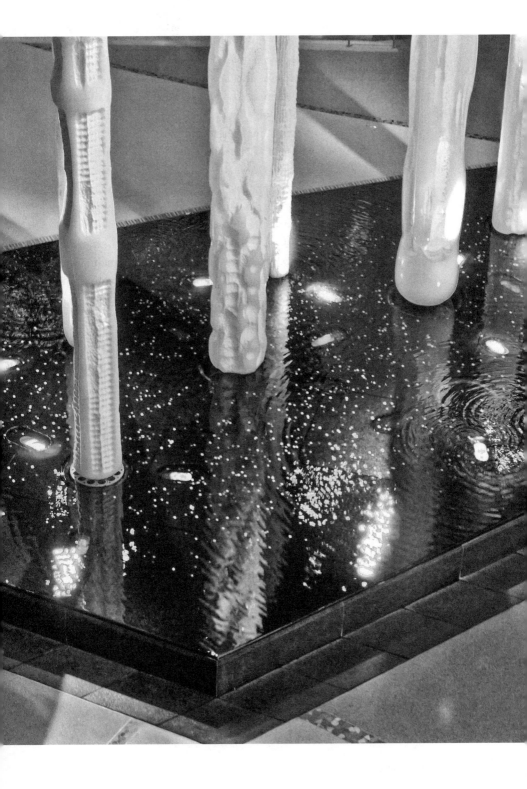

insoluble natural resource removed from its ecological context and instead mediated by entertainment technology.[15] Water, as exemplified in Las Vegas spectacles, is a new vector of mass media society, and when we consume these watery entertainments we are always already engaging in a wide-scale network of H_2O businesses, technologies, and new modes of social communication. The Bellagio fountains were the first, and most famous, of what has become a recent wave of high-tech water features in the city that has changed the face, but also the behind-the-scenes infrastructure, of the Strip. "I love watching the fountains," says a woman as we pass the Bellagio on the Deuce. "They are so relaxing." As hypnotic and calming as they can be, they are driven by a range of high-tech robotics and computer engineering with often militarized language. This isn't just a fountain but a sophisticated next generation of cannons, lasers, and shooters.[16] Lest we think that the dancing sprays across Vegas are simply graceful, peaceful, public installations, consider the introductory quote of the fountain's creator presented on the design firm's web page: "I know the secret of turning tap water into cold hard cash. Click on me to read more."[17]

The vast majority of the recent water marvels on the Strip were designed by WET (Water Entertainment Technology) Design, a Los Angeles–based firm opened in 1983 by former Walt Disney Company Imagineer Mark Fuller. Throughout his educational and professional tenure, Fuller has worked to develop new technologies to control water flow that are specifically applied in the service of entertainment and fantasy. For example, Fuller's extensive and groundbreaking research during his college and graduate school years into laminar stream nozzles was applied precisely to create special effects experiences such as the arching water Leapfrog feature at Disney World's Epcot Center.[18] At WET, Fuller matches his knowledge with that of creative thinkers who are not only civil engineers but also animators and artists, filmmakers and choreographers. Las Vegas is the epicenter of the company's work, condensing the largest grouping of water designs not only in the same city but on the same street, not to bring water to the needy but to provide an H_2O show for consumers and tourists. The webpage for WET Design declares the company's response to the increasingly digital era with a focus on the "authenticity of real human connection," the senses and the emotions. For example, WET's reimagining of the volcano feature at Mirage was intended to offer not merely an iconic spectacle but a "primal experience." The company created 120 trademarked Fireshooters to combine choreographed fireballs with red-lit water above the three-acre lagoon. The music for the show was designed by Grateful Dead drummer Mickey Hart, who, along with tabla master Zakir

Hussain, studied the rhythms and mythologies of volcanoes to set the tone for the water-fire dance. The medium is powerful as a mode of mass communication in large part because of these references to primitive nature, the natural resource at the center of the spectacle. Indeed, advertising for WET Design, as well as repeated press release quotes from Fuller, are quick to note that the company does not create simple water fountains as we may understand them. Instead, the company presents itself as a mass medium where technology meets showbiz. "We're in the emotions business," says Fuller. "We make experiences that draw people in, that make them stay longer and that make them want to come back more often."[19] Irrespective of geographic or environmental limits, water features such as the Mirage volcano or the many airport and shopping mall water designs by WET situated across the globe are, like other mass media outlets, geared toward large anonymous audiences and seek to engage them in ways that encourage social or economic actions.

In addition to the many chances to watch water on show, there are abundant opportunities throughout Las Vegas to actually get wet. My boyfriend Chris and I found ourselves following a sign toward "Liquid" one day while meandering through the hotel-casino Aria at CityCenter. Reminding me once again that this is a very different consumer experience from actual water consumption, the overhead signs ended at the door to the pool. We could do a study of swimming pools in Las Vegas—they are plentiful and diverse. While the pool at the Imperial Palace is rectangular and exposed, the swimming spaces at the Tropicana cover almost two acres and offer curved, secluded inlets with lush landscaping and even a separate adults-only smaller pool. More than swimming, many of these pools allow visitors to splash in waterfalls or waves (such as the ocean-mimicking wave pool at the Mandalay Bay). But pools are not just about submersion in the wet; pools provide channels for wide-ranging consumer activities from food and drinks to swim-up poker—lest our relaxation time detract from our spending.

These water engagements take many forms and encourage different degrees of contact with water and various levels of personal control. At the other end of the spectrum from the swimming pool is the splash zone indicated on the seating chart of Le Rêve theater. As I found out on a different trip to Vegas, the performers of this aquatic acrobatics spectacle demand that you be more than a distanced observer to the show. The movements of the performers in and out of the pool, or the swimming bodies being pulled above you on a trapeze, spray audience members in the front rows, like me and my mom, physically engaging us in the show.

The newly constructed resort CityCenter offers several new WET water features. In the mall, shoppers of all ages weave in and out of plastic tubes of water vortexes set into the floor at varying heights and angles. Passersby brush and rub the surfaces of the tubes, as if causing the water funnel clouds to spin more vigorously and grow in height. As one visitor comments, these are "man-made tornadoes" made into innocuous mall pleasure points. Such controlled vortexes are a far cry from those unpredictable and deadly storms that hit areas like Joplin, Missouri, in May 2011 and Moore, Oklahoma, in 2013. Where much of America sat glued to the television listening to local meteorologists and interviews with survivors, by contrast, in the Halo instillation water is bottled into harmless consumer amusement. This sort of control and manipulation of water has a pacifying effect also on the consumer, leaving the visitor with a sense of playfulness rather than urgency.

Nevertheless, there have been some rare moments during my visits to the city when the political and ecological realities of water were made visible to the more observant tourist. I came across an atypical example of open political and ecological reference to water when I perched to take a rest on the side of a small cement planter outside of the Venetian. There, two small bubbling stone fountains bookended a planter that, in December, was filled with geraniums and sculpted shrubs. A small, unobtrusive placard read, "This feature is operating in compliance with the drought ordinance. A water efficiency and drought response plan is on file with the Southern Nevada Water Authority." The 40 million visiting tourists who come to Las Vegas each year are not, however, accountable to this body, and often they could not do their part if they wanted to.[20] Especially given the research subject of my trip to the city, I attempted to be a bit more of a water-friendly traveler when I found that my towels and sheets were replaced after a single use. I searched my Flamingo hotel room for one of those cards often found in drought regions allowing me to bypass the unnecessary extra water and electricity wasted on my hotel laundry—to no avail.

If the irritating dripping sink in my Harrah's hotel room on a different trip is a subtle reminder of my participation in the city's water ecology, this too is reframed. Vegas culture transforms the leaky sink into lighthearted stage performance. I was once again confronted by the same sound of a watery "drip, drip" while waiting for the lights to dim, signaling the opening of the Cirque du Soleil show *O*, at the Bellagio. This time the leaky drips were scored and amplified throughout the theater like a musical overture. That water became a prop for a clown walking through the seats with an umbrella to the sounds of spectator laughter and amusement. As we lounge in water, or watch the spray move synchronistically to the music, these entertainments are always already

haunted by the necessity of the resources. This is quite unlike at my home, where a very shallow well necessitates a summertime of shorter showers, washing clothing at the Laundromat, and curbing activities that might suggest even moderate water use. In Vegas, my pleasures and experiences as a tourist are marked by not having to confront the darker flip side of water spectacles—the privilege of not having to face or acknowledge the problem.

In contrast to the manufactured water innocence of the tourist is the reality of the Las Vegas worker-resident. While the visitor is free to act within the carefree, no-consequence, "what happens in Vegas stays" experience, the same is not true for those who reside there. At the same time that the Bellagio praises the sustainability of its lake and fountain display because it is run by a self-sufficient (self-controlled) spring on-site, the fountains in the yards of local residents are monitored by a force of local water police. Excessive use leaves owners liable for citations and fines.[21] The categories of water use, and the discrepancy of control, make worker-residents the essential scapegoats for scarcity. Water is zoned and categorized, such that the most water expended is in fact the most invisible, such as irrigation and more domestic uses, while the obvious and showy water exhibits are touted as the most efficient. Residents watch the water levels of Lake Mead sink—made visible by a "bathtub ring" of mineral residue left behind by the sinking water level. The livelihood of locals is reflected back at them in this very different visual spectacle. "The last time I remember [the water] being that high was in 1983," recounted a security guard at the Hoover Dam as we looked out at the thick white band wrapping the lake above the waterline. What interests me about this narrative is a contradictory visual politics, where the show is celebrated while water's necessity for the life of bodies and landscapes, sanitation, and home use (the invisible of Vegas identity) is rendered suspect.

At the dam, water is paradoxically conspicuous and obscured. The National Heritage site perpetuates a narrative of taming destructive nature—of turning the history of devastating floods along the river into a benevolent, managed source of electricity. It is the demand for water, more than electricity, that drives the operation of Hoover Dam, and yet there is only minimal mention of the release of the resource to generic cities and irrigation districts. Though power is a by-product, the electrical power plant, the science of electricity, and the glory of "clean" energy are the focal points of a visit to the site, while water use is downplayed and often completely ignored. Though it is common knowledge that Las Vegas gets much of its water from Lake Mead, the state of Nevada as a whole is listed merely as a beneficiary of electricity, not as a proclaimed water user.

Back on the Strip, casino and government officials are quite adamant about the efficiency of spectacular water features, hyping water recycling programs like the underground facility that services the Mirage and Treasure Island. This so-called reverse osmosis plant reprocesses used water back into Lake Mead—the supplier of 90 percent of the city's water. Here the hotel infrastructure is reframed as an organism contributing to a natural ecosystem. In the model of Shel Silverstein's *The Giving Tree*, which always provides a selfish young boy with what he wants, the business claims itself a benevolent contributor. Highlighting the water treatment plant that gives back, the Mirage and Treasure Island refashion themselves as water producers for the pleasure of the community, not self-interested consumers in their own right.

The visitor to Las Vegas in fact consumes the same water more than once. The sanitary practices of showering and hand washing that take place behind the closed doors of the hotel room provide the raw resources for many of those water spectacles on the Strip. With some exceptions—including the Bellagio pool and fountains, which are fed by an underground well—the majority of those spraying, erupting waterworks are in fact displays of reclaimed greywater. Officials always differentiate greywater from blackwater—no, not the private security firm—the toilet wastewater that is sent directly to the sewer system. While this juxtaposition—wastewater on show—is certainly a sign of water conservation efforts on the part of the city's businesses and regulators, the politics of such practices are not so transparent as the final crystal product. Greywater is currently the stuff of debate, because it impacts the water allotted to the city from the Colorado River. At present, Las Vegas is allocated 300,000 acre-feet of the river, but the recycling programs that put water back into Lake Mead provide the city with "return flow credits" that allow additional water consumption above and beyond the allotted amount. This system is not equal. As the *Las Vegas Sun* has reported, residents have begun to fight for access to their own greywater, which could have valuable uses in the community, for example, to water lawns and gardens. From a conservation standpoint, the practice would save energy used to clean and pump the water from the city twelve miles back to the reservoir. Yet, in doing so, less water would be credited to the city's hotels and businesses. The debate in part hinges on the idea of who owns waste, and whether or not it is equal to the unused, unrecycled, pure, authentic original water. In this case, the Southern Nevada Water Authority supports the status quo, because it allows the entertainment mecca to use more.[22]

Even when at rest, water along the Strip is a billboard of status. The more water and space for water put on show, the more exclusive the institution.

Recall that vacationer who expected to see at Treasure Island a lake similar to the one at the Bellagio. While we have seen that water features are central to the dominant themes of the popular hotel-casinos, large expanses of space allocated exclusively to water are a facet of the more upscale institutions. The two prime examples of this are found at the five-star resorts Bellagio and the Wynn (incidentally, both owned by billionaire businessman Steve Wynn). Is it a coincidence that both resorts also play host to the Strip's two water theaters (home of the shows *O* and *Le Rêve*)? Perhaps more telling, though, are the watery lakes and pools that don't actively appear to make money—the pools that provide elegant backdrops and those "free" shows such as the Fountains of Bellagio and the Wynn's Lake of Dreams, a secluded three-acre lake that hosts the resort's complimentary nightly light show. Along with the 8.5-acre lake at the Bellagio, we should consider how this watery surface offers shows of lush resources that reflect wealth back at us. Additionally, in the tightly developed zone of the center Strip, the allocation of land to nonfunctional open water rather than retail, hotel rooms or condos, gaming, and so on, is an indication of space and wealth to spare.

Water features and entertainments—though seemingly "public"—thus facilitate boundaries of inclusion and exclusion. Where scenery makes water blatant and seemingly abundant, the opportunities for swimming and playing in it are more obscured and hidden. In my visits to Las Vegas I have been struck by the fluidity and often interchangeability of the casinos and shopping spaces. Choosing where to sleep has been immaterial as it concerns one's ability to gain access to the wide range of Vegas activities and spaces. Yet water rights are a different matter. Your ability to access the swimming, wave, or even dolphin pools is what distinguishes a particular hotel's guests from all the casual casino visitors. Lined with fences and foliage, swimming holes are visually obscured, detectable only by the sounds of music and splashing. Getting to the pool at the Flamingo is like going through an airport security checkpoint; alongside ID checks for alcohol consumption, the gate attendants screen privileged guests with room keys from those without. Pool access corresponds in exclusivity to the price and star rating of the hotel, and functions as a sign of inclusion.

Water uses and regulations suggest a disjuncture in terms of which *bodies* are policed. While drunken college students abound and alcohol is liberally imbibed in the streets, structures are in place to control the clandestine water vendor in those same open spaces. Adjacent to a female water seller, a blue-and-white sign greets the people carried up the escalator to the pedestrian overpass from Bally's: "NO table/structures, vendors, soliciting, Handbills,

Skates/bikes on or within 15 feet of pedestrian structures." Like traffic and legal signage, this placard is prominent in this context for its lack of digitization and eye-catching visuals. Clearly intended for something other than instructing or catching the attention of visiting tourists, this signage instead renders illicit the Latina water seller. Why was that teen with the baseball cap looking out over the side of the overpass more captivated by the door and escalators than the Las Vegas view? On another visit I got the answer, as I witnessed an exchange between a woman in hotel uniform waving a walkie-talkie—signs of officialdom—and a group of sellers temporarily driven off by threats of calling the authorities. While the sale of water street-side might cut into profits on the same in hotel-casino shops and retail establishments, the one-dollar water bottle competition cannot account for the antagonism directed toward the vendors. Rather, the bottled water sellers are examples of circumventing systems in place to control water, labor, and trade in the entertainment capital.

Certainly, Las Vegas has many spectacles on offer, from the abundant stage performances to the digital television screens advertising the same. We can feast our eyes on the architectural façades and the plentiful consumer displays of clothing and food. Each of these spectacles functions as an exhibition of social and economic distinction. However, water spectacles are different from this broader Las Vegas pageantry. Water resists the notion of conspicuous consumption. Yes, a casino can flaunt its status by showing off its water access. However, a liquid spectacle is not fixed; it is fluid and appears natural and can thus defy our ability to recognize its cultural, political, and economic meanings. The constant shifting movement of water—like the dancing spray of the Bellagio fountain or the running river through the stationary mammoth the Hoover Dam—offers a substance that resists fixity. In the same way, the social and economic privilege vested by water in Las Vegas is likewise difficult to locate and thus to challenge. H_2O is ordinary and necessary. As such we can easily lose ourselves in its cool wetness on a hot day in the desert and forget that hidden in its seeming transparency is a high-tech infrastructure that provides a consistent current of social distinction.

NOTES

1. Robert Glennon, introduction to *Unquenchable: America's Water Crisis and What to Do about It* (Washington, DC: Island Press, 2009).

2. E.g., Natalie Dicou, "Bellagio Fountains Designer Inducted into Highland High Hall of Fame," *Salt Lake Tribune*, February 2, 2011.

3. For a look at both the invisible infrastructure of water in Las Vegas and the ways in which the value or costs are not visible in the price of water, see Stephanie Ayanian and Mark Cooper, dirs., *Liquid Assets: The Story of Our Water Infrastructure* (University Park: Penn State Public Broadcasting, 2008).

4. "Quenching Las Vegas' Thirst," *Las Vegas Sun*, archive, December 18, 2014, http://www.lasvegassun.com/news/topics/water/.

5. Steve Kanigher, "Once 'Jewel of the Desert,' Sahara Entertains Last Weekend Guests before Closing," *Las Vegas Sun*, May 14, 2011.

6. Steven Solomon, *Water: The Epic Struggle for Wealth, Power, and Civilization* (New York: Harper Perennial, 2010), 334–35.

7. "Quenching Las Vegas' Thirst."

8. "Quenching Las Vegas' Thirst."

9. Solomon, *Water*, 369.

10. Evan Ward, "Two Rivers, Two Nations, One History: The Transformation of the Colorado River Delta since 1940," *Frontera Norte* 11, no. 22 (July–December 1999): 114. For a consideration of the allocations of water to Mexico along with salinity content and changes to water quality because of the Hoover Dam, see Solomon, *Water*, 350.

11. Ted Robbins, "Stakes High for Las Vegas Water Czar," National Public Radio, June 13, 2007, http://npr.org/story/10939792.

12. Jane C. Desmond, *Staging Tourism: Bodies on Display from Waikiki to Sea World* (Chicago: University of Chicago Press, 1999), xiii–xxvi.

13. Desmond, *Staging Tourism*, 218.

14. Desmond, *Staging Tourism*, 190.

15. Walter Benjamin, "The Work of Art in the Age of Mechanical Reproduction," in *Illuminations*, ed. Hannah Arendt, trans. Harry Zohn (New York: Schocken, 1968), 217–51.

16. For more on the next-gen technologies behind these water serenades, see Verne Kopytoff, "Computers Are the Balanchine behind Those Dancing Fountains," *New York Times*, October 21, 1999.

17. "Talent," WET Design, December 18, 2014, http://www.wetdesign.com/#/talent.

18. Richard Berry, "It's Only Water," CNC *Machining Magazine* 9, no. 32, http://web.archive.org/web/20071220110050/http://www.cncmagazine.com/vol_9thru12/v9i32/v9i32c-WET.asp (accessed April 25, 2013).

19. Darrell Satzman, "A Gushing Combination of Showbiz, Engineering," *Los Angeles Times*, March 14, 2010.

20. "Quenching Las Vegas' Thirst."

21. Water waste is defined as any water that sprays or flows off the property as well as water that is used for irrigation outside of designated times assigned to limit evaporation. See "Quenching Las Vegas' Thirst."

22. Alexandra Berzon, "Agency Opposes Water Recycling at Homes: Return Less to Lake Mead, It Says, and We'll Get Less Out," *Las Vegas Sun*, April 13, 2009.

FIVE

Bread and Circuses

In the lobby at Harrah's, Buck and Winnie Greenback greet visitors in white cowboy boots and gold spandex, big hair and bigger jewelry.[*] Bills spill from Buck's suitcase and Minnie's purse, while the couple's manicured French poodle, Chip, begs from below, a wad of hundred-dollar bills in his mouth. This iconic statue of the lucky win is a monument to Vegas tackiness, on par with Big Elvis and Slots-A-Fun: the American couple, their money so obviously new and excessive they lack the luggage and taste to carry it off. Buck and Winnie are a popular site for pictures in Vegas, more evidence that Sin City has long made a virtue of its faults, bad taste chief among them.

These days, however, kitsch competes with more ambitious options, as resorts add art to their stock of entertainment experiences. The Strip's self-promotion as a western mecca for foodies, for example, clearly attempts to catch up with other urban centers, while its mania for art galleries and shows suggests a careful balance between high art and its democratization, at least

---

[*] Jane Kuenz

via the largess of wealthy patrons, such as when Steve Martin exhibited his private collection at the Bellagio in 2001 and Steve Wynn turned the Encore and Wynn into personal museums. Vegas's recently opened Smith Center, a concert hall two miles from the Strip, testifies to the city's desire for the civic monuments it now lacks. Indeed, many of these ventures seem to acknowledge, however indirectly, the limits of an essentially privatized public sphere.

Some of the paintings and sculpture in the resorts function as an element of public decor, but much is promoted as museum art, signaling high rather than popular taste, distinctions that count in a society reluctant to acknowledge class, though it's not always clear how. The Smith Center's opening performance, for example, included TV actor Neil Patrick Harris emceeing a program featuring classical violinist Joshua Bell and former American Idol–turned–Academy Award-winner Jennifer Hudson. Music on the Strip can be a similarly mixed bag. As Susan says in the introduction, even with its nightclubs and growing concert schedule, Las Vegas often feels like "a morgue for Tinseltown has-beens," including stalwarts of radio's "classic rock," circa 1972. Recent efforts seem foredoomed: one can fairly smell the desperation in the press releases describing Britney Spears's two-year deal with Planet Hollywood promising a "cool, hip club-like show" that's "not your father's Shania Twain concert," at least, not yet. There is good music in Las Vegas, much of it happening in smaller venues like the Joint at the Hard Rock Cafe. This is why Planet Hollywood agreed to reduce the size and seating of its theater in order to accommodate Spears's "club-like show." These other venues, along with the daytime pool parties hosted by resident DJs such as the one at MGM's Wet Republic are much of what attracts young people from Southern California every weekend. But Vegas is still a place where certain entertainers past their sell-by date come and take up residence, the way Liberace did in the 1950s and Britney has now.

Whether high or low, new or old, or somewhere in between, the art and entertainment in Las Vegas reflect the stratification of taste in the twenty-first century. Much of it—not just products, but styles and whole experiences—is conveniently branded and franchised so visitors will know what they're getting and can consequently self-select or classify themselves according to what they like or how well they know what is supposed to be good. As in the Smith Center opening, the results are sometimes confusing, such as when an off-shoot of a Canadian avant-garde dance group is repurposed as middlebrow entertainment that supposedly brings a unique and exotic show to Vegas even though every other casino has one; or when the Strip's newest, hippest hotel

promotes its sophistication and élan by reducing books to a projected image of the brand. It's when the city's tackiest performer is remembered by fans as a class act and invoked by more recent artists as a precursor and model.

The McDonald's of Circuses

With eight performances running in eight venues and more planned for the near future, Montreal's Cirque du Soleil is now the most visible and profitable commercial entertainment company on the Strip. Nine thousand people sit down at a Vegas Cirque show every night. In fact, if the tradition of the circus is to travel town to town in search of new audiences, Cirque du Soleil has reversed that relationship completely: now, the town roams the world looking for it, except we're not a town anymore. No longer linked by family, place, or history, we gather together around brand culture we consume, a miscellaneous collection of perpetual tourists in search of entertainment, now housed permanently in theaters built to order, while we move in and out of the hotel rooms arranged around and for them.

"The McDonald's of circuses," Cirque du Soleil specializes in "franchised performances." As Philip Auslander's term suggests, the whole point of branded culture is that we know what we're getting when we buy a ticket: a spectacle of music, dance, and costumes—part circus, part ballet—all of it operating in the liminal space between kitsch and art.[1] Billing itself as "an artistic entertainment company" specializing in "entertainment products," Cirque's avant-garde acrobatics offer spectators the pleasure of consuming something seemingly unique—a high-end cultural commodity—yet consistent and reproducible, like any other global brand.[2] The shows themselves are themed and promoted by Cirque in the kind of mystifying puffery normally reserved for art history textbooks: O at the Bellagio "weaves an aquatic tapestry of artistry, surrealism and theatrical romance in [a] timeless production"; Beatles Love at the Mirage "celebrates the musical legacy of The Beatles through their timeless, original recordings"; Mystère at Treasure Island presents an "exhilarating blend of whimsy, drama and the unimaginable" and "provides the ultimate discovery that life itself is a mystery."[3]

The emphasis on mystery and "timelessness"—either in the shows' themes or Cirque's treatment of them—is one early clue to the general scheme: like the Vegas skyline, Cirque's recognizable brand is "timeless" in that it implies cultural specificity and authenticity while actually erasing both. Though each show has its own theme and rough narrative, all synthesize stories and performance styles, especially circus styles, from around the world. I'm using

synthesize generously. In fact, Cirque cannibalizes everything it encounters, ignoring national boundaries like the global corporation it is, in efforts to uncover images, forms, styles, and whole traditions from across the planet, and remix them into the familiar Cirque look. Besides Asian martial arts at κà, spectators at Vegas shows can see Cirque versions of burlesque and cabaret shows (*Zumanity*). Cirque shows outside Vegas similarly feature a smorgasbord of cultural styles: American vaudeville in *Banana Shpeel*, Chinese circus in *Dralion*, film for *Iris*, and Radio City Music Hall in *Zarkana*. Sometimes the references are more specific—*Amaluna* loosely follows the general plot of Shakespeare's *The Tempest*. The usual plan, however, is more broadly allusive: *Varekai* is based on Greek myths, *La Nouba* on European fairy tales, and *Zed* on the tarot. It's not clear what's gone into the cultural stew that is Treasure Island's *Mystère*, with its giant snail and fifteen-foot ō-daiko drum, so big they had to build the theater around it; it cannot fit through the door should the circus even want to travel. Cirque appropriates childhood fantasy, of both girls (*Zaia*) and boys (*Wintuk*), and scientific theory: evolution is performed as grand narrative in *Totem*.

Now, as though having exhausted its natural resources, Cirque has moved on to new fare, either competing diversions (*Arena* is based on extreme sports) or competing global entertainment brands—the Beatles at the Mirage, for example, and Elvis in the Gold Lounge at Aria. In 2013, a show "based on the music of Michael Jackson" opened at Mandalay Bay. One anticipates future shows based on Cher, Celine, and other one-named Vegas celebrities. Sometimes, national music is highlighted, such as the Brazilian samba in *Ovo* or *Koozä*'s contemporary Indian pop, but the pop is fused with 1970s funk and the samba with the hum of insects. Real difference disappears in production: Cirque treats all musical styles and forms—now, even individual musicians—as interchangeable pieces integrated into a continuous world beat sound. Finally, regardless of the show's theme, it's all the same generic mix of pop and folk, where the pop can be popular music from anywhere and the folk could be anybody's folk, rather than, say, actual people living in an actual place.

Actual people, for example, do not speak the international scat of the typical Cirque clown. The shows' titles, with their insistent diacritics, signify an imaginary ethnicity, a global culture conversing entirely in loan words. When I asked my daughters what they liked about *Mystère*, they both noted the big baby. In bonnet and diapers, bottle suspended from his neck like a medal, he lumbers around the performance space, a kind of global id, alternately menacing and comic, addressing the audience in an infantile babble that occa-

sionally turns into a wail. When asked about the baby, *Mystère*'s original director, Franco Dragone, explained, "A Chinese baby and an American baby are the same. They speak the same language with their eyes and hands. I'm looking for that universal language." Dragone's nod to the fantasy of transcendent community is entirely predictable. Like Benetton before it, Cirque easily appropriates liberal discourse, making social consciousness and "good corporate citizenship" part of the brand. But evoking a universal language by putting accents over every possible vowel cannot deflect attention from the true state of things: the language of Cirque du Soleil is the universally pronounceable language of the commodity, specific and generic, memorable but meaningless.

The same is true of the obviously talented performers, who are conspicuously featured yet practically invisible. Cirque du Soleil employs over five thousand people, a third of whom are visual or performing artists, yet none of them are introduced on stage. As Jennifer Harvie and Erin Hurley point out, this is a striking breach of practice in the circus tradition.[4] Though they are recruited from across the globe, particularly China and Russia, and speak different languages, once they assume their identity as Cirque performers, they all inhabit the same "realm of the imagination," performing in real places—the United States, Europe, and Asia—in shows organized and managed from multinational headquarters in Singapore, Amsterdam, and Tokyo. Like the music and other cultural citations, the performers are moving parts, anonymous and interchangeable, in a global production system where the corporation has replaced the nation and "the show is the star."

More than 100 million people have seen a Cirque show since 1984, 60 percent of them at Vegas shows. In fact, Cirque has been so successful that, after an initial grant from Quebec, it's been able to forego public and private grants completely since 1992. New shows in New York and Los Angeles have been financed with a $50 million fund raised by private investors in the United States and Canada. Cirque's founder, Guy Laliberté, gushed about the company's success, saying, "We could extend this type of fund to real estate. . . . If successful it will give us great credibility in the market without having to go public."[5] Cirque needs this kind of private investment because, while successful enough to maintain its position in entertainment, it does not generate enough internally to grow and expand into other areas, as it would need to do in order to prosper as a corporation. Laliberté's interest in real estate, for example, may derive from the company's commitment to establishing its own permanent venues for its shows and, like Disney World, assuming greater control over the theming and integration of the Cirque brand into new commodities.

This is already the case with the Beatles show *Love* and the Revolution Lounge at the Mirage and the Aria's *Viva Elvis* and Gold Lounge. A five-thousand-square-foot "lounge concept," Revolution "features cutting edge, interactive experiences to create a psychedelic sensory environment." Similarly, the Gold Lounge's black-and-gold furnishings contribute to the "glamorous feel" of this "sleek ultra-lounge . . . inspired by Graceland." Like Walt Disney World, Cirque fetishizes "authentic detail," where copies of originals don't actually reproduce the originals: the Gold Lounge's "modern décor," for example, uses actual "design patterns found within the Memphis mansion" but not the furnishings themselves. The lounge is arranged to "stimulate conversation and promote social interaction" among the Aria's guests, some of whom may then decide to purchase tickets for the show. Since these shows tend to fill quickly, however, the more likely scenario is that the people who've purchased tickets for *Love* or *Viva Elvis* will congregate in these "unique, innovative lounges" before or after so that they can "make [their] Cirque du Soleil experience last just a little longer."

Expanding its brand is not new for Cirque. As Susan Bennett argues, people leaving New York's *Zumanity* can find in the shopping areas right outside the theater outfits with the same mix of "luxury and edgy eroticism" they just saw onstage.[6] Unlike those of the performers, the name of *Zumanity*'s haute couture designer, Thierry Mugler, appears throughout the show's promotional materials. His perfume, Womanity, trades on the show's name as Cirque trades on his. Now Laliberté is extending his company's reach even further: on its website, Cirque promotes "JUKARI Fit to Fly" and "JUKARI Fit to Flex," two branded fitness programs developed in conjunction with Reebok that will offer women "a truly different group exercise experience," perhaps with the "host of international celebrities" who have used a JUKARI fitness program, including "TV personality Kim Kardashian." For the more discriminating, those who expect more than the promise of a chance to consume what TV personalities consume, Cirque offers special event planning, in which the company conceives, designs, and produces "truly unique experiences and prestigious upscale events for an exclusive clientele."

Cirque's aspirations for new ventures have followed the model of vertical integration introduced by Carnegie and Ford, who sought greater control over the production process by controlling the raw materials needed prior to the assembly line. Cirque's form of "forward vertical integration," however, emphasizes managing the product at the consumption stage—for example,

by owning retail stores and distribution sites. This kind of integration is now a standard feature of contemporary corporations, such as American Apparel, which weaves the cloth and runs the retail store. And it is a defining feature of Internet and social media sites: Google, for example, integrates its search engine with Gmail, Google Docs, Google Scholar, and Google Books. Similarly, Facebook has encouraged multiple user-generated—thus, unpaid— applications on the site that encourage and enable its members to integrate their Facebook accounts into different areas of their lives: games, clubs, invitations, even educational pages for high school and college classes. Like a mall with a theater or a casino with a roller coaster, there's no reason to go anywhere else.

The Art of the Motorcycle

Throughout the extensive website promoting its new branded experiences, Cirque du Soleil emphasizes their distinctive character and trades on the hope that these experiences and products will be similarly distinguishing for anyone who consumes them. A Cirque experience is not just "unique," but "truly unique." The lounges are "unique," "innovative," and "cutting edge." Even the fitness programs purport to be "truly different." As for the special events, Cirque promises "original content" and individual service, the company working "closely with each client to ensure their specific objectives remain the priority." Cirque's language of distinction, its promise of individuality and uniqueness through consumption, is rendered in judgments about taste: "innovative," "cutting edge," and "original" all point to avant-garde art, perhaps a nod to the company's origins in Montreal, famous since the 1980s for edgy dance companies like O Vertigo and La La La Human Steps.

But Cirque has cast its net elsewhere, lending its brand to a different kind of art, specifically *The Art of Richard MacDonald Presented by Cirque du Soleil*®. The gallery for *The Art of Richard MacDonald Presented by Cirque du Soleil*® is located immediately outside the O Theater in the Bellagio, where Cirque's *O* plays twice nightly. It's across from the buffet. Another MacDonald-Cirque gallery is in Crystals in CityCenter, between Rodney Lough's oversized landscapes and Dale Chihuly's exquisite glass flowers. This is the same Chihuly whose work is displayed prominently above the reception area in the Bellagio and is for sale down the hall at the Via Fiore shops.[7]

One of the striking things about Vegas today is the obligatory art gracing every new venue. Steve Wynn started this with the opening of the Bellagio Gallery of Fine Art in 1998, which remains at the Bellagio, though Wynn himself has not. It was soon followed by the short-lived Guggenheim Las Vegas, whose first show, *The Art of the Motorcycle*, tried mightily to bridge the gap between serious art and more familiar Vegas pursuits. Today, the Rio furnishes its nine Palazzo Suites with privately owned pieces from one of the state's largest collections of corporate art. While other resorts offer their high-rolling whales bowling alleys, private pools, and theaters, high rollers at the Rio get art and antiques, including original Renoirs, Picassos, and Hockneys.

Richard MacDonald is not Picasso. He's not even Dale Chihuly. His figurative sculptures ostensibly modeled on Cirque acrobats capture the body in motion, but *The Art of Richard MacDonald Presented by Cirque du Soleil®* is what it is: $4,000 stone dancers and mythological figures of varying sizes, perfect, as the ad says, "for your sculpture garden." This is expensive gift shop art for people whose main criteria for art is how they think it will look in their living room. What they want in their living room is Cirque du Soleil.[8]

In fact, if the art in Vegas were placed on a continuum, *The Art of Richard MacDonald Presented by Cirque du Soleil®* would be closer to the end that includes the elaborate junk for sale at L'Art de Paris: full-sized mermaid statues, warring Roman porcelain deities, and Remington and Degas reproductions. There are gilt and marble mantle clocks and garden fountains, green with fake age. In one of them, two nymphs hold up an open clamshell on which two others cavort. In another, a cherub rides a dolphin. It's the worst of nineteenth-century neoclassicism and academic art, though of a piece with the statues of Poseidon in the fountain outside Caesars or the fake oil reproductions in the Paris lobby featuring nobility and their stuff. Eventually, we get to the frank kitsch, assembled around a "50 percent off" sign like sale items at Walmart: souvenir Eiffel Towers and the inevitable religious pieces—wall crucifixes and tabletop Last Suppers. When I took a picture of one of these, the shop attendant asked me to stop, as did the woman outside the Penske-Wynn Ferrari showroom at the Wynn, as though a room full of new cars were a museum or art gallery.

This category confusion is general in Las Vegas, an effect of turning culture into entertainment commodity and vice versa. One version of it works from the top down and the other from the bottom up. At the Guggenheim, visitors would ask if the art was real. Now, over at the Rio, the Michael Godard Gallery is simply listed under "shopping" with other stores. The Bellagio gallery is outside the casino, across from the pool and next to Café Gelato and La Scarpa Shoes. When it first opened, the art was mounted on dark green walls, like precious gems on velvet, the kind visitors could see in jewelry stores elsewhere in the mall. The gallery itself had to be explained in terms of the resort's Italian theme, now barely visible, even less acknowledged in the decor, a patently ridiculous story of a fictitious count of Bellagio who, like all effete Europeans, suffered from asthma and consequently fled Italy, using his fortune from international banking and real estate to build a grand manor house on Las Vegas Boulevard. Wynn subsequently bought out the count, the story goes, rescuing the precious art collection for the benefit of the Bellagio's guests and all of Las Vegas's visitors. He wasn't selling art, he said, but giving people an "art experience."[9]

Like the Rockefellers, Gettys, and Guggenheims before him, Wynn's stated purpose suggests a desire to mediate between the cultured classes and everyone else, but like those earlier "personal museums," Wynn's was eventually revealed as an elaborate tax shelter.[10] As William Fox has shown, the experience Wynn gave them helped drive up the value of art he owned privately and was given in such a way—field trips for local school kids, for example—that allowed Wynn to write off some of the expenses.[11] Like the privatization of sidewalks and other public spaces, the advantages of the deal were in Wynn's favor while the city itself and the locals eventually felt the effects: as money and attention shifted to private casino art, donations to and support for the public Las Vegas Art Museum declined, and the museum closed in early 2009. When Wynn sold the Bellagio to MGM, he removed his private collection to a new gallery in his new hotel, where such an elaborate backstory was no longer necessary. But the Wynn gallery didn't survive, closing in 2006, at which point many of these privately owned works were then displayed throughout the resort, but with no signs to help resort guests identify them. The former Wynn gallery itself is now a Rolex store. I found a great zebra print watch there for $70,000 but didn't buy it.

In his study of Las Vegas, Fox found that early surveys conducted at the Bellagio and Guggenheim suggested visitors were interested in obvious displays of wealth, such as the life-sized jeweled horse in the Bellagio's lobby. Sparkling in silver and gold, it's described by one wit on Flickr as "the world's best disco ball shaped like a horse." When the Guggenheim led with motorcycles, their stated hope was to display something familiar in order to attract a crowd not accustomed to museums. With this tactic, they missed the main point that people who didn't go to museums nevertheless wanted art. Unfortunately, they ended up instead at *The Art of Richard MacDonald Presented by Cirque du Soleil*®.

There's no apostrophe in Caesars Palace. It was left out intentionally to suggest that Caesars was everyone's palace, at least for a few nights. This fantasy of luxury and wealth for all has given way now to something more precise: not money, but taste. The architects of CityCenter understood this: "It's not something that advertises itself on the exterior," says the audio tour guide in my ear at the Bellagio Gallery's CityCenter show *12 + 7: Artists and Architects of CityCenter*. If true, this one detail makes CityCenter conspicuously unlike its counterparts on the Strip. As one early review of Crystals put it, there's "no theming, no gift shops, no gimmicks, no casino. Just pure elegance."[12] Crystals is a mall; it has over forty high-end stores and its own concierge, so "no gift shops" means nobody sells any of that stuff Susan discovered on her souvenir tour of the Strip.

What you can find in Crystals and throughout CityCenter is art of the established and recognized variety. Some of it is integrated into the resort's functions and spaces, like the Holzer installation in the Aria valet exit, where the running text can be mistaken for public signage, or Maya Lin's *Silver River*, an eighty-seven-foot sculpture representing the Colorado River (all of it) mounted behind the registration desk. Lin's snaking silver line is striking, but also abstract; minus a wall plaque, guests are unlikely to connect it to the Colorado River, much less anything Lin might be trying to express about water conservation at a massive tourist complex in a desert. Anyone already interested in or knowledgeable about contemporary art might recognize these pieces, especially the Holzer—while others may notice them while checking in or boarding a taxi without really registering them as anything other than interior decor.

On the other hand, a good deal of the art at CityCenter is clearly on display, again most of it late modern and contemporary. If anything, CityCenter dispenses entirely with the default Vegas traffic pattern ushering everyone through the casino regardless of destination. Here, art gives all routes a purpose. Anyone walking around the whole complex can see installations by Tony Cragg, Nancy Rubins, Peter Wegner, and Anthony Gormley. Outside, on the way to the Mandarin, past the five private art galleries, one passes Oldenburg and van Bruggen's giant *Typewriter Eraser, Scale X* (1998–99) and Henry Moore's *Reclining Connected Forms* (1969–74). Because the Mandarin is set back, unless you make a point of seeking it out, as I did, much of the art there, such as the huge Masatoshi Izumi sculpture at the front entrance, is likely to be viewed only by hotel guests, as though it really were a private sculpture garden.

Does it matter if the people checking in at the Vdara Hotel don't recognize Frank Stella's *Damascus Gate Variation I* (1969) behind the registration desk? If the flashy colors on the wall just seem to be part of the general mix of glitz and glamour, like department store decorations? Over at the Aria,

the only one of CityCenter's four hotels that includes an actual casino, Julian Schnabel's Polaroid portraits of Christopher Walken line the hallway beside the Deuce Lounge. Not the typical celebrity shots, they look damaged, as though they were crumpled up and then framed. Walken himself, the movie star, is almost unrecognizable. Meanwhile, before they even get to see the digital art displayed in the lobby by the main desk, guests arriving at the Cosmopolitan and parking in the garage will find the walls covered with the work of four prominent urban street artists, including one of Shepard Fairey's Angela Davises. Much of it looks like graffiti, as though calculated to confuse anyone still unaware that graffiti can be art.

"Taste classifies," writes Bourdieu.[13] It's also for sale, though as the hipsters have recently demonstrated with their old-school Chuck Taylors and black plastic nerd glasses, what you consume may be less important now than how you consume it. Besides L'Art de Paris, guests at Paris Las Vegas could also visit the Paris Gallerie, which featured a show titled *The Heart of a Woman: Harlequin Cover Art 1949–2009*, the first of a series of joint ventures proposed between Harlequin and Harrah's Entertainment. Unlike L'Art de Paris, Paris Gallerie is right off the casino, somewhere between the lobby and the elevators, a dark and small place, but well suited to the book covers, some of which could have doubled as miniature posters for the Chippendales. The Harlequin show takes mass-produced genre fiction targeted to women, one of the most déclassé of all literary forms, and turns it into art solely through presentation and point of view. With enough irony, anything can be hip. This may be good to know when appraising that Thierry Mugler couture for sale, lest someone decide that those "tasteful yet evocative" Cirque designs featuring "sexy bodices, bejeweled jockstraps, fur and feathers" actually look more like the outfits sported by Barbie's rivals, the Bratz and Monster High dolls, and available in cheaper versions at any Forever XXI store in Any Mall, Anywhere, USA.

Inspired Experiences™

In eschewing any kind of theming, CityCenter and the Cosmopolitan show their hand by marketing a Vegas experience explicitly as an engagement with art. Joking that "opposites attract," the Cosmopolitan aims to "satisfy [the] cultural sensibilities" of guests while they are "sipping on a cocktail" and "splitting Aces . . . all while reaching audiences that might otherwise look past Las Vegas as an art destination.[14] Like CityCenter, the Cosmopolitan is heavily invested in its difference from traditional casinos and traditional conceptions of what people want to do in them. Unlike most places where the slots are lined up and dominate the room and view, here machines and game tables may be sequestered in cabanas within the lounge. The effect is to suggest privacy: gamblers are connected to but separated from the regular nightlife by cords and red fringe. In most casinos you have to buy privacy: access to private gambling rooms is dependent on the size of your bankroll, but these tables had a $25 minimum at night and only $15 during the day, more than some other places, but not all, and not by much. As one reviewer put it, it's "a VIP experience without the VIP expense."[15] Part of the attraction of the cabanas is that it makes it easy to step out of a game and into the lounge. The point isn't that you can get a drink more easily—it's very easy to get a drink in a traditional Vegas casino—but that the gambling is more obviously being treated as only one of a number of entertainment experiences.

Indeed, the Cosmopolitan is neither primarily nor particularly interested in gambling. Unlike many Strip resorts, especially behemoths like MGM, its reach is up rather than out, a smaller vertical and urban footprint, rather than suburban sprawl. Sofas and chairs are arranged in intimate conversation pits for people to sit and talk. The layout encourages congregating and a nightclub atmosphere. It's studiously hip. In fact, sitting in the Cosmopolitan's swank lounge one Friday night, I fully expected to see the entire cast of HBO's *Entourage* walk through. This is very different from stalwarts like the Flamingo and even newer places like Paris or New York, where functions are segregated spatially and it really is hard to find a place to sit that's not in front of a dealer or slot machine. This is why it doesn't matter that, unlike in hotels and bars, there are so few televisions in most casinos: there's nowhere to sit anyway. Where you do find one, people just stand around it as though reading the arrival and departure screens in the airport. It's something you do on your way to doing something else.

People stand around and stare at the Cosmopolitan, but for different reasons. In anticipation of its opening, the resort premiered six videos on IFC and the Sundance Channel introducing its Inspired Experiences brand: *Stay, Nourish, Details, Reveal, Explore,* and, of course, *Taste.* Announcing itself as "a new independent voice in Las Vegas," the Cosmopolitan promised to deliver "a cultivated, curated, real experience."[16] The juxtaposition of terms highlights the challenge and the stakes at play: can an experience be curated and real at the same time? The authentic spray paint high art in the garage suggests one way to do this, but it's not the only way, nor the most dramatic. The developers' goal was not "just another painting or sculpture that blends into the background," but a whole "art program that every guest—from the most novice observer to the most sophisticated critic—could touch, feel, hear and experience." There is an artist in residence you can actually talk to, but the emphasis is more on immersive sensory experience and accessibility, which is why the hotel finally removed the cords around Roark Gourley's oversized stilettos, *Fit to Be Tied* and *Steampump*: too many people simply ignored them in order to climb in the shoes to take pictures. The day I was there, two kids played on the pink shoe as though it were playground equipment.

The real draw is the hotel lobby, where screens wrap around eight columns, with even more running behind the registration desk itself. Using photography, film, and 2D and 3D animation, images on the screens run continuously day and night. Rather than pose a temporary distraction, the lobby screens organize the space and how people move through it. At one point, they're bookshelves, with different books lighting up at different times. At another, they contain exotic plants—they look like upside-down jellyfish floating in an aquarium or Chihuly glass art at the Bellagio store. Though one spokesman says, "It's not marketing; it's just art," each image is linked to the resort brand: for example, the books don't represent books, or literature, or even reading; instead, this is the "master collection of every unique and engaging guest experience" at the Cosmopolitan. Similarly, the plants are "a new species of plant-life, never-before-seen specimens," like the "new notion of luxury" and "new type of guest" at the Cosmopolitan.[17]

If Cirque appropriates cultures and performance styles, the Cosmopolitan appropriates entire realms of human activity and the natural world for the Inspired Experiences available to its guests. Upstairs, several early twentieth-century Burmese nats, with their human faces, antlers, and demon masks, coexist comfortably with Cheryl Ekstrom's *Earth Warriors*, full-sized bronze sculptures, vaguely human if you don't count the feet, which almost suggest a mythological creature like Pan, or the fantasy natives of Pandora in James Cameron's *Avatar* (2009), socially connected, wired to the ground. Put them in the front window of DNA 2050 down the hall and they could model the jeans.

As the name implies, "the new type of guest" at the Cosmopolitan—one of its Identity Members—is at home in the world, free from local attachments and prejudices, a person defined, not by production, nor even by consumption, but by affinity and taste. This largely mythical, transhistorical cosmopolitan guest inhabits a world that produces varied entertainment experiences with limited labor: though there are over four hundred digital displays on the columns and behind the desk in the lobby, all are controlled by one central system out of sight somewhere in the bowels of the building. Once the work is designed and installed, it doesn't require many people to keep it

going, just someone, anyone really, to schedule programs reflecting the hour or the mood required for whatever Inspired Experience is on tap for that day.

Mr. Showmanship

I count myself lucky to be among those who visited the Liberace Museum before it closed its doors permanently. It was located off the Strip, down on Tropicana. I took the Liberace Bus, a long, black affair with "Free Shuttle to the New LIBERACE Museum" emblazoned on each side, along with pictures of the man himself in a fabulous powder-blue costume. After we'd picked up our last passenger, the driver inserted a video for us to watch along the way, most of it clips from old shows, and most of those stage entrances. In one, Liberace takes the stage in a 1962 Phantom V Landau mirrored Rolls-Royce. When the chauffeur opens the door, he accepts the extended crystal microphone and deadpans, "It really stops traffic at the Safeway." Another segment shows Liberace in a white feather cape performing at a grand piano adorned with lit candelabra. In another, he exits the car and flies away, lifted by wires above the audience waving below. Behind me, a woman talked about how much her father enjoyed the old TV show. "He didn't have a word for gay," she said. "So he would just say, 'He's such a good entertainer.'" Across the aisle, someone else nodded and agreed: "He was classy. He always looked good." I was the youngest person on the bus.

The museum was in a strip mall, across from the Aladdin International Market, a Middle Eastern grocery. There were shopping carts in the parking lot. At one time, Liberace had owned the entire complex, using part of it as a studio apartment and what was then the museum as a rehearsal space. Our guide, Howard, said, "He bought the whole place." In fact, most of the Liberace Museum was devoted to things Liberace bought: entire rooms of pianos, cars, and clothes. He had a 1954 Custom Rolls, a rhinestone-studded Duesenberg Roadster, a 1972 custom gold-flaked Bradley, a hot pink VW bug. There were antique pianos, upright and grand, and a mirrored Baldwin.

These exhibits were accompanied throughout by excerpts from Liberace's *The Things I Love*, a kind of coffee table book devoted to cataloging his stuff. In it, he writes, "All these things that I live with have been placed in my care to look after. They don't really belong to me. They belong to the world." Both here and at the King's Ransom, the Elvis museum at the Imperial Palace, a lot of space and attention are given to clothing and things: Elvis's brown suede jacket, the original "crushed velvet bedspread from [his] custom made bed" at Graceland, his favorite peacock jumpsuit. One sign at King's Ransom even quotes Tommy Hilfiger favorably, saying, "Elvis Presley was the first white boy to really bling it up." Yet both museums also share a profound discomfort with fame and wealth, hence the insistence on each man being a real person whose success was genuinely earned. Both highlight what each man gave away.

When I saw the costumes, I regretted immediately not bringing my youngest, a real diva who would have recognized a soul mate and shown the clothes the proper respect: capes with ostrich feathers and mink, a sixteen-foot white llama fur coat, a costume composed of 150 pounds of dyed pink turkey feathers, a King Neptune costume designed for the 1984 New Orleans World Fair, a Czar Nicholas costume that Liberace wore accompanied by two Russian wolfhounds. A glass case displayed mirrored and rhinestone wigs on Liberace-head wig stands; one blue Liberace head sported a white fur wig. Another round glass column held the Glitter Man's glittering shoes: spar-kling gold and white zip-up ankle boots, rhinestone stacked heels, loafers with pink, beaded rosettes. There were capes and canes, flag-blue hot pants, diamond buttons, and, always, the ruffles at the wrists.

Besides Howard, the other people working at the museum, all volunteers, were older women. They told me the story about the "design student from Europe" who spent days in the museum, drawing the costumes, telling every-one "the costumes here were better than any in Europe." He said he was going home to design for Lady Gaga. A sort of keeper of the flame, Howard re-peated the rags-to-riches story told on the museum's walls: how Liberace rose from $45 a week to $50,000, the highest-paid entertainer in Las Vegas. In the museum, this transformation was told explicitly as an immigrant American Dream story with an Italian father, Polish mother, two musical siblings, and an ungainly polyglot name to match, so bad it had to be for real—Wladziu Valentino Liberace. In the photographs, he seemed proudly predigital: unlike the waxed and bronzed Chippendales, Liberace was pasty-faced and scrag-gly, his hairy legs sticking out under the hot pants in his red, white, and blue sequined and fringed drum major outfit with matching argyle knee socks and oxfords.

The whole place felt frozen in time. The man determined not to tell all remains permanently old school. Could he have survived the transition to a world with no secrets? His death from AIDS was acknowledged, but not highlighted, and, otherwise, he seemed locked in the past, always putting on his carefully cultivated public persona like one of his rhinestone costumes. If Cirque offers low culture as high art, Liberace appalled his critics by popu-larizing classics, always insisting he just wanted his audiences to have a good time. Though his fans expressed what they liked about him in the language of taste—he was a "classy entertainer"—his opulent kitsch suffers now next to Cirque's slick acts. Of course, put Cirque next to the Cosmopolitan, and you'll get the same effect. Cher, of course, does drag too. But all of it could find a home in a risqué or comic Cirque show and probably still will since any work of art or culture can be reduced to a clever or sophisticated branded "entertainment product" with licensing tie-ins to Kim Kardashian and another half-life after that as a tax write-off.

I bought my sole Vegas souvenir at the Liberace Museum: a book of Liberace paper dolls, each sporting a different outfit and campy thought bubble. Once assembled, they are the kind of thing that could serve as place cards at a dinner party for one's great-aunts or hip friends. As I checked out, I mentioned to Howard that I was writing about Las Vegas, at which point he pulled me aside and invited me to return Thursday night at 10:50, after the museum closed, to see the Showcase. At that time, the Composers Showcase was held once a month in the other building across the parking lot known as the Cabaret Showroom. It was not an open mic, but a planned program performed by local singers and dancers, many of whom were cast in shows on the Strip. These were not just the headline acts, but the ones who did the singing and dancing grunt work of nightly theater. Here, they performed for each other. The only rule was that all the work had to be original. It seemed too great to miss, so of course I went.

It was a smallish room, arranged with tables and chairs, like a cabaret, with one of Liberace's gold pianos on the stage in front. An open bar was available before and after. The museum sold homemade cookies, wrapped in plastic. Once the program started, the first thing that was clear was that many of these people had just come from working a show and most of them knew each other. Everyone was introduced by name and usually also with a story or joke that indicated the group's shared knowledge and experience. Much of that shared experience concerned their work, their efforts to be successful as artists and performers and make a name for themselves, though usually the jokes were double-edged. "Patti LaBelle was not available tonight," sighed one in mock lament. "So I decided to go her one better." A man referred to himself self-deprecatingly as "one of the copious Frankie Vallis from *Jersey Boys*," the musical at Paris. Another said, "My show closed a year ago," then joked, "What's up? Unemployment?"

Since everything performed had to be original, none of them were able to do any of the numbers they did for work on the Strip, and none of them wanted to. One woman sang a song she wrote for an eighteen-year-old friend's memorial. Another had written a new song, but recruited a friend to sing it for him. There was a duet with a harp and piano. If they sang at work, then they came out here as the songwriters they wanted to be. If they danced at work, they sang here. Occasionally, a joke slipped about the low-common-denominator audiences on the Strip. Clearly, to them, this was the more demanding venue. One man told the house, "I set off the suck meter at *Phantom* several times tonight, thinking of what I would do here." They knew and respected each other and what they did. When my tablemate checked the messages on her phone during one number, someone at the next table leaned over and asked her to stop.

When the Liberace Museum closed, the Showcase did not. They found another place to meet—the Smith Center for the Performing Arts in downtown Las Vegas. On their website announcing upcoming shows, they thank the now-defunct museum for supporting them as long as it could and express regret that the Showcase performances could not save it. When news reports announced the closing, a spokesperson for the museum explained its demise as the result of many factors, chief among them the difficulty of keeping the brand alive. You need a "fleet of lawyers" to do that, he said. Another factor was that, though at one time his name was synonymous with Las Vegas, Liberace never had a hit record. You can still find clips from old shows on YouTube like the ones I watched on the bus—the top ranked one has over a million views—but there is no vertical integration with Liberace, only creative debts, such as the one Lady Gaga clearly owes. Like Cirque du Soleil, Liberace was known mainly for his spectacular live performances, but most weren't preserved in media of any kind. They exist mainly in the memories of all those older women who came to Las Vegas and took the free bus to the museum that honored him, the city's greatest celebrity, and in the shared work and community of those artists who continue to gather under his name.

The last thing visitors saw at the Liberace Museum was a wall of artwork. The pieces were created and donated by past recipients of scholarships from the Liberace Foundation for the Performing and Creative Arts. The foundation is the only thing on the Liberace website that's still active. After the spectacle of the museum's cars and pianos, the drawings were easy to miss, just taking up one corner in the gift shop. The scholarships are awarded competitively to students in accredited programs in art and design. At the age of seven, Liberace himself received a scholarship to study at the Milwaukee Music Conservatory, and he would continue to depend on scholarship aid for the next seventeen years. The museum emphasized this history, saying the foundation was Liberace's acknowledgment of a debt he owed, a form of re-

payment that went directly to support the kind of unique and talented young person he had been.

The art is uniformly sophisticated and first rate. None of these young people would have been confused by the RETNA graffiti in the Cosmopolitan garage. Many of the pieces reference Liberace directly, as though in thanks or, as in the Composers Showcase itself, to acknowledge a kindred spirit. Pianos predominate, such as the drawing sent by a fashion design student of a gown with a keyboard drawn into the skirt. Is it ironic that this work was made possible by the largess of an entertainer who anticipated and celebrated style over art? That other artists gather in his name to perform original work, not for pay but for themselves and each other in his former rehearsal studio next door to his now-defunct museum? That in hindsight he seems finally more real than much of the Vegas culture that overtook him, every costume and smirk suggesting something that couldn't be packaged and sold and will, therefore, not survive? Next to their artwork, some of the students added statements of gratitude to an artist from another era, if not, to them, from another planet. "Until the grant awarding process," writes one, "I never knew who Liberace was."

NOTES

1. Philip Auslander, *Liveness: Performance in a Mediatized Culture* (New York: Routledge, 2008), 54. See also Maurya Wickstrom's significant elaboration of this concept in *Performing Consumers: Global Capital and Its Theatrical Seductions* (New York: Routledge, 2006), especially chapter 3, "*The Lion King*, Mimesis, and Disney's Magical Capitalism," 66–95.

2. I am indebted throughout to Susan Bennett's excellent discussion of Las Vegas in her examination of the role of contemporary commercialism in urban tourism. Susan Bennett, "Theater/Tourism," *Theatre Journal* 57 (2005): 407–28.

3. Quotations about Cirque shows and other products are taken from the company's home page and the promotional copy appearing there and on the websites of the various venues at which they perform: http://www.cirquedusoleil.com, http://www.bellagio.com/o-cirque-du-soleil/o-cirque-du-soleil.aspx.

4. Harvie and Hurley, "States of Play," quoted in Bennett, "Theater/Tourism," 421. Cirque now identifies some of its performers in promotional photos.

5. Christian Sylt and Caroline Reid, "Cirque du Soleil Swings to $1Bn Revenue as It Mulls Shows at O₂," *Independent*, January 23, 2011, http://www.independent.co.uk /news/business/news/cirque-du-soleil-swings-to-1bn-revenue-as-it-mulls-shows-at-o2-2191850.html.

6. Bennett, "Theater/Tourism," 424.

7. The two thousand glass blossoms of Chihuly's *Fiori di Como* covering 2,100 square

feet of the Bellagio's ceiling weigh forty thousand pounds and are cleaned and maintained daily by a staff of engineers.

8. On the role of function or use in class distinctions based on aesthetic taste, such as selecting an artwork according to whether or not it matches one's sofa, see Pierre Bourdieu, *Distinction: A Social Critique of the Judgement of Taste*, trans. Richard Nice (Cambridge, MA: Harvard University Press, 1984).

9. William L. Fox, *In the Desert of Desire: Las Vegas and the Culture of Spectacle* (Reno: University of Nevada Press, 2005), 27.

10. For a discussion of past and present "personal museums," see Joe Day, "Hubrispace: Personal Museums and the Architectures of Self-Deification," in *Evil Paradises: Dreamworlds of Neoliberalism*, ed. Mike Davis and Daniel Bertrand Monk (New York: New Press, 2007), 219–40.

11. "By blurring the lines between profit and nonprofit behavior, and seeking to have the tax laws accommodate them, the Wynns maximize profit, retain control of their personal culture, and foster a libertarian capitalism based on individual rights." Fox, *In the Desert of Desire*, 64.

12. Steve Kaufman, "Crystals, CityCenter, Las Vegas," *VMSD*, February 26, 2010, http://vmsd.com/content/crystals-citycenter-las-vegas.

13. Bourdieu, *Distinction*, 6.

14. "Art," Cosmopolitan of Las Vegas, http://www.cosmopolitanlasvegas.com/experience/art.aspx (accessed January 3, 2015).

15. MikeE, "Necessity the Mother of Invention: The Casino Cabana," Vegas Tripping, December 17, 2010, http://www.vegastripping.com/news/blog/3790/necessity-the-mother-of-invention-the-casino-cabana/.

16. Quotations are from the description of their design work for the Cosmopolitan by DigitalKitchen, http://thisisdk.com/work/creative-agency-year-award/cosmopolitan-las-vegas-digital-installation (accessed May 30, 2013). See also "Inside the Cosmopolitan," promotional video, *Las Vegas Sun*, December 15, 2010, http://www.youtube.com/watch?v=EhcDZStbi5s.

17. All quotations are from the Digital Kitchen's promotional materials for the Cosmopolitan lobby cited above and widely reproduced in commentary about it. See, for example, Alice Yoo, "Living Art at Cosmopolitan Las Vegas," My Modern Met, March 2, 2011, http://www.mymodernmet.com/profiles/blogs/living-art-cosmopolitan-las.

SIX

The Whole World on a Plate

Las Vegas may be in a desert, but it doesn't appear to be a food desert. If water as a resource is threatened by drought and dwindling supply, food on the Strip bespeaks abundance. Just peer into any one of the Las Vegas buffets, and you will see bounty offered up for the taking. The atmosphere textured with mouthwatering carbs and succulent oils, the aromas laced with sugar and spice, the sounds of quiet conversation, cutlery, and chewing—this is free-market capitalism's dream of unimpeded consumption. And I'm ready to dig in—foot-long papaya strips, crab legs that all but walk onto my plate, every pan brimming, begging me to scoop.* Too bad my stomach doesn't have a storage unit, something like a basement or attic, or one of those PODS that people park in their driveways to handle the overflow from their houses. As the epitome of a society built on disposable commodity consumption, the all-you-can-eat Las Vegas buffet bundles the abundance of magically produced goods with the dilemma of oversupply.

---

* Susan Willis

What's more, it fully does away with all manner of spatial or temporal constraints. Put simply, there will always be strawberries—and not just strawberries, but blueberries, blackberries, and raspberries as well. I realize I'm among a dwindling number of consumers still rooted in a sense of seasonality. Fresh berries in winter—or for that matter, in a desert—give me pause. If it's December, and the local Whole Foods is offering raspberries along with the more predictable beets, carrots, and cabbages, I'll see the berries as oddly out of time and place. By comparison, nothing on the Las Vegas Strip can ever stand out as remarkable. This is because everything from everywhere is always available and never out of the ordinary. You can have strawberries every day, with every meal, and never have to consider why the best gift that John Forsythe gave Shirley MacLaine at the end of Alfred Hitchcock's *The Trouble with Harry* is "two boxes of fresh strawberries every month, in and out of season."[1]

Just imagine your local IHOP restaurant on a Sunday morning—the parking lot jammed, people crowded around the cash register, packed into the minuscule waiting area, spilling out the front door—all this just to get a table. Now consider the buffet at the Excalibur in Las Vegas, where three to four thousand eager diners are seated for breakfast every day. The logistics of mass consumption are astounding. Thankfully, I was not waiting in line at the Excalibur. Instead, I had chosen the more modest Harrah's buffet.

Typical of Las Vegas's sixty buffets, the waiting area outside Harrah's Tastes is a dead zone. Unlike the sensory overload of the casino floor, the waiting area is home to a patient herd of docile guests. Even though all anticipate a sumptuous feed, no one pushes or jostles. Many murmur in mooing conversation, barely heard over the casino's busy ringtones. Swaying from side to side, dozens of expectant eaters attempt to ease their weary feet. The wait time will be a half hour to forty-five minutes and there are no in-line distractions like those at Disney World, where video monitors and costumed characters turn a queue with multiple zigzags into an extension of the amusement. Did the designers of the buffet intend the regimented tedium of the line as a way of accentuating the pleasure of the buffet itself? Or did they assume that having learned how to abide airport security, visitors to Las Vegas are immune to boredom? I noticed that no one broke ranks to bail on the wait and return to the casino floor.

As a critic of culture, I've learned to distract myself from tedium with observation. So I turned my attention to those around me. A few were trundling wheeled suitcases—a last meal before takeoff? I guess no one fears a bomb in the buffet, as there are no metal detectors or security checkpoints. A great many diners were trundling disproportionately large bodies. Admittedly, I'm a small person, but I couldn't help but notice the exceptional height and girth of the majority of my fellow line mates. Just ahead, a ginger-haired family of four overwhelmed me with the combined weight of their broad shoulders, thick torsos, and heavy legs. Jovial and chatty, they were soon joined by two more family members—equally big and ginger-haired. Just behind, an African American man and his wife towered over me—both of them double my weight. The man, genial and loquacious, struck up a conversation. He explained that he and his wife were from Cleveland, that Vegas was their favorite vacation destination, and Harrah's their favorite buffet. Then he popped the question: did I know how to eat, lay off the fat and go for the meat? I told him my downfall was the pasta, that I always put way too much of it on my plate and hardly have room for anything else. He smiled in commiseration. Clearly pasta was not going to slow him down.

As I turned to face the head of the line in the vain hope of detecting some movement, I recalled the oft-repeated refrain from my childhood that Americans are growing taller and bigger as each generation outstrips its parents and Old World forebears. The Harrah's buffet line upheld the conventional wisdom. But did my parents' generation realize that rather than a superhuman race of giants, we would just become overweight? Yes, there were those two svelte twenty-somethings to give the lie to societal obesity. Cocooned in shimmering evening dresses, they seemed out of place among the middle-aged and heavy crowd. I later saw them in the serving area gingerly tweezing single leaves of lettuce onto their plates. Giggling, they tried to spear one spaghetti noodle, one broccoli floret, one shrimp out of the gumbo. Unlike the customers who pile and ladle, they had turned the all-you-can-eat buffet into an anorexic's game of pick and choose.

Indeed, the buffet might be seen as a laboratory experiment where consumers have to face the dilemma of what to do when desire is not just met, but satiated. Do we re-create scarcity like the anorexic duo, or do we try to have it all—stuff ourselves to the bursting point? Of course, there's always the gorge-and-purge solution. Or did I misinterpret the reek of vomit in the restroom adjacent to Harrah's buffet? Whether bulimia, anorexia, eat till you pop, or shop till you drop—the dark side of consumerist bounty is the fatality of actually having it all.

Musing over the people in line, I realized I had finally arrived at the cashier only to discover that a second line formed to my left—this, the line to actually be seated. Apparently, the buffet maintains the formality of a hostess to direct diners to designated tables. I suppose if we all just trooped in, the crush would resemble a Walmart on a busy Saturday afternoon. There is also a wait staff charged with pouring our requested beverage and with whisking away our soiled plate, even those still piled with food that we appear to no longer want. Thus, we can speed back to the serving line with a clean plate and an equally clean conscience—no starving Armenians to hold us guilty for un-eaten morsels. If you choose unwisely or choose too much of one thing, don't worry about it. Just choose again. After all, capitalism is all about free choice. And unlike shopping at the supermarket, drug store, or Walmart, where an unwanted purchase can mean a bothersome trip to the customer service counter for a refund, the buffet instantly cancels our bad choices with new ones.

American culture is always new—new products, new applications, new styles, even a whole new you. Over and over again, we get to experience the new as a first-time event. I remember the first time I walked into a Walmart store and nearly keeled over. The elderly greeter all but pushed his face into mine. Behind him, aisles jam-packed with bright packaging extended to the store's horizon, and all about me shoppers maneuvered their brimming carts. My kids, on a quest for new school supplies, tugged at my arms. Apparently, their internal GPS units had already located the notebooks, pencils, and cray-ons, while I, befuddled and unable to read the store's merchandising topog-raphy, feebly sought directions from an employee. Granted, I'm not a born shopper as are my children and their entire generation. So I was not dismayed when my local Walmart was chastised for handing out campaign literature for a senatorial candidate, thus giving me a political reason to drop Walmart from my shopping itinerary. But now, with Michelle Obama touting the benefits of Walmart's produce and organic food options, the politics of shopping have become more complicated. Should I support Walmart for making good food choices more available, or should I join the picket lines out front and protest Walmart's failure to provide its employees a living wage?

I thought I had put Walmart well behind me, but now, faced with Har-rah's buffet, I found myself reliving my initial foray into the big-box store. There was just too much of everything—hundreds of people seated in ever-expanding and randomly situated eating areas, dozens more swarming like ants on sorties to the serving line, while countless others disappeared from view, folded into the line's sinuous curves. Unlike the aisle arrangement of a big-box store where commodities are offered up in regimented fashion, Har-rah's serving line consumes the consumer, inviting each to wallow in sights, aromas, and anticipated tastes.

While I may have been ill prepared for Walmart, I'm no stranger to self-serve eating. In North Carolina, where I live, Golden Corral is the buffet of choice. At half the price of a Las Vegas buffet, Golden Corral herds diners into a bounteous world of tummy-filling fare — mac and cheese, mashed potatoes, hush puppies, fried chicken and fish, steaks and roasts, salads smothered in creamy dressing, puffy dinner rolls, and vats of Cool Whip. Those who choose wisely and begin with soup, salad, and a dinner roll may be finished before the entrée. Really big eaters might begin with the meats and side dishes and never have room for the dessert. Since "all you can eat" is never all that you see, why not just begin with dessert and work backward? Golden Corral makes every meal a Thanksgiving Day spread. Sadly, we can't store the leftovers in Tupperware for a week's worth of refrigerated meals. No wonder so many buffet diners can be seen squirreling tasty items into their coat pockets and handbags. The elderly on fixed incomes are especially adept, like the two women I observed one Sunday afternoon at the Golden Corral near my house. Primly dressed as if they had just come from church, each had a copious handbag stowed on her lap. One used paper napkins to wrap individual food items before depositing them in her purse. The other took a more direct approach. She had lined her purse with a plastic shopping bag and proceeded to drop things in without recourse to daintiness. Both women were mindful of the wait staff patrolling the dining area with pitchers of sweet tea. They cautiously slid items from plate to purse only when they saw the wait staff occupied elsewhere.

The notion of an all-you-can-eat buffet teases consumers with the possibility of beating the system by getting more than we pay for. Because we pay up front and there are no bar codes or dollar signs to mar the foods on offer, everything presents itself as free for the taking. Not so at a cafeteria, which is the historical antecedent of the buffet. Cafeterias offered their bounty on a strict unit pricing system. The more you took, the more you paid. And some items definitely cost more than others. I remember my family's excursions to the cafeteria in the 1950s — a wonderland in chrome and glass where food items beckoned from shelves behind hygienic plate glass windows. Diners reached under the plate glass to secure their choices. Many items were already sliced and displayed on plates, while scrupulous servers ladled up the gooey foods, careful to allot the same amount to every customer. Because each item had its price, the fun of sliding a tray along the line and letting oneself be tempted by every appealing food had to be reckoned against the reality of the cost that the vigilant cashier would ring up at the end of the line. "Your eyes are bigger than your stomach," admonished my parents, whose Depression-era upbringing instructed them in the practice of consuming within their means. No wonder cafeterias have all but disappeared from the landscape.

They represented a moment in the historical development of the consumer when desires still had to be measured against needs. They also predated payment by credit card, a time when consumers had to make choices according to cash on hand. As a child, my eyes were truly bigger than my stomach and they went straight to the chiffon pies at the end of the serving line—lime green, lemony yellow, or deep chocolate—each with a swirl of cream on top. In putting it all on view, the cafeteria was already tempting consumers to want beyond their means. "Would you like a Jell-O?" Clearly, my mother thought she was being extravagant in offering me a dessert. She would never consider a chiffon pie, much less imagine that I might desperately want one. Her eyes could look and not really see.

I think my mother may have eaten at one of history's landmark cafeterias: Clifton's in downtown LA. I know she had a special fondness for cafeteria-style eating, and Clifton's opened its doors in 1935, just about the time my mother's family moved to Los Angeles from Brooklyn. The original restaurant featured a themed environment that lifted diners not only out of the Depression but out of LA itself and dropped them Oz-like into a redwood forest complete with a waterfall and wildlife. While the original restaurant no longer exists, photos of its art deco façade and fantasy interior rival Disneyland for saturation of design, and suggest that Disney's dreams had more to do with Hollywood kitsch than the Brothers Grimm. .

As a product of the Depression, Clifton's boasted the motto, "Dine free unless delighted." Indeed, accounts of cafeterias throughout the Depression, and particularly in hard-hit areas in the South, are rife with stories of cheap food for the destitute masses and leftovers served after hours and out the back door to the penniless.

The origin of cafeterias can be traced to the boom-and-bust economy of the California Gold Rush. San Francisco in 1849 seethed with hungry prospectors—all of them burning calories and none of them producing food. The need to provide quick but substantial food for the laboring masses found its solution in the *Mexican cafeterías* that dotted the city's barrios and side streets, offering simple fare and pots of coffee. Much like the barbecue—derived from *barbacoa*—cafeterias migrated out of Mexico with the Southwest's Hispanic workforce, the one to provide for cowboys on long overland cattle drives and the other to service the urban working classes.

What perpetuated the cafeteria as a cultural form from the Gold Rush to the Depression is as much aspirational as it is practical. Yes, the masses needed to be fed, and no one understood that better than Clifford Clinton, founder of Clifton's Cafeterias, who went on to develop soy as the basis of

The Whole World on a Plate [165]

what he called "meals for millions." His chain of cafeterias provided as much food for thought as for hungry stomachs. The redwood forest conjured lush refuge; the glass and chrome spoke to faith in progress and American industrial might; and the treasure of food on display summoned prospects of bounty. The nation might have been in the depths of economic depression, but the cafeteria—like a space capsule projected into the future—preserved the dream of American plenty.

Now, fast forward into the barren landscape of southern Nevada. This is where the cafeteria comes back to earth and transforms itself into the amazing all-you-can-eat Las Vegas buffet. As if history were repeating itself, the Strip swells with hungry masses prospecting for gold. Every visitor's vacation is a tale of boom or bust played out against the backdrop of the larger U.S. economy that features a recent deep recession and a slow crawl toward perpetual joblessness. Meanwhile, the stock market takes its wealthy investors on a roller-coaster ride toward ever-higher peaks haunted by ever-lower lows. Here, the all-you-can-eat buffet offers respite from worries over financial insecurity and the threat of foreclosure. There may never be enough money in our paychecks or in the government's economic stimulus package to pay down the interest-accruing debt on the nation's credit cards, but there will always be unlimited bounty at the Las Vegas buffet.

Boom, bust, and a burgeoning labor force—these may not be the only factors that contributed to the development of cafeteria-style eating both in Los Angeles and in its later reincarnation in Las Vegas. Los Angeles in the 1930s was one of the most corrupt cities in the nation. It certainly rivaled Las Vegas during that city's mob-dominated period for protection rackets, prostitution, and extortion—all of it run out of the mayor's office and overseen by the city's police. It took a grand jury investigation, a special recall election, and the indictments of a number of police officers to end Mayor Shaw's campaign to turn the city into a private money mill. Was it coincidental that the drive to rid the city of its corrupt bosses was spearheaded by the cafeteria mogul Clifford Clinton? Or did the aspirations of all the common people who dined in his restaurants somehow manifest themselves in his efforts? Clinton's civic crusade was not without grave personal risk. His house was bombed by members of the LAPD, as was the car driven by his private investigator. Narrowly escaping death, the latter testified from a wheelchair. No wonder Raymond Chandler, father of the hard-boiled detective genre, had such a predilection for Clifton's Cafeteria.

Did the mobster moguls of the 1950s who turned Las Vegas into a gambling mecca wholly underestimate the importance of the buffet? Or did they grasp its aspirational value and opt to limit it by sidelining the buffets? For whatever reason, the entrepreneurial casino bosses of the 1950s saw the buffets as a basic pit stop for players who needed a quick calorie fix without the difficulties of casting about the Strip for food. Because the casinos made their real money at the tables and on the machines, the food was cheap. If it was also unremarkable—well, all the more reason not to linger over it.

In sharp contrast, today's buffets are as much a reason for going to Las Vegas as the casinos and the dream of a big win. Diners sample the different buffets and can be overheard offering comparisons. Some write online food reviews and others advertise discount coupons to the buffets for sale on eBay. But no matter how many buffets a particular visitor might have tried, each and every diner I queried always responded, "This one's the best."

Such was the case one evening when I attempted a conversation with a party of four seated next to me in Paris's Le Village buffet. I was with Stacy, who had spent her study abroad year in Dijon, so an excursion into things French seemed a logical choice. The decor summons up a French village of yesteryear complete with provincial storefronts, flowery window boxes, and waitresses dressed in dirndls. National pride infuses the serving area, which offers a pedagogical tour of five of France's regional cuisines. Thus, Brittany serves up coq au vin and crepes; Normandy, quiche and steamed mussels; Burgundy, boeuf bourguignon; Provence, ravioli and ratatouille; and Alsace, fondue and braised duck. As for the salads, cheeses, and desserts, these are set apart, the latter in their own little freestanding Hansel and Gretel–style house.

The four diners seated next to us were reluctant to enter into conversation. Perhaps they were put off by Stacy's enthusiasm. She had just returned to our table after a preliminary excursion to the serving line to announce, "It's marvelous, and totally vegetarian friendly!" Either incurious or unimaginative, the four diners were working their way through platefuls of meat. No braised eggplant or zucchini for them, although one had a few snails rolling about with the beef. Undaunted and trying to figure out why they were so wedded to meat when Le Village tempts its diners with a host of unique possibilities, I chatted on, explaining that this was Stacy's first trip to Vegas. I asked if they came often. A few vague murmurs seemed to imply a "yes." I mentioned that Stacy and I are fans of the buffets and wondered if they had any special tips. Clearly annoyed by two chatty vegetarians, they dove deeper into their plates, stoically chewing to avoid giving a response. Finally, one of the men and a woman I took for his wife began to open up. Between mouthfuls from her second and his third plate, the man said they were all from Rochester and they tried to get to Las Vegas a couple of times a year. Through half sentences and

a fair number of grunts and murmurs, I gathered that the four considered themselves buffet connoisseurs. In their judgment, "Paris is best on the Strip," although "some days are better than others." I found it odd that Paris ranked at the top of their list when the folks from Rochester eschewed so many of Le Village's regional specialties. Gazing at our own plates, I realized that Stacy and I had progressed to dessert and that we had each chosen four, which we divided in half and shared for a total of eight sweet delights apiece. Sugar is definitely the vegetarian's bane.

Why do we choose what we choose? It's true that I have a sweet tooth and can't help but indulge it, especially when tempted with petit fours and chocolate mousse. Does it follow, then, that meat eaters have an analogous taste-driven desire for roast beef au jus? Or are we all just playing *Supermarket Sweep*? Like contestants on the TV game show that premiered in the mid-1960s, we bolt into the serving area. Instead of racing about with a shopping cart, we ply the line, tray in hand. And just like the supermarket sweepers, we don't just grab everything. I remember the televised players racing to the frozen food section—there to toss four or five turkeys into their cart, then on to the meats, where they stuffed T-bones and filet mignons into the nooks and crannies between the turkeys. Some players headed straight to the toiletries, over-the-counter drugs, and Pampers. On the game show, choice was a simple matter of price, with victory going to the contestant whose shopping cart totaled the highest dollar amount at the end of the frantic spree. The show taught viewers and contestants alike that winning means equating taste with expense. In a commodified society such as ours where wanting is channeled into buying, and where value means price, how can we not want what costs the most?

Dinner at Le Village comes to $24.99 per person. I wonder if the foursome from Rochester managed to consume $100 worth of meat between them. Or for that matter, did my daughter and I come close to $50 in sweets and veggies? Is it possible that any of us let ourselves be guided by taste alone? Or did we all heed a system of unseen price stickers—ingrained over numerous trips to the supermarket—that ranks the sweets as extravagant and therefore valuable, and the meats as just plain pricey?

If Paris offers its diners five regional cuisines, the other Las Vegas buffets aim to deliver the whole world on a plate. A trip down the serving line is a little like a themed ride at an amusement park. Diners journey past the well-known food landmarks—the big hams, vats of potatoes, and side dishes—then wind their way through the ethnic offerings, dishes from Asia, Mexico, Italy, and the Cajun bayou. Often the ethnic foods are designated as such, framed with

paper flowers or fiesta napkins. These alert diners to their encounter with diversity. We become what anthropologist Lucy Long has dubbed "culinary tourists."[2] As she sees it, culinary tourism can bridge cultural divides precisely because the act of sampling another's food is by nature an intimate experience. From Long's optimistic point of view, culinary tourism offers the best way to appreciate another's culture because it is multisensory. As she puts it, "Sightseeing is only a partial engagement with otherness, whereas culinary tourism, utilizing the senses of taste, smell, touch, and vision, offers a deeper, more integrated level of experience."[3] It bears noting that sensory engagement is not always voluntary and enacted out of curiosity and openness. As Stacy reminds us in "Gaming the Senses" (chapter 7), an excursion through the sensory overload of the Las Vegas Strip defines us not as agents of our engagement but as unwitting subjects whose senses are piqued and played. Additionally, Long's overall faith in the benefits of culinary tourism allows her to sail over the difficulties posed by the history of colonialism and newer forms of economic imperialism that necessarily impact the practice of tourism. Bear in mind that the symptomatic expression of unequal global power relations is the assimilation of what were once exotic foreign foods, and the flattening of those foods and culinary traditions into the fodder for our fast-food industry.

Not coincidentally, the Mexican food zone in a typical Las Vegas buffet includes do-it-yourself tacos with crisp taco shells and precut fillings displayed in a cluster of serving trays. Then there's the tamale pie—a mound of savory ground beef, layered with corn meal, and smothered in melted and congealed cheese—all of it bathed under the heat lamp's red glow. Chips, refried beans, and guacamole offer the possibility of nachos or a tostada. We all know how to assemble the ingredients and how they will taste because we've all dined at a Mexican restaurant somewhere in the United States.

The Asian food items, unlike the dog-fried rice that Long encountered in Burma, are reassuringly recognizable—egg rolls, sweet-and-sour chicken, stir-fried vegetables with bits of beef, or chicken, or shrimp. Similarly, the Italian offerings strike a familiar chord—fetuccini al fredo, pizza, bowtie pasta salad, meatballs in a rich tomato sauce, and bowls full of grated parmesan to top it all off. So too are the Cajun dishes familiar—a gooey gumbo, dirty rice, and the enormous steamed crab legs. And last but not least, there's the obligatory sushi. In all my trips to Las Vegas, I have yet to encounter a buffet that doesn't include sushi. Even Paris, with its rigorous attention to traditional national cuisines, proudly offers sushi, prepared on the spot by a presumably world-class sushi chef.

Notwithstanding their familiarity, these foods were once foreign to the mainstream American palate. Now they're our favorite ethnic cuisines. Walk into any shopping mall and let your nose guide you to the food court. There you will find the foods of our immigrant brothers and sisters sandwiched in between the Coney Island hot dogs and frozen yogurt treats. Thus, Panda Express shares counter space with Sbarro, Wendy's, N.C. Bar B Q, and Baja Bistro. All vie for the shopper's taste buds and wallet.

What's interesting about buffet-style eating and what distinguishes it from the mall's food court is that the buffet invites us to sample everything and to put it all on the same plate. At the mall we're faced with a choice: do I want a calzone or a burger and fries? At the buffet our choice is cumulative: do I want a taco, and some of that cheesy pasta, and what about a bit of rice and stir-fry? The plate brings it all together. Spoonfuls from a dozen separate dishes collide, then merge. Overambitious diners begin to pile foods on top of foods until their crowded plates threaten to overflow. The plate is a culinary epicenter where all the world's possibilities slide into a homogeneous mass that no one would mistake for fusion food. But, hey, as we probably once told our moms as we swallowed a gluey mound of mashed potatoes studded with peas, "It all goes to the same place."

Besides, everything at the buffet is cooked in the same kitchen—and often by Latinos. The huge kitchens that serve the casino hotels differ only in scale from restaurant kitchens all across America, whose employees are largely immigrant and predominantly Hispanic. In my hometown, the Vietnamese lunch counter greets diners with rich aromas and a demure Asian serving staff. But every pot that emerges from the kitchen is carried by a Latino who doesn't appear to speak English—or, for that matter, Vietnamese—but who has clearly mastered the art of cooking in woks. When I first saw such a man hoist a heavy pot of kung po chicken and pour it into the serving tray, I was struck by what I took as an incongruity. But isn't it the height of ethnocentrism to imagine that the ethnicity of cooks and cuisines must match like the icons in a child's lotto game? Indeed, no one seems to question the thousands of Anglo chefs and their dilettante wannabes who have no qualms about learning and mastering the foods of other people in other places.

After all, hasn't Anthony Bourdain made us all want to bite into some richly grilled organ meat from a street vendor in Lima, Peru? Bourdain has used his popular TV shows like *No Reservations* and *Parts Unknown* as vehicles for traveling the world and bringing exotic foodways into our living rooms. With gusto and bravado, he chomps into feet, eyeballs, snouts, and anuses—animal "parts unknown" to most of his viewers. With reckless abandon, he hurls praise and insults, sexual innuendo and expletives. A self-confessed former smoker and user of every drug under the sun, Bourdain has since turned his unbridled appetites to foods of every culinary persuasion.

No matter where in the world, be it the Palestinian West Bank or the streets of Hanoi, Bourdain is the bwana figure—the Great White Hunter—who is guided by a local (or the local's entire family) into the secrets of off-the-map dining. In body and voice, Bourdain displaces his hosts even while he immerses himself in their foods. The shows speak to the benefits of getting to know other people and their foodways even while Bourdain embodies the macho affirmation of an imperialist emissary for whom the exotic fare he samples will never have to be the mainstay of his diet.

Indeed, Bourdain is just a genteel version of the sort of food othering viewers have long relished on the hit show *Survivor*. In her essay "Gagging on the Other," Stacy Jameson takes on the show's "gross food challenge."[4] She characterizes the competition as a performance wherein subjects clearly defined as representatives of the First World, whose normal diet includes Big Macs and Mountain Dew, are challenged to eat all manner of vermin, bugs, and entrails, which the show defines as representative of the locals' normal diet. Jameson's analysis focuses on the contestants' gagging reflex, which enacts both a real and a symbolic "gatekeeping" against the foreign other, who by reason of the gagging can only be thought of as disgustingly primitive.[5] Unlike the locals in Bourdain's programs, who are shown to have elaborate culinary traditions, the locals on *Survivor* are almost never shown and are, instead, displaced into the embodiment of raw animal parts. Jameson's delineation of gatekeeping provides a model for thinking about America's foodways and our culture more generally. Do we not enrich ourselves with comfortable infusions of the foreign so as not to gag on too big a bite of otherness?

Try to imagine a Las Vegas buffet without its ethnic offerings. Erase those colorful corn kernels and red peppers, stifle the savory aromas, soften the piquant tastes, and do away with the fun of making your own taco. What's left is the rich and bland. How better to express America's dilemma—rich but bland. We want the diversity of palate that comes with our immigrant populations, but we don't necessarily want the bearers of diversity to stick around. "Send them back!" "Keep them out!" Do the vigilante Minutemen who shout these slogans and devote their weekends to building and patrolling sections of fence along the border with Mexico scrupulously avoid pit stops at Taco Bell? Or for that matter, when the residents of Hazleton, Pennsylvania, and Escondido, California, my childhood home, passed ordinances to penalize landlords who rent to so-called illegals, did they remember to decree that tacos henceforth be renamed "freedom sandwiches"?

The daunting task faced by all who rail against immigrants is to assiduously distinguish the foreign from the American. But what the Las Vegas buffet makes clear is that the best of America has been becoming foreign for a long time. If the ethnic foods in the buffet are familiar, it's because America has lived with them for more than a hundred years. They came with the Mexicans who herded cattle throughout the Southwest, the Acadians who migrated out of Quebec to fuse with bayou culture, the Italians who cut the stone for our monumental skyscrapers, and the Asians who built the Transcontinental Railroad.

I've been on the planet long enough to remember a time in my hometown when the now-familiar ethnic still had a tinge of the foreign. I imagine some places in the Midwest are only now beginning to experience what it means to be a cultural crossroads—something I took for granted as a native Californian. Growing up in Escondido in the 1950s, I was pleased that my family frequented the town's two non-Anglo eateries. One boasted a neon sign that glowed the words *Chinese American*. It featured beef, chicken, and pork versions of chow mein and chop suey as well as egg rolls, fried wontons, and, of course, the crackle of crispy fried noodles that you could sprinkle on top of everything. Best of all were the delightful little white paper boxes with wire handles. The packaging made eating Chinese like opening a present.

Lupita's was Escondido's other ethnic restaurant. A Mexican *loncheria*, Lupita's had migrated out of the barrio and across the highway that separated the Mexican and Anglo parts of town. Diners at Lupita's could gaze across four lanes of blacktop and see the pastel houses of the barrio without ever leaving the familiarity of Main Street. The restaurant's A inspection rating stood as reassurance against mental images of the sorts of things sold in the barrio markets, particularly the organ-rich meat market, where spleens, tripe, and enormous beef tongues were commonplace.

Lupita's is where I discovered *huevos rancheros*—a dish that so far hasn't made the transition to fast food. It's just too messy to be eaten in a car. Imagine two fried eggs soon to be pierced by your fork, then stirred into a savory blend of beans and salsa—all of it piled on griddle-warm corn tortillas. For the Anglo population of Escondido, Lupita's was familiar without being assimilated. Other than the A & W Root Beer stand and the car hop drive-in with its roller-skating waitresses, there was no fast food—much less a Taco Bell. Mexican food belonged to the Mexican people. It was ours only as culinary tourists.

Similarly, we took in the language. How could we not, when the speech and music filled the air? It wafted above the groves when the truckloads of workers arrived to harvest the citrus and avocados. Spanish was the language of schoolyard gossip aimed at *jueras* like me, and it boomed out of every other AM radio station.

Sadly, I was an imperfect speaker, never able to decipher the entire story line of *Superhombre*, or the juiciest—if not meanest—bits of gossip whispered about me. So Lupita's smacked of the exotic. And not least because the windowsills above all the booths were lined with giant taxidermy frogs—each holding a musical instrument in its delicately elongated frog fingers, each with its lips coarsely stitched in a grin. I see those frogs to this day—haunting reminders that another culture's kitsch was my ineffably foreign.

Out on the Las Vegas Strip, the architecture pays homage to the foreign. If a plate of food at the buffet can deliver a microcosm of the world, then the Strip offers the world in macrocosm. But have no fear. This is not the world seething with ethnic violence, torn by economic disparity, decimated by famine and sickness, and wounded by war. No, it's the comfortably safe world of pastiche, where everything that's unique and different in the real world is reduced to a quote, much like the Americanized version of ethnic cuisine found in the buffets. At Paris, the Eiffel Tower erupts out of the casino floor, through the roof, and into the Las Vegas skyline. The Luxor condemns its guests to life inside the steeply pitched walls of a pyramid. The Venetian captivates visitors with its version of the famous canals, complete with gondolas and gondoliers. The Bellagio's aristocratic façade is offset by a crowd-pleasing computerized water show set to the strains of popular ballads. Caesars Palace offers the Roman Forum colonized by upscale shops like Prada and Gucci. Mandalay Bay is vaguely and nonspecifically tropical. And Rio features the nightmare wish fulfillment of Mardi Gras every day of the year.

Can any of this be called exotic, or is it all just plain over the top? Clearly, no one who visits Las Vegas is apt to imagine themselves in any of the real places that the architecture quotes. This is true even in the Venetian, where visitors stare spellbound at the ceiling, whose play of light and drifting clouds gives the appearance of an evening sky. Unlike tourists at Disney World's EPCOT, who remark that their sojourns in the park's replicas of France and Germany made them feel as if they were really there without the discomfiture of actual travel, visitors to Las Vegas know they're in Vegas and only want to be in Vegas. In fact, all the references to the world outside merely confirm that it's all just Vegas. Of course, sticklers are apt to remark that some places are absent from the Strip—most notably China and Russia. Others may see the presence of the purely corporate (MGM Grand) and the egotistical (Steve Wynn's and Donald Trump's casinos) as distractions from the otherwise World's Fair ambience. If the Strip subsumes the world, it does so unevenly and incompletely. It has no need to document the world in its entirety because it is the world.

In writing on the simulacrum, Jean Baudrillard asserts that simulation "is the generation by models of a real without origin or reality."[6] He has in mind the way that a map of a particular territory comes to precede and eventually supplant the world that it references. Baudrillard's formula can be readily translated to the Las Vegas Strip, where the degree of simulation goes beyond the map's relation to its referenced territory. Indeed, the built environment of the Strip seems to be modeled on the postcard images found in countless gift shops on the Strip. What can we say came first when referentiality is circular and any association with the so-called real Eiffel Tower is merely iconographic?

In imposing itself on the desert, marooned in a sea of sand, Las Vegas suggests a world unto itself. A night flight into the city confirms its apparent isolation—an island of light ringed by the void-like dark. It's a conceit born of hubris that is wholly contradicted by the city's absolute dependence on the wider world, whose riches flow into Las Vegas in a steady stream like plankton sucked down the maw of a giant whale. Here, the wealth of the world's production—the meat, the fish, the fancy out-of-season fruits and vegetables, the butter, eggs, milk, and ice cream, the coffee, sugar, and don't forget the chocolate—really does all "go to the same place," drawn into the city on supply lines made of concrete that function like feeding tubes attached to a disproportionately huge stomach. The Bellagio alone runs up a food tab of a million dollars a month for its rich buffet that includes a thousand pounds of prime rib per day.

Most visitors to Las Vegas never see the city's backstage feeding area, as was my lot during one of my research trips. I had been walking on the Strip and decided to take what appeared to be a shortcut to Caesars Palace by way of an upscale mall named Fashion Show. I wouldn't call the mall labyrinthine, but its internal space seemed to expand with every step I took. With Caesars Palace nowhere in sight, much less an egress back to the Strip, I opted for an emergency exit. Hoping for sunlight, I was dismayed to find myself in a narrow fluorescent green corridor where I'm sure no shopper has ever trod. With a few twists and turns, I finally arrived at a door. Dismayed once again, I emerged into sunlight but not on the Strip. Instead, I stood perched above a massive loading dock with other docks to my right and left. A maze of arterial service roads snaked in multiple directions, none of which led to the Strip. Like a port where massive container ships disgorge their cargo, this no-man's-land of loading docks and truck routes embodies the topography of global-

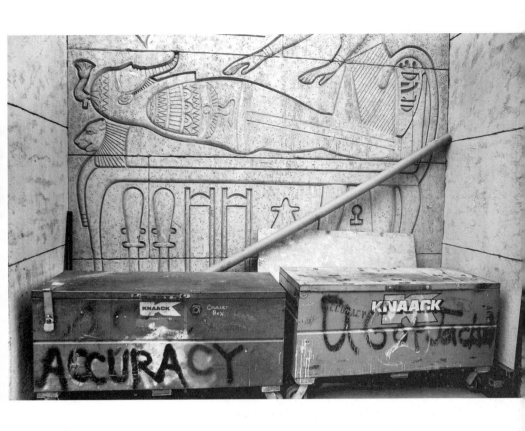

ized production wherein most of the food items we buy travel a minimum of 1,500 miles from farms to our plates. Las Vegas, once a vernal meadow, now a concrete desert, is the epitome of global capitalism's irrational supply chain, which wholly and precariously depends on the uninterrupted flow of cheap fossil fuel.

Indeed, as Eric Schlosser points out in *Fast Food Nation*, the food service industry that defines our consumptions in the First World works its influence down through the chain of production to reshape the food infrastructure of distant and economically disadvantaged food-growing regions. Schlosser primarily takes aim at McDonald's and other icons of the fast-food industry, whose establishment in foreign countries occasions the importation of "entire systems of production."[7] Such systems sweep aside small agricultural holdings and ecologically sensitive habitats in the process of carving out large-scale monocrop production sites. The Las Vegas buffets may be a cut above McDonald's, but the massive bounty on offer depends on the same worldwide monocrop production process. This puts food crops on a par with other extractive industries. The iceberg lettuce grown for McDonald's in southern India, like the blueberries grown in Mexico for Whole Foods or the Las Vegas buffets, are raw materials not unlike the rare earth metals mined in Congo. Systems of exchange based on extraction neither replenish nor sustain the economies of their origin even while they create tremendous bounty elsewhere.

In an effort to take a stand against the inequalities inherent in globalized systems of production and consumption, various communities and collectivities have banded together to support local businesses, particularly when it comes to food. Farmers' markets, CSAs, and restaurants that source their ingredients from local farms are growing in popularity. Nevertheless, it would be tough—if not downright impossible—to be a locavore in Las Vegas. Unlike other towns and cities across America where eating local is becoming commonplace, the Strip vaunts the far-flung. Imagine dedicating yourself to the 100-Mile Diet popularized by Alisa Smith and J. B. MacKinnon in their book *Plenty*.[8] Smith and MacKinnon developed a locavore regime in the food-rich environs of Vancouver. Granted, March was difficult for the couple. With only beets and potatoes as fully local foodstuffs, Smith and MacKinnon survived on borscht and potato pancakes. But spring brought plentiful greens and summer its bounty of fruits and vegetables. The couple's dietary experiment dramatized how regional economies that were once self-sustaining have been decimated by market-driven systems of production and distribution. Thus, the environs of Vancouver that once produced wheat could not provide its dedicated locavores with a single loaf of bread. Even fish were scarce, as the dockside markets boasted catches from Latin America and Asia. Where the Vancouver locavores trolled independent markets and backyard gardens for the makings of a meal, a locavore in Las Vegas would truly be hard pressed and perhaps doomed to a repast of mirages, not unlike those drought-crazed prospectors in the movies.

Luckily, there's RC Farms right in northern Las Vegas ready to provide any dedicated locavore with a "porkatarian" option. A perverse twenty-first-century realization of Clifford Clinton's dream of providing meals for millions, RC Farms feeds its hogs with recycled waste from the Las Vegas buffets—thirty tons per day to be exact. Just imagine all that food brought out to the serving line but left to languish under the heat lamps, not to mention all that food left on your plate. It's all dumped together, then stirred and raked by patient RC Farms employees, ever on the lookout for stray utensils. The whole world, now no longer on a plate, gets churned into swill and trucked out to the farm, where it's steam sterilized and served up to the happy hogs. Fortunately, hogs have a digestive system very like our own. I wonder, though, if the five thousand hogs at RC Farms are up to the task. If four thousand humans stuff themselves at the Excalibur breakfast, can a mere five thousand hogs finish off the leftovers? And what about the garbage from all those other buffets? Shouldn't there be as many pigs as people?

Maybe the distinction between pigs and people is moot. After all, the pigs feed us and we feed the pigs. "It all goes to the same place"—from pig to pig, not unlike the Bible's "from dust to dust." Maybe Charlton Heston had it wrong and "Soylent Green is pigs!"

This rumination on how the buffets impact the diners' waists has come full circle to a consideration of recycled waste that again impacts the diner's waist. While the recycling of some of the Strip's food waste into pig production represents a step in the right direction, it falls short of the full-scale town- and citywide food waste composting projects currently mandated in Seattle and San Francisco, where compost derived from household dinner tables and restaurants has become a valued soil amendment now used in the vineyards of Napa and Sonoma. The success of food waste recycling in these cities and throughout Canada has precipitated a number of pilot programs in other states including Pennsylvania, Massachusetts, and Colorado. Indeed, Mayor Michael Bloomberg closed out his tenure with a call to add New York City to that list. Imagine the Las Vegas Strip as a great, but undeveloped, waste recycling resource capable of supplying incalculable amounts of agricultural compost and biogas.

If we conduct a thought experiment wherein the United States becomes a utopia of sustainability, we would have Ernest Callenbach's landmark science fiction novel, *Ecotopia*. Written in 1973, the heyday of the counterculture, the novel documents the practices of a utopian breakaway nation, composed roughly of present-day Washington, Oregon, and Northern California. (The actual food composting cities of Seattle and San Francisco would be at the heart of the novel's imaginary independent nation.) *Ecotopia* follows the fact-finding experiences of a journalist sent into the breakaway state some twenty years after its separation from the United States. Not coincidentally, the journalist wants to know how Ecotopians have managed to feed themselves, especially since all trade with the United States has ceased. The novel essentially asks the same question currently taken up by the locavore movement; that is, can a finite region sustainably feed its population? Imagine the journalist's dismay when his interview with the assistant minister of agriculture begins with a tutorial on sewage: "The first major project of his ministry after independence, he said, had been to put the country's food cycle on a stable-state basis: all food wastes, sewage, and garbage were to be turned into organic fertilizer and applied to the land, where it would again enter into the food production cycle."[9] It's only after a detailed lesson on sewage that the minister takes up food itself and explains that Ecotopia meets its food needs by learning to produce less—hence, eliminating the sorts of wastes that accrue to surplus.

The distance between Ecotopia and the Las Vegas Strip yawns wider than the Grand Canyon. Nevertheless, Las Vegas gives rise to many of the same desires for a better life that fuel the utopian imaginary, not the least of which is the desire for a bounteous life. From within the stable-state economy of Ecotopia, plenty is simply a way of life. Contrariwise, bounty in Las Vegas is as driven by the desire for excess as it is tortured by the fear of scarcity.

Boom or bust, such was the lot of those who flocked to the California gold fields as well as those who fled the Great Depression–era Dust Bowl. Boom or bust?—these are the terms that shape many a tourist's visit to Las Vegas. Indeed, boom or bust may well be the motto of our larger, out-of-kilter economy, where 99 percent of the population sees itself precariously hovering on the verge of bust while a minuscule 1 percent enjoys an unprecedented boom. In the context of the uneven distribution of wealth—now on a global scale—the all-you-can-eat Las Vegas buffet is more than just an opulent spread. As a cultural signifier, the buffet bespeaks the desire for plenty even while it embodies inevitable scarcity elsewhere and the dead weight of its own waste.

1. Alfred Hitchcock, dir., *The Trouble with Harry* (Los Angeles: Paramount, 1955).

2. Lucy M. Long, "Culinary Tourism: A Folkloristic Perspective on Eating and Otherness," in *Culinary Tourism*, ed. Lucy M. Long (Lexington: University Press of Kentucky, 2010), 21.

3. Long, "Culinary Tourism," 21.

4. Stacy M. Jameson, "Gagging on the Other: Television's Gross Food Challenge," in *Food and Everyday Life*, ed. Thomas Conroy (Lanham, MD: Lexington, 2014), 11–40.

5. Jameson, "Gagging on the Other."

6. Jean Baudrillard, *Selected Writings*, ed. Mark Poster (Cambridge, MA: Polity, 1988), 166.

7. Eric Schlosser, *Fast Food Nation: The Dark Side of the All-American Meal* (New York: Houghton Mifflin, 2001).

8. Alisa Smith and James MacKinnon, *Plenty* (New York: Random House, 2007).

9. Ernest Callenbach, *Ecotopia* (New York: Bantam, 1981), 21–22.

SEVEN

Gaming the Senses

"Submerge the senses," coaxes an advertisement in a tourist magazine for Cirque du Soleil's O.* This long-running production at the Bellagio presents a 1.5-million-gallon pool as a stage into and out of which a dreamlike cast of characters, objects, and even landscapes plunge and surface. The literal watery submersion of the characters functions as metaphor for the audience experience — and for the Vegas tourist more broadly — suggesting a saturation of physical and emotional stimulation. In the model of water, O purports a sensory splash back, the movements of the actors on the water stage causing a spray of feelings and sensations to douse the audience. Encountering this advertisement while sitting at the side of the Flamingo hotel pool as people splash in the water, lounge in a crammed milieu of beach chairs, indulge in the unavoidable supply of large, colorful mixed drinks, and attempt to converse over the blasting music, I wonder: did I really need to buy the $100 ticket

---

* Stacy M. Jameson

to submerge my senses? Indeed, I was experiencing an unavoidable sensory overload right there at the pool side.

The city is more than just a place to visit—it engulfs and even gets inside you. My visits to Vegas are marked by this constant and dense overtaxing of all of my senses. Where the language learner might strive for cultural immersion, as a tourist and researcher in the city I instead struggle to gain a degree of distance. "Overload" seems to be the constant refrain of visitors after they return home from a trip to the Nevada city. The buildings, lights, and video screens, both on the street and in the casinos, compete constantly for our attention, offering an inescapable visual barrage that demands we "look over here," now "over here!" The visual cues seem unidentifiable en mass, hailing us incessantly from all angles simultaneously. Unlike the relationship between the television viewer and the screen, there is no clear sense of orientation for the tourist to this city. There is no way to step back and get one's bearings within such a flood. Identifying an autonomous standpoint or singular frame of reference—like a museumgoer viewing a painting—is impossible within the Las Vegas show that just seems too overpowering and all encompassing. We should not be fooled, however, into thinking that the city thus encourages many diverse points of view and varied perspectives or ways of experiencing its spaces and their pleasures. Considering some of these complex pluralistic stimuli of Las Vegas suggests a more restrictive message. The inundating smells, sounds, and other sensory inducements condition consistent modes of orientation, playing on and even in our bodies in ways that control and limit our interactions and experiences.

Navigating your way on foot through the city is a challenge. Like the food store channeling you past many other tempting products before you can pick up your necessary milk from the back aisle, casinos place diversions along the path to possible exits or amenities such as gaming opportunities, or staff members hounding you to buy show tickets. Signage is hard to locate, confusing, and often misleading. "Where are we?" asks my boyfriend, Chris, as we try to find our way out of Aria, the newly built casino in CityCenter. "I think I'm going to have to start using my compass," he concludes, highlighting the way the city spaces can distort one's bearings.

Vision has long been privileged within a Western Enlightenment tradition as a means of knowing your surroundings. However, in Las Vegas visual signals are deceiving markers of both direction and proper behavior. Standard expectations of scale are altered: enlarged like the faces of Marie and Donny Osmond occupying the entire side of a hotel building, or shrunk like

the model of the Eiffel Tower that competes with the singing sibling duo for visual dominance. Visual perspective is not to be trusted. Indeed, what tourist hasn't attempted to walk the length of the Strip because it seems as if the Stratosphere is right next door?

Here façade becomes a mode of life, not just an architectural style. The constant screens, murals, and false fronts draw you into illusory surroundings while confusing your sense of direction and perspective. "That's a projection," I told Susan as she walked off in the wrong direction toward a wall of swimming fish during our search for the Mandalay Bay Aquarium. Similarly, a series of painted panels lower into the water, offering an illusion of three-dimensional canals and alleyways to pedestrians at the Venetian, suggesting vistas and opportunities where there are none. How do we make sense of our surroundings when the eye is so bewildered or absorbed in pretense? Like a plunge underwater, the visual onslaught has an ironic muffling effect that bewilders and disorients. I found myself, as if visually disabled, turning to my other senses to find some degree of purchase, only to find that these other modes of orientation also encourage our bodies to react in ways we may not intend. By thinking beyond sight and examining Las Vegas through touch, taste, sound, and smell, we can begin to understand the embodied multiplicity of the pulls, temptations, inducements, and mandates on the visiting tourist.

Though Las Vegas purports to be a place for free play, open to bending mores and varied opportunities, a look at sensory engagements suggests a different story. Like the body adjusting to an air-conditioned space, the atmospheres of Las Vegas regulate visitors' experiences, naturalizing modes of behavior and commercial engagement through an overwhelming appeal to sensory and bodily processes. Much more subtle than the traffic signals and crosswalks that direct crowds along a designated path across the bustling Strip, our sensory engagements with the objects, people, and spaces of the city become incorporated; eventually, we are acclimatized to them and thus do not even know they are at work. Structured auditory and olfactory atmospheres trigger nerve endings in our fingertips, journey up our nostrils, and impact our guts. Thus are we oriented to and away from spaces, objects, and people, conditioned at every turn to the consumer paradigm of Las Vegas.

Las Vegas is identified (inside and out) as an entertainment capital with a plethora of games and diversions. Bodily sense suggests a distinct perspective on the modes of interaction and engagement in such a play space. I am reminded of a contemporary trend in performance studies in which spaces (table settings for teatime, industrial zones, and costumes) are wired for sound or light that become triggered by individuals' contact and motion. The performers "play the space," unintentionally, but actively, generating unique and irreproducible artistic concerts. Las Vegas—from the dinner tables and casino floors to the shows and architecture—offers a reverse of this paradigm. While we play (in more or less structured ways), the space in turn *plays us*. As cultural theorist Arjun Appadurai has argued, the body is an "intimate arena for the practices of reproduction," upon which social disciplines can be inscribed. That is, the temporal structures of everyday life, especially bodily necessities like eating, which must be repeated daily, are important models for the habituation to more complex patterns of consumption.[1] Las Vegas gambling sites and retailers naturalize modes of commercial engagement through an appeal to mundane sensory and bodily processes.

Let's compare the Las Vegas paradigm to another common model of sensory discipline: an electric fence used to condition a dog to stay within the boundaries of a yard. The lesson we as a society can learn from the example of an electric fence—and one that Vegas in turn teaches us—is how our sensory experiences can be channeled into the management of our movements, behaviors, and feelings. One model is Pavlov's dog, describing a person conditioned to react automatically without using critical thinking. Ivan Pavlov is famous for the concept of the conditioning reflex, in which ringing a bell, shocks, whistles, or even visual stimuli can be used to signal meal times and promote real unconscious physical responses, like the anticipatory production of saliva. While we ought to be somewhat critical of the animalistic, viscerally driven automaton this phrase invokes, what we should draw from it are the ways in which we respond physically and often predictably to sensory stimuli. In Las Vegas, when we hear the "bing, bing, bing" of the slot machines, are we physically quickened to come over, to spend, to play? To answer this question, I will embark on a multisensory tour of Las Vegas, attempting rather artificially to disentangle individual sensory cues that actually occur mixed, blended, and fused with others. In isolating single senses, we can start to get a feel for how systematized sound, touch, taste, and smell condition specific modes of orientation to the city and its pleasures, and by extension we will gain insight into the organizations of a broader American mass cultural sensorium.

Sound

From the moment you step off the plane—in what could visually be any other airport waiting room—the sounds of slot machines function as geographic and ideological markers. The sounds identify the destination, set the lively mood, and guide the newly arrived tourists to gamble. Indeed, my most lingering "image" of Las Vegas is in fact auditory. The name of the place and the ideas it inspires is inextricable from an unavoidable recall of a chorus of those slot machines. My head fills with that characteristic cheerful sound, "bing, bing, bing."

In comparison, I was aware of the urban noises on a recent trip to New York City: cars that whoosh by pedestrians, honking horns, shoes hitting pavement. Vegas has many similar sounds and yet what becomes muted in Las Vegas is the sound of everyday urban life: barking dogs, teens headed to school, sirens, and so forth. These missing sounds draw attention to the condensation of entertainment and consumer spaces and the absence of interruptions in the landscape by residences, grocery stores, or office buildings. Sounds are one of the many factors that make walking along the Las Vegas Strip both distinctive and at times arduous. The city defies the possibility of experiencing its scenes as a mere stroller, a loiterer or a window shopper: that is, like the nineteenth-century Parisian flâneur.[2] In contrast, the sounds of the Vegas Strip generate a physicality that can quite literally move you. Noises call people into spaces, such as the cheerful sounds of a lively restaurant or lounge that "must be good," or they can drive you off like the bass-blasting Rockhouse Bar and Nightclub with its doors open and speakers turned to the streets assaulting the passersby. Sounds declare that "it is time" and call us to attention, like the bonging bell of the Bellagio belltower just before the fountain show begins its dance. There are sounds that set the mood, like the croaking frogs and chirping crickets that get louder just before the eruption of the Mirage volcano, transporting the listener away from the urban space into tropical nature. There are sounds that sell, like the continuous looping advertisements playing outside of Casino Royale for Cinnabons and other mass food items, the man dressed as a leprechaun broadcasting O'Sheas beer pong, or the smutters "click-click-clicking" their stacks of girlie cards. When you are visiting Las Vegas, these sounds not only shape the tone of the city, but physically move you in and out of establishments and push-pull you to action: to party, to purchase, to game.

Standing on the bridge in line to take the elevator up the Paris resort-casino model of the Eiffel Tower, I listen in one ear to Peter Gabriel's "Sledgehammer" issuing from speakers along the blue sky-like ceiling above. Meanwhile, the other ear registers an overwhelming wash of "bling bling" and the thundering voices of Heath Ledger and Christian Bale reverberating from the video accompaniment to the new Batman slot machines on the floor below. Together these overlapping dins and echoes produce the sound montage that characterizes the casinos of the Strip. I am perpetually confronted with varying and multiple sounds that do not always fit smoothly together. As within the Paris casino, the sounds clash in tempo, key, and tone, creating a discordant collage effect. These discrepancies are important in that at one moment, your body can tune in to register individual elements that accelerate you either toward or away from that Batman slot machine or push you toward other activities like shopping or relaxing. Additionally, these combinations produce single heterogeneous assemblages that characterize Las Vegas as a whole. It is that "sound montage," to use film terminology, that you carry home with you in recollection of the Entertainment Capital of the World.

Variations in the sound montage across the different zones of a resort complex mark divisions between public and private spaces (boundaries that are often very fluid in Las Vegas under the "what happens here stays here" mantra). Indeed, noises buffer our interactions with strangers in open communal spaces. Walking around Madame Tussauds Wax Museum, where very loud music provides cover, you feel free to behave in ways you might not normally in public. The noises shield your conversations and create a bustling, distracted atmosphere in which strangers won't register your getting fresh with a celeb, dancing, or even singing your girlfriend "Happy Birthday" alongside your favorite musicians.

Given this formula, the shocking quiet of an elevator in Las Vegas can be startling. This is a break from the American norm, where a tradition of elevator music, often soft-rock mood music, traditionally soothes the awkwardness of these transitional spaces where strangers come together briefly before being dispersed on various floors or to different offices, businesses, or shopping spaces. Vegas alters this paradigm, such that elevators are often shockingly silent, in contrast to the jingles and resonances of the casino floor and "public" zones more broadly. Instead, the startling silence of the elevators at the Flamingo transition me out of the public forum and into the private zone of the hotel. The silence of the space marks a shift in my identity from my role as tourist and gamer to guest.

This transitional quiet zone also works in the other direction. I set out from my Flamingo hotel room for breakfast at the Paradise Garden Buffet. The doors open on the way down, letting other visitors in and out of the elevator.

As in many other parts of the casino, the signage surrounding the elevators, marking the building level, is difficult to see. Small black numbers hang on the door frame at each floor, invisible to the passenger looking straight out of the open doors. When the door opens on the lobby level, the view doesn't tell me much about where I am. Rather, the doors open onto a wall of mirrors. The mirrors are cut and arranged like stained glass with inlaid panels and beveled edges, creating the disorientation of a fun house. Such a visual motif is thus bewildering rather than informative. When the doors open, it is the noise instead that tells me where I am; the sounds are what can lead me past the casino floor with its characteristic chimes to the buffet entrance.

If sounds create some spatial and psychological partitions that distinguish the casino from the hotel, they do not orient you to the time of day. From 1:30 AM, when I first arrive at the Flamingo, until noon the next day, the slot machine cacophony offers a consistent blurring of one's sensibility to day or night. Not unlike a torture technique in which detainees are played a steady stream of children's music, the sounds of the Strip can be both joyful in tone and at the same time maddening in their unending onslaught. The most exaggerated example of this is found on each casino floor, where the cheerful sounds create the impression of activity no matter the hour and even if many of the seats in front of the machines lie empty. Craps tables are always particularly loud, lively, and surrounded by a crowd. In comparison, the mechanical bells and ringing are technology's answer to the more singular individual experience of staring into the screen as you play the slots. The noises unify disparate gamers and facilitate a communal sense of activity even when games like the slots only require a single person and the nominal push of a finger. The sounds are thus vital to the sense of play. For example, despite the fact that one Star Wars slot machine at the Venetian seemed to be on a roll, we walked away because the sound was disabled or broken: "This is no fun," said Chris. The noises of the slots are a consistent brand for the city, one that persuades us not merely psychologically but physically as these noises work on the body of the tourist. On each of my trips, I match time spent in the city with a reprieve in nature (the Grand Canyon, Zion National Park). It seems to take a day or two for the ringing in my ears to subside even though I cannot forget the sounds entirely.

In thinking about the sounds of Las Vegas as a homogeneous brand, it is worth reflecting on the variations between one casino and another. From Treasure Island to Excalibur to the Wynn, each hotel-casino constructs its own thematic feel, and yet with my eyes closed listening on the casino floor, the establishments seem indistinguishable. That distinct consistent soundscape is part of the fabric of Las Vegas as a whole.[3] However, an auditory distinction is produced between one casino and another in at least one way: volume. Each gaming floor makes use of similar types of sounds and participates in that ubiquitous Vegas soundscape, and yet the volume of the sounds in each establishment can variously generate a feeling of reserve or carnival. You may not be aware of the volume button if you play the slots in Harrah's or the Tropicana, where the noises ring freely, like the dinging chimes and call of "Wheel of Fortune." Here the special sounds marking slot play achievements—like reaching a bonus round or hitting a jackpot—are never muted. Indeed, the blaring, honking party horns call the attention of everyone in the area to your "jackpot party!" Conversely, sitting down to a machine at the upscale Bellagio or the Venetian, you can heed propriety in the low volume of the machines. In these casinos, the sounds are more attuned to the individual than the crowd. I can map the number of stars attributed to each hotel-casino in the tourist guidebook through the volume, and thus the respectability, of its sea of slot machines.

There is also a sliding scale that corresponds with whether or not the points of origin of sounds are more or less hidden or flaunted. On my last trip to Las Vegas, I was engaged in a scavenger hunt, seeking out the sources of music and noises that so shape and condition my experiences. Particularly in places where music is central to the creation of a celebratory environment, as in the Rockhouse, visible, identifiable speakers are part of setting the stage for the festivities. In contrast, the Bellagio infuses and blends sound more covertly into the architecture. Speakers are literally embedded in the architectural features, shaping the ways in which we experience public space. Through speakers hidden in lampposts, the low continuous music filling the pathways along the lake seems natural rather than constructed—a part of the fabric of the place. Depending on which fountain show you catch, you may be quickened to patriotism by "The Star-Spangled Banner," incited to dance by Michael Jackson, or moved to tears by Celine Dion. When in Las Vegas, my body accommodates itself to these various sounds, driven and tugged by the seemingly inborn natural effects of the noise.

Smell

What's that smell? Opening and walking through the doors of the Venetian, I am hit by a cloud of what seems like jasmine perfume. The scent doesn't just waft by me gently; it is so powerful it seems a physical emanation, a structural characteristic of the building. The powdery floral aroma lingers in the air, fill-

ing each corner, hallway, and alcove. The distinct fragrance hangs over the blackjack tables and travels with the singing gondoliers down the canals and throughout the shops. On a hot day in June, the smell even occupies the passageways outside, following me as I cross the bridge to Treasure Island. This scent is unique to the Venetian and perpetuates a distinct ambiance that is indicative of not merely a nostalgic Italian culture, but one of wealth, leisure, and status. Certainly, the architecture and material layout of the space, including design details such as wallpaper and furniture or even the style of background music, can set the tone. But there is another design component that is more subtle and at the same time more invasive: the fragrance. I am always physically struck by the feel of air conditioning that marks entry into a hotel-casino on a hot Las Vegas day. As to the temperature-controlled air, visitors become acclimatized to an olfactory atmosphere. The scents play a significant part in the realization of each imagined world but further highlight the constructed nature of each space and how we adapt to and experience it. Aroma is architecture and decor, yet unlike the brick belltower or Venetian gothic façades along the canal—this aromatic scene is invasive; it gets up your nose and inside you.

Las Vegas offers a pastiche of *smellscapes*, the term used by geographers to describe the ways in which spaces and landscapes can be ordered and recognized by aromas. Smellscapes are temporally, as well as spatially, specific. We can historically and culturally map attempts to both create and eradicate *smells*, a term generally associated with the negative characteristics of aroma, those that suggest a stench or stink. Geographers Gram Dann and Jens Jacobson, for example, recount modern efforts to banish or erase smells from urban environments—to create a sense of sterilization that in turn reverberates back to social distinctions of people and neighborhoods. The banishment of smell distinctive of the modern era is typified for them in the supermarket, an olfactory wasteland.[4] Las Vegas today, by contrast, illustrates the postmodern shift from antiseptic to branded; aroma becomes not a problem to be eradicated but instead the answer to specific cultural needs.

The production of controlled scents in casinos is in part a continuation of efforts to regulate smells in the negative sense; rather than dissolving or sterilizing, this is an act of cover-up. The branded aroma becomes an answer to the seemingly uncouth, unhygienic, or disgusting. When I ask fellow tourists about the smells of their visit, cigarette smoke is inevitably one of the first things mentioned. To most of us, for whom smoking is increasingly banned from the indoor spaces of our daily lives—apartments, office buildings, theaters, and other entertainment spaces—the inevitable confrontation with cigarette smoke in Las Vegas spaces is a shock. The smell of smoke lingers on the gaming floor; it is soaked into the carpets and chairs, and hangs onto the clothing of many of our fellow gamblers. While smoking is becoming increasingly curtailed around the United States, Las Vegas seems to put the cigarette on par with cocktails and gambling, exempting all floor spaces in major casinos (meaning those with more than a dozen or so slot machines) that do not serve food from smoking bans. Ashtrays are commonplace adornments of those gaps between one machine and another, permitting and inviting you to smoke, even as they threaten to drive customers like me away. Inevitably, a woman sits down next to me at the penny slots in Harrah's holding her cigarette in her left hand while pushing the "repeat bet" button with her right. The appealing, relaxing quality of smoking makes its flagrant consumption in this retreat destination understandable, and yet unlike alcohol, which perpetuates individual affects, smoking generates an atmospheric cloud that inculcates others in the act.

I do not mean to invoke the long-term health effects of secondhand smoke (though indeed this is a concern for Las Vegas workers who physically inhabit these spaces daily), but rather I am thinking of cigarette smoke in more experiential and affective terms: that is, the meanings of the smell. Indeed, attacking cigarettes from the perspective of the "smoke stream" allows opponents of smoking to bypass the political and advertising rhetoric that posits smoking as a privilege of individualism, an idea reified in the images of the independent Marlboro man and the liberated woman smoking a Virginia Slim.[5] Smoking as affect in Las Vegas gets at this tension between individual and society in a different way. The act of smoking permeates the environment, leaving an olfactory trace that is distinctly negative and alienating (even at times to smokers themselves). Indeed, what we come in contact with is not so much the cigarette itself but rather the waste product of smoking, the debris left behind and lingering, often long after it has been expelled from the bodies of the smokers themselves. We might consider that the discourse of risk surrounding smoking is in some ways appropriate to the context of gambling in Las Vegas, and yet in the culture at large the "choice" to smoke demonstrates that the engagement in this risky behavior is becoming increasingly stratified and disproportionate along social class, education, and racial lines.[6] Does the "smell" of cigarettes, the lingering leftover stench that hangs over the casino floors, which might have indicated a social glamour in the 1950s and 1960s, instead suggest today an uncomfortable proximity to waste and the masses?

Rather than curtailing consumer behavior, Las Vegas casinos have a new way to compete with unwanted and undesirable smells like cigarette smoke—

a new way to get you to hang around and play another hand. The answer is a branded, individualized air freshener for the whole establishment. "Banana boat" is what the Flamingo casino smells like to me. "Clean and warm," says my companion, describing the air in Aria. Though you may not even notice it, each hotel-casino complex has its own scent beyond the cigarette odor or the tempting, wafting food smells of the restaurants and buffets. Las Vegas is at the forefront of a new trend in aroma branding and scent marketing. Founded in 1991, the company AromaSys counts MGM-Mirage Resorts and Casinos and the Wynn, Bellagio, and Venetian among its many clients. This emergent industry blends fragrances to create unique bouquets for each space. Companies like AromaSys not only generate a signature scent to identify the hotel-casino, but, further, they control the levels of distribution, thus, in the words of their website, "enabling your brand to be the most effective with your chosen environment." The company's signature scents are designed and proven to "stimulate appetites," "stir emotions," "improve relaxation," and "stimulate environments and memories."[7] Casino scents are most noticeable to visitors at thresholds when they are experienced for the first time, before the brain stops signaling and registering their presence. Though you may become aware of the scent only in liminal spaces where competing hints of aroma cause your brain to register the trademark scent anew, the brand nonetheless follows you around the gaming floor and into the gift shops, its essence pumped around you through the HVAC system. Gaming floors are one of the specific targets of companies such as AromaSys, whose studies prove increased time spent by gamers at slots (and thus increased takes by casinos) in environments with fragrance.[8] Smell is a business and an art that stimulates and moves the subject behind the nose.

In the book *Fast Food Nation*, Eric Schlosser considers the construction of the hamburger in part from the perspective of its aroma—a central part of our identification and enjoyment of the food. Schlosser recounts how contemporary mass production, preservation, and cooking processes leave foods tasteless, and how smells and flavors must be created chemically and reinserted back into the foods. When you enter a restaurant and smell French fries, what you actually smell is not the food but the top-secret formula developed and branded in a lab in the "scent corridor" of New Jersey. The test tube can produce food seemingly more authentic than the grill.[9] Though they might object, given the distinction they try to cultivate between high culture and mass culture, we might compare contemporary hotels to fast-food retailers in their efforts to make their establishments unique and seemingly unprocessed. To accompany the imported landscapes and themes of Las Vegas businesses, a

EXIT

similar behind-the-scenes scent construction industry is at play to reproduce a sense of reality in these imagined environments. The glass flowers in the lobby of the Bellagio—*Fiori di Como* by sculptor Dale Chihuly—are experienced within the manufactured air doused with a soft floral scent that makes even these glass blooms on the ceiling smell fresh and alive. Smells are a way of inserting mood and tone back into even the generic hotel. Indeed, what better way is there to signal "relaxation," "retreat," and "vacation" than the smell of cocoa butter, that sunscreen smell demanded by Steve Wynn for the tropical-themed hotel Mirage.[10] Scents can invest a place with an air of "sophistication," "cleanliness," or "hominess," or can provide the impression of the "exotic," as was my experience at Mandalay Bay, where I was reminded of hot chai tea.

I spent a lot of time trying to identify the distinct scents of different casinos, and the most resounding characteristic is their often elusiveness and a malleability in the face of very personal and individual olfactory impressions. Engaging in a bit of nose training that took me from space to space sniffing and identifying, I thought I had correctly labeled the aroma of Mandalay Bay, only to receive a different accounting of the same scent from another person: a floral bouquet rather than a spicy tea. Indeed, our discourse for identifying and describing the smell qualities of these localities is limited, and often we fall back on nouns of origin (specific flowers or spices, for example) rather than identifiers for the scents themselves.[11] Two things stand out about the pastiche of Vegas smells: first is their commodified nature. Though we may resort to using the seeming origin of smells to describe them, they are in effect disconnected from any actual site, action, or source of origination. We do not need to bake an actual apple pie to create the aura of American domesticity throughout a home—we just need that Glade candle. Taken to the next level, aroma systems harness technology to apply this on a massive scale. Additionally, the specific scents that typify the Vegas smellscape are often nostalgic for nature. Though they rely on sophisticated HVAC systems and advanced laboratory science, the smells themselves reify the garden, the beach, and the open air.

Cinema scholar Laura Marks has argued that efforts to construct common, symbolic, or branded distinctions of smells by entertainment industries and retail businesses can be somewhat undermined by our personal memories of and experiences with smells; "unless we have strong, shared collective memories associated with a smell, our associations will be resolutely particular." In the case of smell, memory can be "at odds with communication."[12] This is because olfaction is the most "primitive" of our senses. Aroma, unlike touch or taste, travels to, and is processed in, a unique location in the human brain. Smells do not stop at the thalamus (a sort of sensory way station or processing center on the way to the brain) but rather travel to the limbic system and the cerebrum. As such, our noses orient us to spaces in ways that seem to bypass thought for pure feeling; we can respond to smells without being very conscious of doing so. Precisely because of these personal connections, the powerful potential of this sense is not lost on the smell-savvy marketer trying to entice passersby to a quick sale. At the same time, because of this unique sensory trajectory to the brain, smells, more so than touch, sight, or sound, are emotional and psychological stimulators. Memories, like smells, are processed in the brain's limbic system—creating an overlapping and entwined quality by which aroma can transform one's moods by triggering memories of people, places, or events. "It smells like Grandma," says my partner, Chris, as we push open the glass doors and pass into the perfumed cloud of the Venetian. For him, one whiff was enough to recall his departed grandmother; in particular, her purse with its consistent collection of bingo markers. While studies have shown that humans do not experience smell with the same degree of accuracy as vision, the ways in which we experience the world through olfaction can have a more lasting impact, a detail not lost on Vegas hotels and casinos.

Las Vegas businesses are leaders in this emergent scent industry, forging ways to make physical and emotional responses with scent consistent with both a common lexicon and synonymous with their unique services and products. Guess what: if you like the scent, you can take the essence of your vacation home with you—a reminder at home to retrigger that connection to the vacation destination. The resort shop Apothecary, selling bath, beauty, and pharmaceuticals, also distributes Essence di Palazzo, a spray bottle of that unique Venetian *arancia* (Italian for orange) scent. We should notice the effort of hotels, then, not merely to brand their own scent but to brand in your memory, by way of aroma, the connection of their hotel with the very notion of vacation.

Taste

Eating and drinking are often presented in the popular imagination as magical avenues of transport. As in *Alice in Wonderland*, Las Vegas offers its own commands to "eat me" or "drink me" as gateways "down the rabbit hole." In Las Vegas, the opportunities for delight and adventure via taste seem bountiful. Mimicking the physical, sonic, and visual collage of the city is a broad smorgasbord of tasting experiences typified by the buffet dining experience, where, as Susan Willis explains in "The Whole World on a Plate" (chapter 6), sushi can accompany pizza in the same meal. Alternatively, we can embark on a tasting tour of the upscale signature restaurants of Las Vegas–based artist chefs, wherein the physical sensation more clearly elucidates taste in terms of class distinction. And yet what interests me most about the possible tasting adventures in this entertainment capital are the more mass-market experiences, where eating and shopping, physical taste, and consumer practices often merge—or, in most cases, where actual tasting is made secondary and at times even inferior. As with Schlosser's account of how technology leaves food somewhat tasteless, our physical experiences with flavor in the city are not located solely on the tongue but are more often mediated by a broader perceptual environment. Indeed, the sense of taste is often subsumed into, and altered by, our perceptions via other senses, such as smell and sight. This complex, tangy mix of food merged with souvenirs is best savored at two adjacent establishments at the south end of the Strip: M&M's World and the Coca-Cola Store, where visitors are presented access to whole "worlds" via the act of consumption (in both senses of the term).

At M&M's World and the Coca-Cola Store, taste is not just a sensation in the mouth, but a quality infused into both the architecture and inedible material commercial goods. As *Learning from Las Vegas* explains, the city's architecture has evolved "consistently toward more and bigger symbolism." We are not greeted at the Coca-Cola retail store with merely that iconic red, cursive logo, but instead a giant soft drink bottle blending into the building's façade. Robert Venturi and his colleagues draw a relevant distinction between two iconic structural forms: the "duck and the decorated shed," or the ways in which architecture makes use of symbols. They suggest that "the duck is a special building that is a symbol; the decorated shed is the conventional shelter that applies symbols."[13] The Coca-Cola Store is both in that the bottle on the front is an exaggerated billboard for its wares with a functional zone of retail behind, while at the same time the interior space submerges the shop into a physical experience of being inside the bottle of Coke, such that you can look out from the escalator in the midst of a sea of merchandise through the glass windows of the bottle. That the building enacts the edible pushes our physical engagement with architecture and space a step further. I feel like Mickey in Maurice Sendak's *In the Night Kitchen*, who, in his dreams, swims his way through a vat of cake batter. Though we are not in danger of being baked into the "morning cake" by three tyrannical chefs, visiting the Coke store offers the sense of being bottled up into, and swimming through, a branded consumer package. Like Mickey, who emerges from the bowl literally wearing the cake batter, you can adorn yourself with your favorite food product via Coke T-shirts, hats, and pants, and even lather your lips with Coke-flavored lip balm in case someone tries to taste you. Walking around the shop, I feel submerged in Coke products—edible and inedible—that leave me declaring in protest, like Mickey: "I'm not the Coke and the Coke's not me!"

Next door in M&M's World, the architecture is even more obviously food-like. The store rooms are round in mimicry of the chocolates themselves. The decor follows the primary M&M colors, with red tiles creating large spheres on the otherwise white floor. Recessed ceilings follow similar curves painted in the classic M&M yellow and blue. The colorful candy products are displayed on curved and circular shelving that reflects the candy, reminding us that we are there to buy. The second floor features the main attraction: an arching wall of clear tubes filled to bursting with the candies. All the possible chocolate colors (primary colors and pastels, as well as black, white, and gray) and combinations (milk, dark, coconut, peanut, peanut butter, etc.) reach to the ceiling like columns. The pillars are candy dispensers that never appear empty. One little girl turns to her dad, who wears a rather troubled expression: "Dad, look how many rainbow ones I got in two seconds!" If not actually providing structural support for the space, these candy columns are the economic foundation of the business.

In addition to taste accesses through architecture, souvenirs, and design, our experiences of food tastes blur with the sense of smell, and indeed the smell of chocolate permeates all four floors of the store. Whether a by-product of the store's tasty contents or an artificial construct, like a Glade candle used by realtors to create that domestic aura of cookies baking in the kitchen—the scent awakens a craving and compels you to buy. In these spaces we become like the food-deprived Hansel and Gretel confronted with the edible ginger-bread house: driven by a "primitive" drive to incorporate (and which the story teaches can lead to our potential destruction). In this world, taste/smell, display/consumable, edible/inedible, shopping/eating all mix, such that we are consuming the products via the nose before we either purchase or eat.

On my last visit in January 2012, both spaces were filled with an overwhelming number of people—predominantly children—tasting/buying their way through the stores like kids in Willie Wonka's chocolate factory. Where Wonka offers that edible wallpaper—interior decor offering a feast of visible, lickable, tastable fruits—Coke gives you Sniff-Its apparel, encouraging visitors to "enjoy wearing the flavors" of Coke and other soft drinks. A sign in the middle of this wall of T-shirts encourages passersby to "sniff me," that is, consume me. I pick up one of each "flavor" T-shirt and hold it to my nose to take in the soft drink selections in turn: root beer, grape cola, Fanta, vanilla Coke, and so on. The bright green shirt features a cartoon image of soda in a bottle that declares, "Here's Sprite: Taste It! Tart and Tingling." Later on, I watch amused from the other side of the store while other consumers browse the merchandise by burrowing their faces into the fabric. Where some retailers might post signs against handling their wares before buying, Coke demands physical interaction, even incorporation, as a vital component of shopping behavior.

This adventure through consumption is then meaningful in a different way than, say, the Rainforest Cafe, located in the MGM Grand, which bills itself as "part adventure, part restaurant and wholly entertaining for the whole family." At the Rainforest Cafe, eaters are immersed in a jungle environment, a drastic departure from Nevada at large. You eat among the trees, surrounded not just by the impression of lush tropical vegetation, but also by "indige-nous" animals and misty waterfalls. You enter through a 10,000-gallon arch-way aquarium, into a tropical world constructed via sounds and animation as well as static decor. The difference I want to draw between this dining context and the Coca-Cola Store is that at the Rainforest Cafe you are encouraged to commune with, rather than to become, the jungle turkey simultaneously served to you in a wrap. At the Coke store, the adventure or transport is ac-cessed not through the impression of being there, but via tasting (which is always both eating and buying) and through which you literally incorporate and become an embodied part of the brand.

M&M's and Coke offer more than the services of a generic retail store, but rather an "experience business," one that charges for the "feeling" cus-tomers get by engaging with it. In these examples, memory itself becomes a product for sale.[14] But additionally, physical and sensory feeling—in this case taste—is another important vector of retail practice. These businesses mar-ket not merely a branded product but a physical effect on the body: a sense that is molded by the entire environment such that consumers are tasting even before they eat a single M&M. In being moved to taste, the consumer body becomes as Mickey: his body and identity indistinguishable from the cake batter.

A more traditional opportunity to taste can be found in the midst of the shopping experience at the Coke store: a soda shop. Here, in addition to floats and sodas, tourists are offered Tastes of the World. While the Vegas casinos at-tempt to bring the feel of a distant place to the tourist—realized when people in Las Vegas exclaim that "now they don't have to go to Paris" proper—Coke promises to transport you to other parts of the world through taste. Scholars refer to this process as "culinary tourism"—the active engagement in eating and drinking experiences (consumption, cooking, or the activities surrounding them) that diverge from your normal culinary practices.[15] In the soda shop, the ubiquitous red-and-white motif of the Coke store is broken by clear cups containing a selection of bright orange and even green bubbly liquids stacked on trays and passed from person to person across tables. Paying for the experience, tourists "travel" to sixteen different countries from the comfort of the metal chairs in the Coke soda shop. They sample sixteen different regional sodas representing distinct cultural traditions: Vegitabeta from Japan, Beverly from Italy, Ciel Aquarius from Mexico, Mezzo Mix from Germany, Sparletta Sparberry from Zimbabwe, and Sunfill Mint from Djibouti, to name a few. Cups are arranged on trays with sheets of paper identifying each drink. Kids, teens, and adults alike turn into Food Network experts tasting and berating the qualities of each drink: "Ugh. What is that? That tastes awful!" "Mmm, lemony." Through the music you can hear the dares and the accompanying laughter that ensues after someone convinces a friend or relative to try a particularly disliked soda flavor. Of these, Beverly is one of the more notorious. Described by one worker as a licorice-flavored drink used by Italians as a palate cleanser, in the cafe of the Coca-Cola Store Beverly instead seems to promote American disgust. The Tastes of the World facilitate a physical sense of the place from which each drink is said to originate, in a context that demands valuation, assessment, and occasionally gags.

At the same time that Tastes of the World suggests the patina of the exotic, the tasters don't actually leave the comfort of the American establishment. Each of the soft drinks on offer is in fact partially or fully owned by the Coca-Cola Company. Further, tourists' tasting experiences—what we perceive to be a generally impartial, comparative taste test—are in fact mediated by their own local and social expectations. Each of these sodas unifies a common fizzy sensation with the flavor of sucrose (and we should note that this can be distinct by country given the preferred sweetener). But our perceptions of taste cannot be disentangled from expectations about sugariness based on details such as color, which are culturally determined. Charles Spence, of the Crossmodal Research Laboratory at Oxford University, has studied the impact of such things as color and shape on our perceptions of taste. The visual palette of the food—as established by marketing and packaging traditions, color associations with mood or emotion, distinctions in nature, and so on— can quite literally shape our experience of things like sweetness.[16] In this way, we expect the color of drinks to conform to cultural traditions where, for example, brown soda should taste like Coca-Cola, and if it doesn't we experience an unpleasant physical disconfirmation. In the sea of red and white in this store, the greens and oranges of the flavors "from around the world" tell us, in fact, more about our national perceptions than the tastes of a foreign other. Our adventure in world sodas becomes instead an act of re-creating our common subjectivity or culture back home.

Overall, opportunities to consume at the Coke store and M&M's World teach children to discriminate even as they perpetuate fun, innocent narratives about Coke polar bears and talking chocolate. Despite the fact that M&M's are milk chocolate flavored whether the shell is red dye number 5 or not, throughout the store children are encouraged to identify variations in taste specifically with color. A sign flashes in lights over that great wall of chocolate dispensing tubes declaring "My Color!" Rather than settling for the prepackaged assortments (even though these do come in custom dispensers like trucks and Star Wars robots), visitors inevitably buy from the wall, allowing them to choose their own individual flavor and color combinations. While that young girl mentioned earlier carries her hefty bag of rainbow-colored M&M's, another girl walks around sporting her selection of pure pinks. The majority of the store is quite traditional in its color scheme, producing M&M figure mugs, pillows, shirts, pencils, socks, and so on, in a selection of primary candy colors: red, yellow, blue, and green. Over these choices a sign asks the shopper/eater, "Who's your favorite?"

Colors are not simply aesthetic but rather become associated with personalities and identities that change over time. As you travel up the escalator the different-colored candy personas are shown evolving over the twentieth century in a mural timeline. It is hard not to follow this progression with an eye for social integration. The timeline concludes at the top of the escalator with the establishment of the green "female" M&M, adorned by long lashes, luscious lips, and high-heeled boots. This "spokescandy" has been known since her introduction in the 1990s as "the sexy one," whose catchphrase is, "I melt for no one." The connection of color to a particularly seductive gendered persona builds upon popular rhetoric since the 1970s that posits "the green ones" as a modern-day aphrodisiac. The character of Ms. Green reflects and reproduces long-standing associations of the color green with fertility as well as youth culture mythologies about eating this colored chocolate to get in the mood. Former lawyer Wendy Jaffe even built an entire competing candy business on this very association of food and sexual feeling, selling bags of only "the green ones." Consequently, this taste of the color green has been branded by the Mars Company, who sued Jaffe for trademark infringement.[17]

Thus, we cannot set aside the notion of taste and the bodily experiences of food as isolated from and innocent of social, cultural, and economic texts as well as spaces such as M&M's World that give the foods meaning. "I want the red one," says one young boy to his mom, as we move off the elevators and into the stands of consumables, thus laying claim to the outspoken sarcastic candy. Through the personas attributed to each color, our act of eating/shopping is likewise an incorporation of implied identity mores. Considering this, I can't help but note — despite the never-ending options offered by the M&M's dispenser tubes — how hard it is to find a brown T-shirt in this place. Is it so hard to imagine that someone might want to wear brown proud? I should note that my last visit to M&M's World preceded the unveiling of the new brown character in television commercials in 2012. "Brown" is constructed by the new commercial as "naked" — that is, as the chocolate itself — and the eroticization, as well as the primitive racialized connections of chocolate to a description of black and mixed skin tones, should not be missed. Taste, in this context, is made inseparable from an aesthetics of conformity and difference, as the colors of candy and merchandise are imprinted with identities and genders, and shoppers are taught that color counts. At the same time, the natural physical sensation of taste offers authority to those seemingly "personal" "aesthetic" choices.

Touch

The motto of Madame Tussauds Wax Museum in the Venetian is "It's OK to touch." Unlike history museums, where the artifacts are distanced from viewers with glass cases or barriers, the wax museum invites you to feel, caress, and engage. In what is billed as an interactive experience, visitors are encouraged to narrow the distances between their bodies and the constructed wax forms of celebrities. On the one hand, these physical touches are structured and managed exchanges bounded by the settings and poses of the different figures; the space tells us what to do to and with the wax bodies, how to play, and even how to respond. However, it is the visitor's body, not the wax figures, that becomes the primary feature and medium of the exhibit. Though we may seem to play the space, the wax museum works because it plays us, by structuring how we move, feel, and personalize our physical experiences with the bodies on display. A microcosm for Las Vegas more broadly, a stage is set, but it is the tourist's body that provides the performance in response to the many physical stimuli.

Our sense of touch is the means by which we check *reality*. Visitors to the mall in CityCenter stop to admire the series of fifteen-foot towering ice pinnacles rising from a pool of water and bathed in cool-toned colored lights. One of the icicles in the feature, Glacia, is purposely placed close enough for passersby to reach out and touch. Pushing each other forward, tourists can ensure that it is made of ice through the verifiable wet, cold feel on the fingertips. The act of physical examination in turn leaves a mark on the ice pinnacle, slightly altering its shape with the warm residue left by hand after hand. Similarly, the opening gallery of Tussauds is a staging ground for first encounters—a space where tourists stare up close into faces, walk 360 degrees around the apparent bodies of celebrities, and of course reach out and touch their waxy skin for the first time. The act of feeling is somewhat empowering—as in minute altering of that ice sculpture or as in the case of Chris, who pinches the nose of former president George W. Bush. These physical encounters are a process of aesthetic appreciation (of the skill or failings of Madame Tussauds' crafters) but also cultural judgment (expressing your praise or criticism of the idols represented). But at the same time, reaching out to touch is also a moment of disenchantment, when the illusion is broken and you feel firm cool wax instead of warm skin. Likewise, the moment of touch is also two way—hinting at the change the contact may leave on the skin of the visitor.

Touching (and specifically having these encounters captured on camera) is the mode of tourism in Tussauds. Visitors are coaxed to stroke and handle. Indeed, Elvis Presley holds out his hand to the tourist while a sign reads, "Touch the 'King's' hand and hear him speak." When you reach out to take his fingers, a sensor above triggers a selection of responses from the singer such as "Thank you very much!" and "You've sure gotta lot of nerve, baby!"

Each of the figures on display is structured in ways that encourage particular modes of physical interaction. Props signal things you can do to and with the celebs, as when Chris and I pick up a pair of swords from a box like a kid's dress-up chest and collectively mime the decapitation of Johnny Depp, aka Captain Jack Sparrow. The staging and posing of the bodies of the wax figures invite you to put on bunny ears and get into bed with Hugh Hefner or join Beyonce in midshake on the dance floor. In this way, our touches follow a road map set out by the exhibit. The figure of the once infamous bachelor George Clooney is posed in a tuxedo at an altar, hand outstretched for his bride. In turn the visitor is provided the bouquet and white dress to don and enact a wedding scene. Photos on the walls feature anonymous women with the actor in professional-style wedding portraits. These road maps thus set a normative path (in this case heteronormative) of interaction, but a course made intentionally to be toyed with (at least within the limits of damaging or altering the statues and scenes themselves).

In fact, the engagements with the figures always invite behaviors and forms of touching that might normally be taboo, and, as Karen Klugman suggests in "Framing Las Vegas 'Reality'" (chapter 1), carnivalesque scenes invoked precisely for the purpose of a souvenir photo. A girl whispers to her friend after posing alongside Jessica Simpson as Daisy Duke, "I pinched her nipple!" Throughout the museum, television screens play a sample video on a continuous loop encouraging visitors to "get interactive." The video showcases past tourists with the proper guts and audacity as they poke, pinch, and rub up against the celebs. There is a touch learning curve. One man I judge to be in his fifties sits down to take a very composed photo next to the mostly naked body of porn star Jenna Jameson. He sits a few inches removed, giving the blonde woman some space as a woman takes his photograph. "You need to get closer, much closer," calls a Madame Tussauds employee from nearby. "Don't be shy!" the worker adds. A neighboring male visitor, part of the crowd around Hugh Hefner, echoes this sentiment: "She won't press charges." People are pushed to get in and touch: to interact in ways that violate either personal, cultural, or even legal rules about space and behavior. This visitor complies. Though still clearly uncomfortable, he inches over and takes another photo with his hand resting on a naked thigh.

A younger man on his own turns to me and asks me to take his photo with the same suggestive female body. "My girlfriend's going to kill me," he says with a smile. These sorts of comments abound throughout the museum. A trio of thirty-something women in the Clooney exhibit proclaim, even as they perform, "This is so *wrong!*" Like the city at large, Tussauds plays with the boundaries of propriety and taboo. Madame Tussauds, and Las Vegas more broadly, depend upon what Gregory Bateson calls a "play frame." Within this space—this city—we collectively agree, "this is play," and this assertion sets the rules and procedures by which we understand each other's behaviors and actions. This frame of play is always defined in relation to the "everyday frame" creating inversions and decentering, for example, what we define as right and wrong.[18] In this way we cannot wholly read our engagements at Madame Tussauds as isolated, fleeting "what happens here stays here" experiences, but rather they impact the taken-for-granted, natural ways in which we respond to everyday life.

Like the other sensory experiences throughout Vegas, touching in Madame Tussauds is a mode of self-orientation and self-construction. In this case, we are encouraged to map ourselves in relation to the bodies of stars, politicians, and Vegas performers. Most obviously, the interactive attraction encourages physical mimicry. You watch as people of all ages contort themselves into the postures and perform the body language of diverse bodies, such as the thuggish face-off pose of Tupac Shakur or the slightly over-the-shoulder ditsy blonde posture of Jessica Simpson.[19]

In part, such actions demand an extreme scrutiny of the celeb's body. Indeed, we do not actually do these things to the real people, and yet the creation and display of a wax portrait is an invasive practice with which our touches make us complicit. The museum features a behind-the-scenes exhibit in which Beyonce walks us through the creation of her wax double. The surveillance necessary to produce her wax portrait does not end with hundreds of photographs of the star taken at different angles. Her body is subject to detailed, scientific measurement. Samples are taken of her hair and casts are made of her teeth. The skin tone and colors of the irises of the eyes are matched to the living body. More than the honor and infamy it professes to be, the process of creating these wax bodies is not unlike a contemporary popular-culture version of nineteenth-century pseudoscience practices like craniometry and physiognomy that map identity in head, face, and body shapes and sizes. Is the figure of Jennifer Lopez, who reportedly blushes when visitors touch her famous assets, the new mass-culture Hottentot Venus?

"I want to see how tall you are," says a young woman to her boyfriend. She pushes him toward Shaquille O'Neal, whose height is even more exaggerated by his pose; he reaches almost to a basketball hoop as if to dunk a ball. The physical interactions with these wax bodies always encourage individual (as well as social and cultural) acts of comparison and positioning. One of the King's repeated phrases makes it plain: "I'm sure you're looking at me thinking, 'I thought he would be bigger than this.'" Height—so easy to manipulate on the silver screen—is a major subject of commentary as visitors put themselves at eye level with their favorite stars. I remember going to the zoo as a child and comparing my hand size to the large mitt of a gorilla set in a cast outside of the enclosure. Tussauds instead has a wall of musicians' hands, including casts for Eric Clapton, Little Richard, Paul Simon, Janet Jackson, and more. As if judging musical aptitude in the fingers, Chris puts his hand onto of one of them: "Boy, Gloria Estefan has small hands. I could totally palm hers!" The act of touching is an act of assessment, and a process invested with a sense of worth and ability.

Lest we think that the visitor has the upper hand here, these physical encounters bear a warning. Wall-mounted dispensers for hand sanitizer puncture the play frame and highlight the potential consequences of getting up

close and personal with the figures. These are reminders of the dangers of secondhand touching in public spaces: in touching the figures, we come into contact with others who have touched. Another clue of the dangers inherent in physical contact—that these acts of touching are not transferable to other arenas and might have potential health or social consequences—can be found toward the end of the maze-like museum. Scream is the counterpoint to Madame Tussauds; it begins our transition out of the space where "it's OK to touch" back into a world where one ought to think twice. Included in your price of admission is the opportunity to walk through this second interactive space—a containment facility for victims of nuclear experiments gone wrong. Warning against the sort of active engagements with other bodies in the wax museum, the officiator of Scream, dressed in a mad scientist outfit, proclaims, "If you don't touch anything, nothing will touch you." In fact, you do have to touch—you place your hands on the shoulders of a stranger in a line and proceed down tight corridors, where instead of stationary wax figures you meet real bodies that breathe down your neck and leap into your path. In a sense, these bodies do in fact touch you: with sound, breath, and the feel of uncomfortable proximity. The tables are more blatantly turned on the tourist; we move from an illusion of free rein with our touches, to instead having the sense of control over what we experience removed. Unable to move easily between these two different sorts of physical encounters with bodies and spaces, one woman takes the pent-up touches from her walk through the Scream facility out on her partner instead: smack! smack! On the receiving end of the smacking, this man stands as a reminder that the sites of Vegas play are not in fact the wax figurines, or the gyrating physiques of the Chippendales, or even the mechanical forms of the slot machines, but instead our bodies.

IN READING THE SENSES in Las Vegas, I do not wish to revive, in the case of sensory stimulation, that old criticism leveled against mass media that people are cultural dupes who take in messaging automatically and thoughtlessly. Indeed, media theorists have come to resist the notion that mass consumers passively absorb the dominant meanings of television.[20] Similarly, Vegas tourists are not physical automatons that inevitably and predictably respond to the smells, sounds, tastes, and touches of the city. Rather, I suggest that these mundane impulses are powerful and active vectors of the commercial environment, and their influences on bodies and subjects often go unnoticed and unremarked. I began this essay with my visit to the Flamingo pool and the feel of sensory submersion—that muffling and at the same time overloading effect that happens when our senses go into hyperdrive. Within this sensory deluge it is easy to be unaware of how each sense is operating individually in a given environment, to push and pull and effectively acclimatize us to the many spaces, activities, and consumer experiences on offer. Hotels, restaurants, shops, and casinos regulate and naturalize modes of behavior and consumption by effectively gaming the senses. In offering a false isolation of one mode of sensory engagement from another, we can begin to identify some of the ways in which each mundane touch or sound can function as the stakes and the dice, or the subject, pleasure, and means, of a game. Might it be possible then to play our own way?

NOTES

1. Arjun Appadurai, "Consumption, Duration, and History," in *Modernity at Large: Cultural Dimensions of Globalization* (Minneapolis: University of Minnesota Press, 1996), 67–70.

2. Walter Benjamin, "The *Flâneur*," in *Charles Baudelaire: A Lyric Poet in the Era of High Capitalism*, trans. Henry Zohn (London: Verso, 1997), 34–66.

3. *Soundscape* is a term that considers how sounds generally (especially music) structure space and characterize place. See Susan J. Smith, "Soundscape," *Area* 26, no. 3 (1994): 232–40.

4. Gram Dann and Jens Kristian Steen Jacobson, "Tourism Smellscapes," *Tourism Geographies* 5, no. 1 (2003): 15. See also J. Douglas Porteous, "Smellscape," *Progress in Physical Geography* 9 (1985): 356–78.

5. Allan M. Brandt, "The Cigarette, Risk, and American Culture," *Daedalus* 119, no. 4 (fall 1990): 155–76.

6. Brandt, "The Cigarette, Risk, and American Culture," 172.

7. "Creating Your Bespoke Fragrance," AromaSys, http://www.aromasys.com/bespoke/ (accessed May 25, 2013).

8. "Gaming," Brandaroma, http://www.brandaroma.com/gaming/ (accessed May 21, 2013).

9. Eric Schlosser, "Why the Fries Taste Good," in *Fast Food Nation: The Dark Side of the All-American Meal* (New York: Houghton Mifflin, 2001), 126–27.

10. See conversation with Mark Peltier of AromaSys in Lawrence Rosenblum, *See What I'm Saying: The Extraordinary Powers of Our Five Senses* (New York: Norton, 2010), 79–80.

11. Dann and Jacobson, "Tourism Smellscapes," 4.

12. Laura Marks, "The Logic of Smell," in *Touch: Sensuous Theory and Multisensory Medium* (Minneapolis: University of Minnesota Press, 2002), 121.

13. Robert Venturi, Denise Scott Brown, and Steven Izenour, *Learning from Las Vegas* (Cambridge, MA: MIT Press, 1972), 106, 87.

14. The phrase *experience business* refers to a now-popularized concept first con-

ceived by B. Joseph Pine and James H. Gilmore, *The Experience Economy* (Boston: Harvard Business School Press, 1999).

15. Lucy M. Long, "Culinary Tourism: A Folklorist Perspective on Eating and Otherness," in *Culinary Tourism*, ed. Lucy M. Long (Lexington: University Press of Kentucky, 2010), 21.

16. Charles Spence, "Visual Display of Food: Historical Reflections," paper presented at Thinking about Dinner seminar, Jackman Humanities Institute, University of Toronto, Toronto, March 1, 2013.

17. Lena Williams, "Can a Green Candy Make Love Sweeter," *New York Times*, March 17, 1993.

18. Gregory Bateson, "A Theory of Play and Fantasy," in *The Games Design Reader: A Rules of Play Anthology*, ed. Katie Salen and Eric Zimmerman (Cambridge, MA: MIT Press, 2006), 314–28.

19. For an examination of gender and body language (particularly variants in advertising depictions of men, from "leaners" to the "face-off" pose), see Susan Bordo, "Beauty (Re)Discovers the Male Body," in *The Male Body: A Look at Men in Public and Private* (New York: Farrar, Straus and Giroux, 1999), 168–225.

20. Stuart Hall, "Notes on Deconstructing 'the Popular,'" in *Cultural Theory: An Anthology*, ed. Imre Szeman and Timothy Kaposy (New York: Wiley-Blackwell, 2010), 75.

EIGHT

Nature in Vegas: Cultivating the Brand

"I would never go to Vegas because I love Nature." This quote from a horticulturalist in Seattle who studies invasive species is typical of the population that hates Vegas.* What these nature purists might be surprised to learn is that the Las Vegas Strip loves nature too. In springtime, one can barely see the Sphinx for all of the blossoming trees. White tigers play, lions cuddle, and llamas lounge in Siegfried and Roy's Secret Garden while nearby a volcano erupts on a programmed schedule. Flamingoes and swans luxuriate in freshwater streams behind the Flamingo Hotel and Casino only half a mile from twelve hundred marine species in the Mandalay Bay Shark Reef Aquarium. Palm trees along Las Vegas Boulevard endure sweltering summer temperatures, while artificial blooms thrive under faux skies in air-conditioned malls. On the sidewalks between these fantastical ecosystems, we are reminded that wilderness is only a helicopter ride away, but the sun-bleached images of the Grand Canyon plastered on sandwich boards and mobile trailers have the sad, ragtag feel of a going-out-of-business sale. Meanwhile, the newer resorts

* Karen Klugman

along the Strip have forsaken all corporeal forms of nature — the real and the fake — in favor of art and technology that promotes simply the idea of nature. Referring to the development on sixty-seven acres of prime real estate along the Strip, Cindy Ortega, MGM Mirage senior vice president of energy and environmental service, gushed, "We were able in CityCenter to really breathe the idea and respect of nature into the largest sustainable project in the United States."[1] With Vegas's dependency on the rapidly dwindling water supply of Lake Mead and predictions that global warming has set in motion irreversible feedback systems that will continue to warm the earth and threaten water supplies for the indefinite future, Ms. Ortega's statement reads less like an airy celebration and more like an attempt to resuscitate a dying concept.

If we define nature as all things that have not been affected by humans, what the environmental journalist Bill McKibben calls "that separate realm that has always served to make us feel small," we can forget about Las Vegas, of course, but also dogs, farms, English gardens, second-growth forests, ecosystems in which we have introduced nonnative species, and even national parks, where our species has been responsible for such systemic changes as wiping out the wolves and then bringing them back.[2] Even tree huggers might concede that a day on the farm is a day spent with nature. Venture farther from unbridled wilderness to consider man-made inventions such as grass lawns, zoos, fish farms, genetically modified corn, cloned animals, hydroponic gardens, and Labradoodles, and now you have the kind of nature experienced by middle-class Americans on a daily basis. The nature that we've grown accustomed to is the sprawling lawns and occasional trees of housing developments where second-growth forests were bulldozed to create flat palettes for the economical construction of subdivisions. In my town in Connecticut, citizens protested the impending demise of a row of mature trees that impeded power lines and posed a safety risk for people on the sidewalks. CVS Pharmacy, which owned the land, responded by displaying signs assuring the public that a newer and "better" landscape was coming, which, to no one's surprise, turned out to be a row of equidistant saplings and pruned shrubs in several islands of wood chips. Defined by the Dutch philosopher Koert Van Mensvoort as "hypernatural," our designed nature is "a simulation of nature that never existed. It's better than the real thing; . . . always just a little bit prettier, slicker and safer than the old kind."[3] During the recession, vast swaths of barren land in Vegas that had been cleared by bankrupt developers provided a view of what the Strip itself must have looked like before the construction of the themed resorts and their companion lush hypernatural environments. Not restricted by local topology, soil, temperature, or moisture, the new and improved nature provided visitors with extravagant ecosystems that defied the old Mother Nature. Instead of architectural design decisions having to conform to preexisting site requirements, the ecological site itself was a design decision. When it came to naturalizing the themed hotel-casinos of Vegas, planners left no rock unturned. Every detail, including whether to put potted plants in the lobby and what type of plants they should be, was as much a part of the brand as the font on the stationery. And in Vegas, the planners would naturally also consider whether those plants in the lobby should be real or artificial, a decision that might sound trivial but actually reveals some thorny issues about cultural attitudes toward nature, conservation, and philosophy.

The simple question, "How do you feel about artificial plants?" provokes gut responses that begin to root out how people define nature and how those responses divide along economic lines. People with incomes sufficient to insulate them from the vicissitudes of Mother Nature, not only in their everyday lives but also when they visit national parks with their Patagonia gear, reflexively recoil in disgust at pairing the word *artificial* with anything from the natural world. Those whose lives depend on responding to nature on a daily basis—farmers, the homeless, disaster victims, people living in poverty—welcome any effort to control nature. My farming grandmother would never put a real plant that required care inside the house and would never spend her egg money on artificial plants. Yet when she received a bouquet of plastic flowers as a bingo prize, they were placed along the top edge of a picture frame, where they would remain until she died. The blue-collar sector, which does not need to deal with Mother Nature on a daily basis except to mow the lawn, and whose idea of wilderness comes mostly from TV, responds with answers that include some calculus of labor cost. My hairdresser's feeling about artificial plants summarizes the view of many Americans: "I only wish they wouldn't get dusty."

Just as the species-rich islands of the Galapagos enabled Darwin to develop his theory of evolution and natural selection, the Las Vegas Strip, rich with specious nature, is a convenient laboratory for studying our evolving attitudes toward nature. Where better to begin that study than in a tropical garden in an air-conditioned lobby in the desert? In the Mandalay Resort and Casino at the southern end of the Strip, broad-leaved plants and succulents, some of them two stories high, line the staircase that leads from the convention area to the casino floor. If these plants are real, then the hotel supplies their moisture needs and at the same time keeps the tourists moisture free with central air conditioning. Certainly elsewhere on the Strip, spectacular water displays and state-of-the-art HVAC systems perform this kind of juggling act to main-

tain competing microclimates. For many years, the Wynn Hotel ran a nightly show called *Le Rêve* that featured a million-gallon-plus pool as its stage. Not only were the pool and the immediate air above the pool heated to keep the performers from getting chilled, but the audience was protected from the heat and humidity caused by the evaporation of the heated pool as well as the moisture caused by an eighty-foot nightly rainstorm, water cannons, and a culminating ring of fire.[4] Although the water needed to maintain the oversized plants at the Mandalay was a mere drop in the bucket compared to the many extravaganzas involving water on the Strip, artificial plants would be more sensible environmentally and economically.

Since architectural features prevented me from checking out the reality of the twenty-foot-high *Monstera deliciosa* plants, I had to rely on the power of observation. Some of the leaves were torn as if eaten by insects, some bent into unflattering positions, and some were tinged with brown as if they had gone through a period of drought. Was it possible that companies manufactured foliage that, like stressed denim, arrived from the factory with a fashionable amount of wear? The imperfections in the leaves, like the ornate designs of the carpets on casino floors, revealed no discernible repeating pattern. I was about to conclude that the flawed plants must be real when a hotel worker appeared with a plastic spray bottle and rag and climbed into the plant beds. I couldn't tell the difference between real and fake plants, but I had no problem identifying the logo on the bottle; she was misting the plants with Fantastik spray cleaner.

From the Mandalay Bay, one can walk to the Luxor via an indoor shopping mall, where the vegetation reflects the drier climate of its Middle Eastern locale. The stiff architectural leaves of *Sansevieria trifasciata* have such tough, smooth skin that even those on my more commonly called mother-in-law's tongue plant at home seem to be made of plastic or rubber, so it was difficult to determine their authenticity by looking or feeling. Even the white fibrous material revealed by a broken stem gave no further clue about the plant's reality. Hoping for ooze, which would have settled the matter, I was exploring another break in the stalk near the base of the plant when I cut my finger on a large nail that was acting as a splint. And when I inserted my finger into the pot to check if the soil was moist, I jammed it on concrete.

I had hit upon an important discovery, and I sat on a bench in the mall under the shade of some "trees" to think it over. Moments earlier, I had not known whether the plant forms were real or not, so, in a pragmatic sense, their veracity had made no difference. They had been artfully constructed like the ones advertised online by Quality Silk Plants, "with nature in mind, mimicking every detail that [the manufacturer] could think of," including simulating the feel of real leaves.⁵ If one cannot tell the veracity of a plant by casually looking, feeling, or smelling, does it matter whether it is real or not?

In 2009, two scientists from the Norwegian Institute of Public Health analyzed fifty empirical studies on the visual effect of nature and concluded that merely seeing plants, whether through a window or in a pot in one's work environment, can have a positive effect on psychological and physical health.⁶ Never mind that in trying to distinguish the purely visual effects of plants in the office place from the possible stimulation of their olfactory or oxygen-enriching properties, the experimenters had not thought to use artificial plants. For me, the sight of the greenery in the Luxor had distinguished this area near the bench as a haven from the bustle of the mall. Even as fabricated sculptures, the plant-like forms had the power to invoke at least some of the experience that we associate with nature. Like the cloth-covered wire surrogate mothers in Harry F. Harlow's monkey love experiments of the 1950s, the plastic plants at the Luxor stood in for the real and I had clung to them as signifiers of Mother Nature.⁷

Yet something was missing. Designer watches, sunglasses, and purses—I couldn't tell if they were fakes and I didn't care. But knockoff plants seemed to be in a different category where the stakes are higher. Real plants clean the air. In our visually oriented culture, we can easily forget that plants supply us with oxygen and remove carbon dioxide. The particular species that had drawn me to the bench in the Luxor shopping mall also scored high in NASA's list of plants that also remove toxins, such as benzene, formaldehyde, and trichloro-ethylene. Not that one would normally care about these obscure elements, but in the bowels of a Vegas resort, much like a space station, air-purifying plants might alleviate what architects call sick building syndrome. Real plants surprise. Seeming to have a mind of their own, real plants occasionally send shoots at strange angles or over the side of the pot, challenging our sense of normal, not only for plants but, by extension, for people as well. There was no possibility of discovering a truly mutant stalk among this field of uniformly stalwart fakes. Any mutation would be an intentionally planted one—a clever trompe l'oeil based on a recognizable variation of the species. Also, real plants change. If a plant happens to be especially healthy or if it happens to be in bloom, we might feel lucky to have seen it in the prime of its life. But knowing that a plant form is immutable, one would feel neither good fortune in experiencing its beauty nor a pang of remorse about the transience of that beauty. After all, real plants die.

In the outdoor areas of the Mandalay—the porte cochere and the pedes-

trian walkway—live green plants dominate, but ersatz blooms are sprinkled among them, presumably to liven up the gardens by adding year-round color. Like fresh bouquets adulterated with plastic ferns, the miscegenation of real and artificial varieties in the plant beds offends me. A fresh-flower bouquet is a bittersweet reminder that lovely things do not last forever, and when the blooms die, their surprising stench adds potency to their message about mortality. But this powerful cycle of life is tainted when one must endure the disgusting process of separating plastic fronds from putrid slime in order to practice modern-day recycling. The undisclosed mixing of real and unreal nature crops up in more and more places, and as we get better at making copies of things, it is getting harder to spot. Among the Easter lilies on sale for $19.99 at a Stop and Shop was a single "*Phalaenopsis* in Ceramic Urn" for $39.99 with no indication that it was fake other than the bottom line on a tag strung around a branch indicating that it was "made in China." If any plant signifies death and the subsequent resurrection of life it would be an Easter lily, but this fake orchid, with more elaborate blooms than the live lilies, offered the possibility of eternal life for an additional $20—a tempting, if idolatrous, alternative.

As John Lienhard states in *Engines of Our Ingenuity*, "Our capacity for replicating, and even distorting, any reality is outrunning our ability to tell what's real."[8] As we get better at replicating natural objects, their inherent messages about the interconnectedness and processes of life are eroding and what has grown up in their place are subjective notions of perfection and design. A five-star review of a faux landscaping rock by Brookstone offers this sad commentary on our changing attitude toward nature as a reminder of the cycle of life: "We covered the stump of a newly-fallen 50-year-old *arborvitae*. It can decompose out of sight thanks to the attractive faux stone over it. Thanks for carrying such a nice product!"[9]

The more that we adapt to the convenience and design sensibility of invasive artificial species, the less likely we are to recognize or even believe in real nature when it happens. The Bellagio Conservatory and Botanical Gardens, located at the end of the carpeted trail through the hotel's casino, presents five floral extravaganzas annually. In one such display, a "typical New England" scene, a life-sized replica of a cider mill was surrounded by hundreds of uniformly shaped red and green apples that had spilled out of harvesting buckets, while oversized falling leaves made of glass hung on invisible wires from the ceiling. Even though most people would assume the gigantic squash on display were too enormous to be real, I live in a small town in Connecticut where local farmers showcase pumpkins at the town fair that would put up a good contest against these Nevada *grandes*. The caretaker at the Bellagio insisted that the thousand-pounders were indeed the real thing, but here's the catch—in the context of Vegas and under six-foot-long glass leaves suspended from the ceiling, it is difficult to believe in supersized vegetables.

To Andres Garcia, horticultural manager at the Bellagio, it is essential for the resort's projected ethos that the "the Bellagio cannot use plastic flowers."[10] And the blooms must be "perfect." An estimated 5 million visitors each year walk through what is essentially a 13,000-square-foot version of a Rose Bowl parade float designed by a team of artists who use large numbers of identical plants to create mass color effects. A seasonal show will display thousands of flowers at any given time, but it might require 100,000 plants to keep the exhibit looking fresh for an entire season because every couple of weeks the entire display is replaced with flowers in their prime. In one seasonal show, the bromeliads were not doing well and so workers rotated them out at 4 AM every day, assuring top-notch blooms by the time the first of the expected 18,000 daily visitors arrived. The Bellagio Resort and Casino prides itself on using only real flowers, yet they are presented in a way that, like digitally manipulated magazine images of models, celebrates uniformity and eternal youth.

To learn more about the source of the Bellagio flora, I took a side trip to Bellagio Horticulture, located about a mile from the Strip, which I had thought was a public display and salesroom for their flowers. Instead, I entered what looked like a Walmart workers' lounge, where a young woman was sitting near a snack machine. Assuming that I was there on official business (which, in fact, I was), she led me through an industrial hallway into an immense greenhouse where two caretakers wearing plastic gloves were chatting with a woman dressed in business attire. With thousands of rows of look-alike plants and what appeared to be an infinite number of empty metal troughs, the regularity broken only by a couple of sinuous hoses on the floor, this was obviously an off-site warehouse for the Bellagio Conservatory. The woman, who introduced herself as the horticultural manager, was clearly upset by my presence and quickly escorted me back to the office area. She was cordial and chatted about my visit to Vegas, but would not say a word about what I had just seen, needing the advance permission of the public relations manager at MGM, who was not available by phone at the time. In this atmosphere of surveillance, those plants seemed to be up to no good. Was it that they harbored the secret to eternal youth, which is to keep replacing aging organisms with clones?

Unlike the Bellagio supply house, Plantworks, also a few blocks from the Strip and a supplier of plants to many of the casinos, was indeed an actual public showroom for plants, although not of actual plants. Plantworks makes artificial plants that "render to reality." In the back room of Plantworks, I had expected to find rows of look-alike plants, much like those in the Bellagio bunkers, but instead it resembled a real working greenhouse with piles of plant debris and cuttings strewn on the floor. A twenty-five-foot *Washingtonia* palm for $6,700 towered in the middle of a large hangar-shaped room. In one section, there were what appeared to be hundred-year-old bonsai plants with Latin classifications, such as the *Pittosporum bonsai*. A manager helpfully told me how the plants are sold as either standard forms, where the leaves and branches are made from factory molds, or as custom varieties, with individually shaped silk leaves (with optional stress marks) made by "plant designers" and inserted into dried bamboo, curly willow, or manzanita stems. Recent advances in materials designed to block UV rays mean that outdoor artificial plants are more colorfast than their more primitive ancestors, and Plantworks was proud that at the Cosmopolitan Resort a fire retardant was injected into (as opposed to sprayed onto) the leaves. According to Tom Lias, vice president of sales and operations at Plantworks, "Safety is our number one priority when developing artificial plants and trees for our clients."[11] Good to know. Lounging at the pool deck of the Cosmopolitan, you won't have to worry that the UV-rated jasmine topiary balls will catch fire.

Besides Vegas hotels and casinos, Plantworks' clients range from local homeowners to all manner of businesses throughout the United States. In fact, their most popular seller is *Dracaena marginata*, which is surprising since its real-life counterpart is a hardy breed that can survive for years under the fluorescent lighting of office buildings or in dark hallways and is available for sale year-round for a much cheaper price at Walmart and Home Depot. Learning that I was from the Northeast, the manager told me about a current project to supply plants to camouflage a parking garage in White Plains, New York. Everybody and everything about the place was open, friendly, and welcoming. In the place where I had expected perfection and secrecy, there was messiness and an eagerness to explain how fake plants are made to look so real.

Plantworks supplied Planet Hollywood Towers (PH Towers) with four hundred feet of planters holding "permanent artificial bamboo" for its valet area as well as de rigueur potted plants for the lobby. But the hotel's vanguard foliage, offering a twist on rank-and-file artificial plants, is a phalanx of palm trees that extends inside the main lobby through a glass partition into the pool area. Both the indoor and outdoor plants have discolored and torn leaves, and the boles of the palms are irregular and bruised. I told the Plantworks manager that it had taken some work for me to discern that the plants inside were fake and that the ones outdoors were real, although I didn't tell him that in my research I had extracted tiny bark samples from the palms. I asked if he knew that the outdoor palms were losing fronds on the windy side of the pool area. "Ah yes," he lamented, "the problem with mimicking existing plants is that the real ones keep changing." Even before PH Towers opened, the hand-carved trunks of the indoor palms had to be repainted several times as the outdoor ones continued to be stressed by weather conditions and kept changing colors. Plantworks had probably not signed a contract with PH Towers to keep up with nature indefinitely and yet, only one year after the opening of the hotel, the lack of visible natural environmental effects on the artificial plants had begun to show. Frankly, the outdoor palms looked downright straggly on their windward sides, and I doubted that PH Tower nature designers had ever meant to mimic such lopsided versions of real nature. What would they do if the palms were blown over in hurricane-force winds — topple their indoor stand?

Vegas resorts choose a signature brand of nature that fits not only their theme but also their budget and, by extension, the budget of their targeted clientele. The Bellagio, where "contentment and opulence are the hallmarks of your Bellagio luxury hotel experience,"[12] employs a staff of nearly 120 horticulturalists. Its regular guests can afford and quite possibly expect the kind of nature that is perennially in its prime — landscapers to manicure the grounds, vases of fresh flowers, and cosmetic procedures to replace their own aging bodies. Planet Hollywood Towers, which offers vacation villas distinguished in part by the size of their flat-screen TVs, also caters to the high-end market, but speaks to a glitzier aesthetic. When Westgate Resorts opened PH Towers, it boasted of having "the largest letters of any hotel sign on the strip. The Westgate brand is now the brightest light in Las Vegas."[13] The clientele of PH Tower villas opt for "comfort and convenience" and the wonders of technology; they would be likely to keep silk orchids on the table back home and appreciate the continuous stand of palms where the artificial indoor trees mimic the real outdoor ones. In Mandalay Bay, the guests tend more toward an income bracket that may not be able to afford actually going to the tropics. The nature back home might be what has defined success in suburban America since the 1950s — a lawn with a few trees and evergreen shrubs that hide the foundation of the house. With limited vacation time and limited savings, who would even want to know if the blossoms were real?

Why did so many of the resorts built in Vegas bother to include flora in any form in their designs? One can imagine the Luxor pyramid in a real desert

locale surrounded by fake dunes with perhaps a simulated sunset. Surely the greenery was not intended to satisfy what Edward O. Wilson describes as a universal instinctive desire to connect to the natural world and thereby feel humbled.[14] In Vegas, it's a stretch to believe, as Wilson does, that all people possess such desire. Do the urbanites seeking the nightlife or the card sharks looking to make a big win really mind the long trek through barren casinos to get to the luscious gardens at the end of the trail or even the potted plants in the lobby? Instead, the nature of Vegas resorts provides what Thorstein Veblen identified in 1899 as "conspicuous consumption."[15] Never mind the environmental or economic cost, the more difficult and expensive it is to maintain lush gardens or fresh flowers for our leisure, the more bang we get for our vacation dollars. The constructed nature on the Strip, like most of the nature that we experience in our everyday lives, is a celebration of our ability to outdo real nature with a better product.

The newer resorts, designed to attract an international and ever-richer clientele whose consumption of nature might include African safaris and cruises to see Alaskan glaciers, use technology to mimic the idea of nature, rather than trying to copy an objective look or feel. In a "forest" in a hallway in Crystals mall, the chichi shopping area of CityCenter, the "trees" consist of hundreds of low-maintenance philodendrons in layered planters arranged around metal boles. And the wisteria-like flowers never drop their blooms, since they are actually strings of tiny LED lights that continually stream from top to bottom in quick patterns from flower to flower to seem as if the blooms are blowing in the wind.

Several other high-tech displays in Crystals also challenge the notion that constructed nature does not move, change, or surprise. In the exhibit *Glacia* by WET Design, the company that is responsible for the Bellagio fountain display, columns of frozen water below floor level gradually rise as the ice builds up and just as slowly melt away. As Heraclitus famously said about rivers, the ice monoliths never take exactly the same shape twice. In another exhibit, *Halo*, vortices of water rise and fall within slanted translucent tubes sprouting up like a big unruly garden in the mall. Unlike older natural-extravaganza counterparts, such as the regularly scheduled eruptions of the volcano at the Mirage and the hourly thunderstorm in the Middle Eastern wing of Miracle Mile shops in Planet Hollywood, these computer-driven water phenomena at CityCenter simulate the unpredictable nature of nature. The water patterns of *Halo* are either so complex as to be indiscernible or they are run by a random generator, for kids and grown-ups alike believe that when they touch, rub, or even hug the tubes of whirling water, they are actually controlling the rise and fall of the vortices. Like a favorite slot machine that if played long enough will probabilistically confirm its lucky quality, the water in a caressed tube will eventually rise to meet expectations.

These high-tech displays invite a different kind of wonderment about natural phenomena than the multitudes of perfect blooms in the Bellagio display or the mix of real and man-made palm trees in Planet Hollywood. They invite wonderment about where all of this techno-nature is leading us. For some time now, cell phone towers have been posing as trees, such as the one along the Jersey Turnpike that from a distance looks like a freakishly tall fir tree transplanted from the Pacific Northwest, but up close looks exactly like a cell phone tower scantily camouflaged with branches. This camouflaging of technology seems like a fun game, but someday we might see whole forests along roadways that look like real trees and are actually power generators. A company in England, Solar Botanic, developed realistic-looking artificial trees with leaves that contain solar panels to capture the sun's energy and that swivel to generate power from wind.[16] Yet other varieties of artificial trees remove carbon dioxide from the air, although they do not transform it into oxygen as a real tree would, but instead pump the carbon dioxide into underground storage.

If artificial plants could truly perform photosynthesis, we might evolve into a society where we would never see real trees again. But as Richard Dawkins reminds us in *The Greatest Show on Earth*, with the exception of some underground microbes, "all of the energy that drives life comes ultimately from sunlight trapped by plants."[17] In ever more complex man-made "natural systems," this humbling message of our very real dependence on other forms of life gets lost in translation. The carbon dioxide pumped into underground storage by tech-savvy fake trees stays there, until, well . . . it doesn't. As the science writer Elizabeth Kolbert explains, the carbon dioxide and the even stronger greenhouse gas methane, created by the incomplete breakdown of plants in the Arctic, have remained trapped in the permafrost since the last ice age, but as the permafrost has been melting, those gases are escaping and consequently accelerating the global warming that caused their release in the first place.[18]

Even if unaware of the science behind the irreversible feedback systems that are effecting climate change, the international elite are certainly aware of global warming, and the newer resorts use technology and art to supply feel-good conservation messages. As I was walking by the Cosmopolitan Hotel, a monitor screen sixty-five feet in the air—much like the ones that cycle through advertisements for tequila, Facebook, or entertainment—was broadcasting a video of trees whose leaves gradually changed shape and color. True to Cosmopolitan's commitment to provide art that is accessible, the video was noticed by people on the sidewalk, in part because its slow pace was out of sync with the images quickly flashing on Jumbotron screens elsewhere in Vegas and also because it was shocking to see such a wholesome image as trees in Sin City. Like Cosmopolitan's tree video, Maya Lin's eighty-seven-foot-long sculpture *Silver River* over the registration desk at the Aria hotel has a quiet, unexpected presence, depicting the sinewy form of the Colorado River over a backdrop grid of windows. Nancy Rubins's immense and colorful sculpture *Big Edge* seems only remotely related to nature in that its shape suggests that of a flower petal. However, both sculptures are touted for their use of recycled materials—reclaimed silver for the river and old canoes for the flower. Yet in spite of the environmentally themed art and the fact that CityCenter garnered six Leadership in Energy and Environmental Design gold certifications, the highest award for conservation awareness in a building project, the very existence of such a large complex of shopping centers, hotels, and pools in a region threatened by a dire water shortage makes a powerful statement that denies climate problems and contradicts the conservation messages it promotes.

Within CityCenter, the Rodney Lough Jr. Gallery offers "visitors the ability to step into the wilderness even though they may be traveling the fast lane of Vegas."[19] Like other photo galleries on the Strip, this one offers high-priced, large-scale, supersaturated images of wilderness that are enhanced by a special process that makes the prints glow. My first encounter with this wow factor was at Peter Lik Gallery, where a salesman invited my daughter and me to sit on a sofa in a side room off the main gallery. This being Sin City, we felt a little nervous when he closed the door and began to slowly dim the lights, but of course he intended for us to feel on edge so that we would be relieved when he directed our attention to a particular photograph, in which the sun appeared to be setting under his control. "All you need is a dimmer switch and you can achieve the same effect in your living room"—a dimmer switch and $10,000.

I asked the salesman at the Lough gallery how one would choose what to buy when so many artists photographed the same places in similar styles. The gallery host explained that the work of one artist is more desirable than another, not because of its inherent message about landscape or even for the quality of the print, but because one could get rid of it for a higher price in some future year. I learned that Rodney Lough signs his photographs, whereas William Carr uses a signature stamp. "If William Carr were to die

tomorrow, his photographs could go on being produced and signed, whereas if Rodney Lough were to die tomorrow, the value of his photographs would rise significantly." Forget the life span of the artists. I wondered if the value of my purchase would go up or down if wilderness itself were to disappear. Having personally made multiple hiking trips to many of the wilderness areas whose two-dimensional reproductions were being sold for much more than the cost of visiting them in person, I thought of the crowds waiting for the perfect moment to capture the sunlight at Antelope Canyon, the long lines of people hoping to win the auction at the Bureau of Land Management to visit the Wave, and the day that my family and I had to evacuate our lodge at the Grand Canyon because there had been a bomb scare.

In a wide hallway in the shopping area of Caesars Palace, five immense vertical photographs of wilderness areas filled a display window of the Peter Lik Gallery, while across the hall a video from a clothing store depicted fashion models parading on a catwalk. I sat on a bench between the two and noticed that the video was reflected in the glossy prints so that the models appeared to be walking toward me in a streambed one after the other, all with the hard stare and pouty expression of people sporting expensive clothing. The pairing of fashion and nature happens all the time in advertising, of course, yet this mesmerizing multimedia coincidence seemed like a metaphor for the erosion of wilderness. It reminded me of the complicated mixture of despair and relief I had felt when, moments after experiencing the adrenaline rush of encountering a rattlesnake in a wilderness area along the Utah-Arizona border, I discovered that I could still orient myself by the jet trails visible over two hundred miles away pointing to McCarran Airport.

From the vantage point of the Las Vegas Strip, however, it is difficult to feel one's relationship to the rest of the planet. It is as if you exist in a black hole, where the consequences of your actions don't matter because light cannot escape and where some non-Euclidean geometry allows you to walk from Egypt to New York. So mind-bending is this alternative reality in which the reality of everything is dubious that leaving the Strip can be a disorienting experience, as if one is an astronaut reentering the atmosphere and having to adjust from weightlessness to the familiar forces of earth.

In a taxi headed to the Vegas suburbs, my driver and I laughed about how he had once told some foreign visitors that the surrounding mountain ranges were just a fake backdrop and those innocents, probably having spent days under the influence of faux skies in the resort hotels, had actually believed him. As we headed farther away from the Strip and I gazed at the deep blue sky with cirrus cloud formations over the distant mountains, I thought of the three helium birthday balloons that had been stuck for days in the trompe l'oeil evening sky inside Paris, an ironic twist on the escape into an infinite sky that was the climax of the French film *Red Balloon*. Then poof—my balloon fantasy was punctured by the realization that I, much like those gullible visitors, had been staring blankly at the distant panorama as if it were an image on a flat-screen TV. Aware that I had fallen into regarding nature as something with finite boundaries and apart from myself, like the painted sky that prevented those balloons from their instinctive desire to achieve equilibrium, I forced myself to ponder the vastness of the sky and the volume of the mountains and to experience that sensation Emerson referred to as losing oneself in nature.[20] True, I had just spent three days on the Vegas Strip, where ecosystems are man-made, where meteorological phenomena occur on the hour, and where nature is often packaged and sold. But this lapse of feeling a connection to the natural world is not just a symptom of Vegas vision; it is becoming more and more common everywhere.

I was riding in the taxi that day on my way to visit the Springs Preserve, a 180-acre plot owned and operated by the Las Vegas Valley Water District with trails, gardens, museums, and educational facilities designed to "commemorate Las Vegas' dynamic history and to provide a vision for a sustainable future."[21] Unlike the experience on the Strip, which confounds any sense of history, geography, or current social events, my visit to Springs Preserve began with a film, *The Miracle of the Mojave*, that informed me where I was located on earth at that moment, then took me through a period when my seat in the auditorium had been underwater, when dinosaurs had tromped in the theater, when the entire valley had been a lifeless desert, and finally to the high point of the movie, when underground forces caused water to spurt to the surface, giving birth to the Las Vegas Springs, allowing vegetation, animals, and finally human civilization to flourish. As the music turned a little sad, I learned that the last vestige of the springs dried up several years ago and that the future of Vegas, a harbinger of the future of the world, depended on man changing his ways and finding a solution to the problem of population growth and limited resources. For a few seconds, the screen filled with a blur of neon lights, rushing traffic, and megaresorts. I was the only person in the theater, and while I was learning how to survive in the face of rapidly depleting limited resources, I thought back to the Strip, where police cruisers equipped with bullhorns broadcast directions to hordes of tourists about when it was safe to cross the street. "Yes, there would be challenges ahead for the Valley," the deep voice in the film intoned, but we all had to find a way to live together by using good conservation practices.

In 2011, Patricia Mulroy, manager of the Southern Nevada Water Authority, was quoted in the *Economist* as calling Vegas "a canary in a mine shaft" that could signal the end of a water supply to other western states.[22] Vegas gets 90 percent of its water from Lake Mead, which has been steadily drying up. The rock face that lines the lake has developed a white layer that is dubbed "the bathtub ring" and serves as a visual aid for understanding the dwindling water supply. Demonstrating a heroism that is a kind of reversal of the Dutch boy who put his finger in the hole in a dyke to save the country from drowning, Ms. Mulroy is supervising the drilling of another bore lower down in Lake Mead to keep the supply of water to Vegas going for a while longer. Nevada is helping to pay for the emergency drilling to keep the water flowing even as Nevada taxpayers are shoring up the eroding income of the Springs Preserve, which has not attracted enough visitors. Meanwhile, for the millions of visitors to the Strip, there are few references to the conservation-minded Springs Preserve. The concierge at my hotel had not even heard of it. As Stacy Jameson observes about Vegas, "Sustainability and environmental politics are structurally obscured for the visiting tourist in favor of a carnival-like water exhibition" (chapter 4).

Many exhibits at the Springs Preserve, however, refer to the Strip by acknowledging its reputation for excessive use of natural resources, but then discrediting that reputation as a myth. In one exhibit about water usage, people are asked to guess the answers to a series of questions, such as how much water is consumed by a person taking a ten-minute shower or how much water it takes to water an acre of lawn for an hour and then given an answer, which is always surprisingly high. One question stood out from the others because it was repeated and interspersed with the others: "What percentage of water in Vegas is used by the resorts on the Strip?" The repetition was probably meant to quell the concerns of anyone who had seen the fountain shows in Lake Cuomo at the Bellagio, the water extravaganzas by Cirque du Soleil, the fountains at Caesars Palace and Paris, the Grand Canal in the Venetian, the waterfalls at the Mandalay or the Flamingo, and the marine tanks of Shark Reef and Dolphin Habitat. Thinking that I could use the facts I had just learned at the previous stations, I tried to calculate how many ten-minute showers are taken by 36 million visitors to Vegas each year. Not to worry—the answer was indeed reassuring: Vegas resorts and casinos consume under 10 percent of the Vegas water supply. The message of this exhibit matched that of all the others at the Springs Preserve: it is the homeowners and small business owners in the town proper who need to change their habits. They need

to take shorter showers, practice xeriscaping, and install low-pressure toilets and faucets.

In another, more tongue-in-cheek reference to the Strip, colorful oversized slot machines enticed people of all ages to press a big button in order to line up the cartoon icons with labels such as energy, xeriscape, Dewey (the water drop who is a relatively new element in educating children about water conservation), and bitterbrush. When three or more of the symbols lined up, bells and whistles indicated that you had "won" a lesson in conservation (along with the more insidious lesson that one can learn anything simply by pressing a button and that what one learns is a matter of luck). Thanks to my matching cacti, I won a lesson about xeriscaping—the practice of growing plants indigenous to the area, plants that could live in desert conditions, requiring little water. The desert plants along the nature trail in the Springs Preserve pretty much summed up the options for home gardens in Vegas—grasses, cacti, and succulents—small plants in various shades of brown, yellow, and light green. Nothing like the rich green foliage described in advertisements for the Mandalay Bay weddings that ask us to "imagine exchanging vows in an enchanting chapel set within a grove of exotic island foliage, built on the shores of an 11-acre tropical lagoon."[23] I recalled the time when, wanting to know more about the geographical location that was the home of the plants at the Mandalay Resort, I asked the concierge where Mandalay Bay was located and he responded in a congratulatory tone, "Right here. You're in it!" But no, I corrected, I wanted to know if there was some other place in the world called Mandalay Bay. Surprisingly, neither he nor any of the people working at the front desk had any idea of where this place might be. Along the Strip, one is always blissfully ignorant of one's actual location on earth. Otherwise, the complete promotion for the wedding locale might read: "Imagine exchanging vows in an enchanting chapel set within a grove of exotic island foliage that might or might not be real, built on the shores of an 11-acre tropical lagoon in the middle of a desert."

The wildlife collection in the Springs Preserve is equally homespun, consisting of a fox, small rodents, lizards, and spiders. In dioramas that replicate local environments in which everything is in shades of brown and green, it is hard even to find the camouflaged fauna. But there is a valiant attempt to generate excitement about the small mammals and insects that are important to the ecology of the region. Proud of this collection of native wildlife, staff members relate a story (although some people wondered if it was true) that the caged fox is sometimes visited by a free-roaming fox that lives on the pre-

LAST CHANCE!
NOW
$ 149⁰⁰
LAST CHANCE!

serve. It is a poignant love story about the boy next door and a testimony that the animals in this particular preserve really are locals.

Back on the Strip, the animals are wild and exotic. In Siegfried and Roy's Secret Garden at the Mirage, white lions weighing hundreds of pounds and as well-groomed as the stuffed miniatures in the gift shop romp in an area of lush grasses and boulders large enough to fit the entire Springs Preserve wildlife collection. There will be no nighttime rendezvous with neighborhood lions here. Rare even in their native habitat of South Africa, these lions live mostly in breeding programs in zoos worldwide. A short walk from the lions, llamas pose in picturesque desert settings, complete with ruins of buildings and a miniature statue of a person that, when photographed with a llama, looks like a distant shepherd. The Secret Garden, like its namesake in the Frances Hodgson Burnett book, is indeed difficult to find, for it is located at the end of the carpet trail that meanders through acres of casino. It used to be that one could view tigers pacing around a glass-enclosed lake within the Mirage resort for free, but they were moved out of their casino habitat and into a more eco-conscious setting, the remote Secret Garden, where one can now view them for the price of admission. In the lobby of the Mandalay, an enormous fish tank advertises the real attraction — Shark Reef, where over two thousand animals swim in 1.6 million gallons of water. Like the Secret Garden, Shark Reef requires an admission fee and, for an extra cost, a souvenir photo — one's picture Photoshopped onto a scene with the exotic animals along with the scripted words "Las Vegas" to verify the authenticity of the experience.

My taxi driver, Franco, had agreed to pick me up after my visit to the preserve, and on the trip back home to Planet Hollywood, I asked him about what kinds of plants he grew in his yard. "Not much," he replied. "Just a couple of small cactuses. Mostly I have rocks. It's cheaper that way. I don't have to water them." After a pause, he said that he felt sorry for people who lived in dangerous areas of the city because they couldn't even have rocks due to the vandals. I expressed surprise that things had gotten so bad in the city that people actually stole one another's rocks. "No, no," he corrected me, "the vandals throw the rocks at windows and break into houses." "So," I wondered aloud, "what do these people have in their yards if they can't afford to water plants and can't have rocks?" The answer, delivered in a matter-of-fact tone, as if it were the most natural thing in the world: "Fake rocks."

1. Aleeza Freeman, "Save the Earth, Hug a Hotel: Vegas Is Greener Than You Think," December 23, 2009, http://blog.vegas.com (under "Hotels").

2. Bill McKibben, introduction to *The End of Nature*, 2nd ed. (New York: Random House, 2006).

3. Koert Van Mensvoort, "Real Nature Is Not Green," 2006, http://www.nextnature .net/2006/11/real-nature-isnt-green/.

4. "Wynn Hotel Aquatic Theater Presents Major HVAC Challenge," *Air Conditioning, Heating, and Refrigeration News*, February 26, 2007, http://www.achrnews.com (under "Exclusive/Manufacturer's News").

5. "Silk Trees," Quality Silk Plants, http://www.qualitysilkplants.com (accessed March 2013).

6. Bjorn Grinde and Grete Grindal Patil, "Biophilia: Does Visual Contact with Nature Impact on Health and Well-Being?," *International Journal of Environmental Research and Public Health* 6 (2009): 2332–43.

7. Harry F. Harlow, "The Nature of Love," *American Psychologist* 13 (1958): 673–85.

8. John Lienhard, "Image and Reality," *Engines of Our Ingenuity*, no. 1449, http:// www.uh.edu/engines/epi1449.htm (accessed March 2013).

9. Review of "Faux Landscaping Rock Pump and Utility Box Covers," Brookstone, July 30, 2013, http://www.brookstone.com.

10. Richard Abowitz, "The Moveable Buffet: The Bellagio's Horticulture Director Makes the Desert Bloom," *Los Angeles Times*, September 26, 2010.

11. "ValleyCrest Chooses Plantworks for Cosmopolitan Hotel and Casino Project," press release, Plantworks, Las Vegas, http://www.plantworksnow.com (accessed March 2013).

12. The Bellagio, http://www.bellagio.com/hotel/ (accessed December 2014).

13. Westgate Resorts, http://westgateresorts.com/ph-towers/ (accessed December 2014).

14. Edward O. Wilson, *Biophilia* (Cambridge, MA: Harvard University Press, 1984).

15. Thorstein Veblen, *The Theory of the Leisure Class* (New York: Macmillan, 1899).

16. Solar Botanic, http://www.solarbotanic.com (accessed March 2011). See also Ranina Sangiap, "Artificial Tree Harvests Wind and Solar Energy to Power Houses," *International Business Times*, 2011, http://www.ibtimes.com.

17. Richard Dawkins, *The Greatest Show on Earth: The Evidence for Evolution* (London: Bantam, 2009).

18. Elizabeth Kolbert, *Field Notes from a Catastrophe: Man, Nature, and Climate Change* (New York: Bloomsbury USA, 2006), 21.

19. The Shops at Crystals, http://www.theshopsatcrystals.com/rodney-lough-jr (accessed December 2014).

20. Ralph Waldo Emerson, *Nature* (1836), in *The Annotated Emerson*, ed. David Mikics (Cambridge, MA: Belknap Press, 2012).

21. Website for the Las Vegas Valley Water District, http://www.lvvwd.com/about /facilities_springs.html (accessed December 2014).

22. "The Drying of the West," *Economist*, January 27, 2011.

23. Five Star Alliance, Best Destination Wedding Resorts 2014, http://www.five staralliance.com/worlds-best-hotels-2014/2188/best-destination-wedding-resorts-2014 (accessed December 2014).

NINE

The Shipping Container Capital of the World

In the peak bubble years of Las Vegas real estate and home building, the locals joked that they had to watch out when driving on the roads and parking lots of the area's newer subdivisions and accompanying malls.* If they weren't careful, the story goes, they would drive right off the edge of the concrete and into the desert. Like the protagonist in *The Truman Show* (1998), the danger, or the hope, was that one day they might just reach the edge of the stage and fall off. This is a city where one can be forgiven for walking into a projection, as Susan did, or misjudging the distance to the Stratosphere, as almost everyone has. As Karen argues, the "culture of picture taking" (chapter 1) on the Strip encourages this confusion of the real and the constructed illusion, exemplified by the "specious nature" of the synthetic plants and fake rocks that decorate the casinos tourists visit and the surrounding homes of those who serve them.

Moreover, as we have tried to show, the glaring visibility of the Strip's mismatched surfaces belies the less visible infrastructures and strategies that hold

* Jane Kuenz

the whole thing together and make its illusions possible: the hidden tangle of delivery roads and bays that signify the global and racially marked system of food production and distribution visitors experience as the bounty and variety of the buffet; the history of environmental politics and class divisions that are simultaneously announced and obscured by water's twin capacity as basic need and entertainment commodity; the creation and deployment of branded entertainment and even sensory experiences as part of marketing strategies that envelop and enter the body; the physical arrangement of cameras and surveillance equipment within casinos and other tourist and work areas; and the digital networks that enable gambling and exchange yet are apparent to most people only as another rewards card in their wallet, something to insert in the penny slot to buy a bit more time. As Stacy points out (chapter 7), the electric fence restrains the dog by letting it run around. Similarly, the vibrancy and apparent freedom these systems offer are inseparable from the limitations and control they exert: you can choose sushi or pasta at the buffet, but both will be cooked by immigrant Latinos.

In the same way that the buffet's multiethnic offerings provide cover for the uniform logic of global wage labor, the mix of themes and styles on the Strip tries to deflect attention away from the underlying sameness of the Vegas most contemporary tourists already know and probably recognize: an especially colorful interconnected web of "non-places." This is Mark Augé's term for the provisional sites for travel, communication, and consumption that make up the geography of "super-modernity."[1] From airport to hotel-casino, restaurant, shopping mall, theater, and back again, we need never leave the conditioned atmosphere and ambient music of spaces marked by both excess and lack: too many signs pointing to nothing. No longer "post" but "super," this world is increasingly wired and networked, yet still anonymous and temporary, rendered familiar and navigable by brands and logos, smartphones and data. We're resident aliens at home, relieved to recognize a fast-food franchise, like travelers abroad.

The characteristic mode is movement. To get from MGM's Signature Hotel to the main resort complex, I had to take an elevator, two moving sidewalks, and an escalator. This does not include walking through an enclosed mall of shops and restaurants along the way or the additional escalators and halls necessary to access the pools or get out to the street or monorail, where the effect continues, including the music, to the sidewalks and parking lots, shuttles and buses. If you don't move, on the other hand, nothing happens; hence all those YouTube videos that consist solely of a tracking shot of the Strip as someone walks up and down Las Vegas Boulevard. Sometimes the resorts demarcate interior space as though to make the otherwise arbitrary distinctions meaningful: walk around the outer edges of New York, and you'll pass through SoHo, Staten Island, Times Square, and Chinatown, but, as everyone knows, this city circles around the casino and its Center Bar.

The local tourist bureau insists Las Vegas has an actual history rooted in a specific locale. Besides the obligatory Hoover Dam excursion, visitors can see the Indian Center and the National Atomic Testing Museum, a testament to the area's past ties to the defense industry. But the Strip today has a global identity; it's what the world looks like when local culture finally disappears and history returns as still shots at the Mob Museum or the wax figures at Tussauds. This transformation can be traced in the recent evolution of resort architecture and decor after the first flush of themed development in the late 1980s and early 1990s produced Treasure Island, Excalibur, the Luxor, and the MGM Grand in its *Wizard of Oz* guise. Since then, the trajectory has been toward international destination cities (Paris, New York, Monte Carlo, Venice), to places marked more broadly in terms of generic culture, whether high European (Bellagio) or popular American (Planet Hollywood, Hard Rock Cafe), to resorts identified by brand-name moguls (the Wynn), and, finally, to the nameless and universal CityCenter and Cosmopolitan. The movement is away from places rooted in geography and history and toward a "global city" built on brands, inhabited by transnational, roaming, cosmopolitan populations, and organized, through them, by the movement of capital and labor.[2]

On this point, CityCenter is exemplary. "The next step in the evolution of Vegas," as one engineering firm puts it, CityCenter is the joint project of MGM and Dubai World, the investment arm of the government of Dubai, "that other desert arcade of capitalist desire" on the Persian Gulf.[3] The audio tour guide accompanying the scale model on display at the Bellagio Gallery describes the mixed-use urban complex as a "participatory engaging event" where visitors will find the "energy of the city" in one building. This is the point: to relocate the center of the Strip by creating a city within a city right in the middle of it. A seventy-six-acre swath of luxury shops, hotel rooms, and condos, CityCenter takes up everything on Las Vegas Boulevard between the Bellagio and the Monte Carlo. People trying to get from New York to Paris will spend their entire time walking past or through it. There's no easy way to do that either, though anyone actually living there will have to try. This is a "city" unwelcoming to anyone who also has to work or eat on a regular basis: there are 2,400 condos but no grocery store, a tram that takes you to the center's periphery but nowhere else. You can find a spa but not a pharmacy. The

multiple venues for luxury and leisure consumption underscore CityCenter's distance from what most people consider necessary to live in a real city, because it's not a real city and most people aren't really welcome there, except to service the wealthy or to look. It's a vision of an urban center as a high-end mall inside a gated community. At least MGM had the honesty to name its exclusive hotel within a hotel the Mansion.

Like CityCenter, the Vegas Strip itself is an oasis of useless luxuries in a desert of lack, fueled by foreign money and unencumbered by regulations. Here, the core ethic of privatization and economic inequality leads directly to the kaleidoscopic sights and sounds that replace the regional and ethnic cultures now flattened by commodity and entertainment branding, for which Cirque du Soleil serves as chief example. Similarly, the wall-to-wall gaming and forced hilarity merely underscore the more general torpor and angst that follow the transformation of labor into an international army of contingent workers, whether in the kitchen or at the slots, always putting in time even at play. All of this is tracked and monitored by a pervasive and insistent surveillance apparatus in the form of networked spaces, cameras, and rewards cards, and an ideological discourse of freedom, security, individualism, and choice. The obvious parallel is the Internet, which also assumes total surveillance and, like the Miracle Mile shops flanking Planet Hollywood, is ever more a continuous wall of advertising and consumption, increasingly private and fully monetized, free to everyone with a password, profile, PIN, or credit card.[4] Yes, what happens in Vegas stays in Vegas, but the great irony of twenty-first-century privacy is that you have to show an ID to get in and out of the spaces where it exists. "Home," of course, is a tab on my browser.

As Augé notes, we get around this world by accessing and processing text and data, some of it personal, all of it bureaucratic: exit signs on the interstate announcing towns we never see; instructions about where to go, what to do, what not to carry, when to get out our tickets, when to take off our shoes. It is all rather like search engines recommending sites, telling me what I want, what my friends want, what I might eventually want at some later time. Each time I log on to Facebook, I'm prompted to say something about myself: "What's on your mind?" it asks, like a conscientious friend. It prompts me to connect with current colleagues and distant family members, people I knew twenty years ago, or complete strangers it thinks I must know now because other people I know do. (However, when I browse Mark Zuckerberg's page, it tells me, "You and Mark aren't friends.") It encourages me to update my profile with my name and relationship status; the names of my spouse, children, siblings, and parents; of my grade school, high school, college, and graduate school. It wants my religious affiliation and political philosophy. It asks about places I've been, where I work, my favorite movies, music, books, television shows. Is there a favorite quotation I want to share? Am I an organ donor?[5] It even supplies a ready-made list of emoticons from which to choose so I can let my friends know my mood, though the list of preapproved emotions is only slightly less jarring than the constant prompting to display one for public consumption.

In Las Vegas, public address similarly mixes personal invitation and general command: the signage directs me through the casino to the buffet, like travelers through the terminal, reminding me to use my player's card, suggesting where to eat, what to buy, how to act at the pool. "Go outside to the real outside," says a woman in the Luxor to her companion. It sounds like a koan or a line from the TV, the language of advertising, where interpellation is always the promise of individual distinction and authenticity (the real outside) and the apparent intimacy of the implied "you" that is, nevertheless, a directive: (You) go outside.

Thus, Jenny Holzer's *Vegas*, an LED installation at Aria's north valet exit, is entirely at home. Commissioned by Michele Quinn, who managed the placement of the Aria's extensive art works, *Vegas* creates a "seamless visual environment" connecting the hotel's interior lobby to its immediate outside where guests waiting for cabs are themselves hailed by seemingly random statements selected from Holzer's *Truisms* scrolling continuously overhead:

It's crucial to have an active fantasy life.
If you have many desires, your life will be interesting.
It's better to be alone than to be with inferior people.
Ignoring enemies is the best way to fight.

Like the fortune in the cookie, what is written as an observation easily starts to feel like an expectation or instruction, if not a command:

It's important to stay clean on all levels.
Overeating should be criminal.
If you live simply, there is nothing to worry about.

Many of Holzer's truisms can be taken as comments on Vegas, and occasionally one appears that seems intended as a joke: "It's not good to operate on credit." But the text is too big and moves too slowly for anyone in a hurry to read, so many will see the display just in flashes and pieces, as part of the environment and decor, like any other screen or sign on the Strip inviting you to play or announcing that night's show. For those waiting, however, it's hard

not to stand and stare, following the scroll, waiting slowly for the break that signals the end of one statement that, in any case, does not lead to anything following nor refer to anything that came before, each presented instead as an isolated announcement or injunction directed to no one in particular, which means to everyone in general. The effect is like the crawl below the news or the steady advance of status updates in the newsfeed. It's like Twitter:

> Let others have their own opinions on their idols and stop bashing
>   them for no reason.
> People should stop what they're doing, run out, and get me a tiara.
> Just get out of the way when you're trying to move set pieces.
> Buy me something off my wishlist!
> How many people are in jail and live in fear over a plant?
> What's god's plan for me?
> I smile for no reason.

I copied these verbatim from a trending hashtag in my Twitter feed. They are typical of the snippets of chatter and images that run continuously across the screens of our phones, tablets, and computers, each requiring attention yet brief enough to be consumed in the spots of time between the endless, repetitive tasks at home or work, between stops on the bus and during commercial breaks, or while we sit behind the wheel waiting for the red light to turn green. "Facebook is a distraction machine for the dispossessed," writes philosopher Jason Read. He wrote it on Facebook.

As in much of her work, Holzer's *Vegas* superimposes text onto public spaces, often in monumental ways. The political potential of this gesture has not been lost on subsequent groups, such as the Occupy Wall Street movement, which projected "99%" and other movement slogans onto the side of the Verizon Building during a march over Brooklyn Bridge in November 2011. More recently, Egyptian protestors demanding the departure of President Morsi used lasers to project "Game Over" onto a government building overlooking Tahrir Square in Cairo.[6] For both groups, projecting text was a way to reclaim public space, by demanding it back from either private enterprise or corrupt government. The powerful images were then circulated widely on Twitter and other social media, which begged again the same question posed by people using privately owned sidewalks for strikes only then to be escorted off the premises: what kind of political agency is possible when the apparent space of public interaction is in fact private property and our actions there are already inscribed within its rules?

For Las Vegas is more than the "city-sized supermall" Mike Davis identi-

fies as the new "dreamworld of neoliberalism."[7] Like other global cities, it is increasingly governed by a different kind of protocol, one coded into the city's very walls much like the terms of use of all those social media platforms where people go to share their political ideas and images.[8] These are the terms that no one reads but everyone must agree to in order to advance; otherwise, you never get to pass go. And they're the terms of neoliberal enterprise and subjectivity required of the new working-class precariat in a global economy of networked non-places.[9] "Game over," after all, is the phrase that appears at the end of every computer game when your avatar finally succumbs to the laws of probability and dies for the last time. It's not what the player says to the game, as the Egyptian protestors seemed to think, but what the game does to you.

Gamespace

When Barack Obama's 2008 inauguration was broadcast on the 130-foot Jumbotron atop Planet Hollywood, people gathered outside to watch. On the street, his face appeared above Trader Vic's and Urban Outfitters. CNN's shot of the Capitol dome mixed in with the Eiffel Tower next door and the Statue of Liberty and Luxor pyramid down the Strip. Miss America contestants, in town to compete for the opportunity to wear a crown for a year, assembled in front; they stood in a line, as if in formation. Inside, the casinos shifted from their usual broadcasts: like Elvises on the Strip, Obamas multiplied, as the overhead screens all flashed the same image in different directions. Since casino TVs tend to show only professional sports, this substitution had the effect of turning the new president into an anchor for ESPN. There above the slots, part of the general flash and chatter, Obama's historic presidency began, so much white noise about change amid the constant time and temperature on the floor.

Besides the Jumbotron, Planet Hollywood includes the Miracle Mile shops, which cover an entire block with electronic signs. By linking screens typically showing different images, the repetition of Obama's face, inside and outside the casinos, highlighted a key feature of contemporary cities, especially in its hotels, malls, entertainment centers, and airports like McCarran, where arrival and departure screens compete for attention with LED ads for Cirque du Soleil. These are dynamic and rich multimedia environments defined by and experienced through technology that relies on digital networks. It's hard to know what the new president could have said in his inauguration speech that would have indicated a more significant change in daily life than the way his audience on the Strip received it. Of course, people have been

watching inaugural addresses on TV for over sixty years; what's different now is that they're watching them not just on the side of a Vegas casino, but on their phones.

If the long history of the city begins with the first shift from walled castle to crossroads market, then Las Vegas's status today as a global entertainment destination is one endpoint of that trajectory, a place impossible to imagine without the ever-faster and more interconnected networks for trade, communication, and finance that define global capitalism. These digital networks constitute an invisible landscape inseparable from the streetscapes we can see, though the distinction between observable and hidden is increasingly moot since we experience them together. A century ago, automobiles fundamentally changed cities and our experience of them. For better or worse, mobile digital devices are doing the same thing now: we no longer use phones merely to connect with each other or document what we do, but to do the doing itself. It would be a mistake to assume this constitutes a false rather than different relation to the real world really out there.

For example, the Strip's jumble of buildings pitched at various perspectives is overwhelming and confusing only if I presume that the best way to orient myself in relation to something else is to look directly at it. In fact, if I want to figure out how far away the Stratosphere really is and what's the best route to get there, I will have better luck not looking up at the street at all but down at my phone. My phone is more likely to be right because it reconceives orientation altogether, using GPS or GIS coordinates to position me on a grid of data that also includes the Stratosphere. Here, my own line of vision matters less than my access to a network capable of retrieving, manipulating, and reporting my whereabouts. Don't miss that the network that helps me find my way around the Strip is the same one keeping track of my bets, purchases, and comps in the casinos, shops, and hotels lining it. These technologies are inseparable; they are designed to work together. This is why an entire city dedicated to gaming and play is simultaneously one devoted to surveillance and work.

Thinking through how we digitally inhabit or experience a place seems counterintuitive in Las Vegas, where, as Stacy and Susan write (chapters 6 and 7), so much emphasis is given to the body and physical sensations—eating, drinking, sex, the shifting sights of the Strip and insistent sounds of the slot machines. But not everyone experiences Las Vegas as a shock to the senses. Indeed, anyone who has spent much time with the Minecraft game my twelve-year-old plays will immediately recognize the suspension of the normal rules of physics and perspective. Of course, looking at my phone while I'm moving around may still make me more likely to walk into walls, but for a completely different reason. Once the walls are themselves wired and made visible digitally, that problem will disappear. At that point, the distinction between real and digital will be less useful since, as the Stratosphere example suggests, things in the physical world will increasingly appear, not just as themselves, but as material representations of the data digitally encoded in them.[10] On this point, consider again the Bellagio fountains and all those other Water Entertainment Technologies installations in CityCenter. As Stacy shows, transforming water into spectacle requires a complex and generally hidden infrastructure, a central element of which is obviously digital: the water's movements make manifest the computer program governing them. For people lining up hourly on the Strip to watch the dancing fountains, the real is the sign of the code.

By occupying a defined part of a larger space, both the fountains and the Holzer installation foreground digital infrastructure as art, but many places now come with layers of embedded data and wireless networks to access it, and not just built structures: you can get Wi-Fi in national parks. As more places get Geotagged, these enhanced or augmented spaces will be readily visible to anyone with the desire and the smartphones to see them. The applications for doing so are already available and increasingly sophisticated. People across the planet, for example, play Geocache, a GPS-abetted game of international hide-and-seek that has participants surveying the environs guided by the compass on their phones, reading and charting the digital landscape as they go.

In Las Vegas, digitally savvy visitors can use their phones to check comps or check out of their hotels without leaving the blackjack table, though eventually the dealer will ask them to stop. This assumes they can get a cell signal inside the casino. Service is famously bad and may be blocked, but the more Vegas properties move poolside for concerts and events, the more they will want to extend the reach and quality of their Wi-Fi, since more Internet access means more free marketing and publicity as guests tweet their whereabouts and update friends on their Sin City decadence.[11] Most resorts are already fairly hysterical about promoting their apps and social media presence. The Bellagio, for example, encourages website visitors to download iPhone and Android apps, sign up for mobile text offers, and sign an online guestbook. At some point, however, the desire to make the digital map cover the entire territory so that everyone can access and be accessed from all places at all times will collide with the need to control gamblers at the card tables by limiting cell service.

Augmented space is not virtual reality. The person retrieving data in an augmented space is actually in that space, not somewhere else, and the data is there whether or not anyone shows up to read it. Augmented spaces can sometimes feel like virtual spaces, though the difference is often of scale. Watch a movie at the IMAX in the Palms, and the effect will be immersive, like being inside virtual space. Watch the same movie on your iPad in the Luxor Starbucks, and the effect will be quite different: there, the movie adds to whatever else is going on in Starbucks but does not replace it. Pause the movie long enough to post a picture on Instagram of your best friend next to the *Bodies* exhibit sign outside the coffee shop and now you are fully using the augmented space, sending and receiving data by accessing the networks to stream the movie to your device and to transmit pictures back.[12]

With their extensive digital architecture, the Cosmopolitan and CityCenter beg the difference between virtual and augmented spaces. Both are explicit about this. The Cosmopolitan's designers muse that resort guests and visitors will "spend their time wandering in the [lobby], just looking in amazement at this experience they're engulfed in."[13] Similarly, the Rockwell Group that designed CityCenter's mall specializes in immersive environments. The term comes from computer games and virtual reality. Unlike other two-dimensional digital interfaces, an immersive environment surrounds the user, often using three-dimensional sound and large video screens that can encompass direct and peripheral vision, which means you're never really not seeing them. Objects in the space may be interactive like the Revolution's psychedelic decor, or they may simply respond to people as they walk past, like the water installations in Crystals, one of which moves to the sounds of a tone poem. Because the equipment required to engulf people is necessarily hidden, the effect of an immersive environment is like being inside a computer game without knowing it.[14]

In *Gamer Theory*, McKenzie Wark argues that the particular theme or narrative of any one computer game matters less than the fact that, like the Bellagio fountains, everything in all of them has to be rendered in digital terms.[15] It's this digitality—the translation of the material world into quantifiable bits of data—that makes computer "gamespace," like the non-places Augé describes, analogous to the rest of the "real," now augmented, world ostensibly opposed to it. In other words, rather than entertaining alternatives to or diversions from everyday life, computer games actually reproduce and extend the world, or, alternately, the world outside extends the space of the game. In both, work and play involve the same rounds of competition and accumulation—another level to attain, enemy to defeat, point to win, person to friend.

Like walking from hotel to mall to theater without ever really leaving one resort, this is movement without progress: you die, and then you get up and do it all over again.

The quiet desperation of life inside a digital world with no outside is hinted at in the columns in the Cosmopolitan lobby. Here, the wraparound screens organizing the space capture the experience of the contemporary city as the wired, multidimensional space its designers envisioned: we're in it, watching it, and being watched in it at the same time. This new fact of twenty-first-century life is captured in the most riveting of the digital images on the lobby columns. "Seduction" shows people, both men and women, naked but not explicit, occasionally together though usually alone. Sometimes they stare out at us directly before turning away. Other times they run their hands along the screens as though looking for a way out. Although only flat screens, the four-sided columns convey depth and volume. However, unlike the books or the plants that appear on the columns at other times, when the figures shown are human, the effect is unnerving, like there really is something inside: a person who isn't a person pressing against a wall that isn't a wall—exposed, naked, trapped.

Vegas 2.0

LETTUCES @BannedAtHooters 5m
@woahchillbro: at home wondering why you wouldn't be getting hookers if you're in Vegas right now

CATH DOOD @woahchillbro 4m
@BannedAtHooters: i found some but they're no good

LETTUCES @BannedAtHooters 3m
@woahchillbro: oh, so they're more like lookers than hookers

CATH DOOD @woahchillbro 2m
@BannedAtHooters: Yup. *sigh*

LETTUCES @BannedAtHooters 48s
@woahchillbro: #thestruggle is real

On the escalator up to Madame Tussauds at the Venetian, three young men ahead of me laugh and tease each other. I'm too far below to catch more than the general drift of the joke (beer and craps), but the form is clearly recognizable: the three huddled together, each staring at his own phone, apparently responding to the same thing someone posted online. This is a typical scene; versions of it take place all over Las Vegas and pretty much everywhere else. It's visible here especially in the liminal periods, when the contrast between the connected and unconnected is more pronounced, such as the time between Friday morning and evening on any weekend in January and February when the winter retirees in residence retreat into their timeshares to avoid the influx of young SoCal refugees in town to play. I read their intimate conversations on Twitter and watch them take pictures of their breakfast at the Paris buffet. I see them at the Gun Store, though it's not just the young men. Everyone is posing and posting, safety goggles in place, rifles at the ready. After my instructor, Adam, took my picture, I promptly uploaded it to Facebook. Everybody liked it.

If capitalism produces the kinds of subjects it needs, then, clearly, what it needs now are people on display, willing not just to be recorded every time they step out onto a public street or log in to a network, but to have their every act, feeling, and preference be seen by others. No longer a threat, the assumption of constant visibility integrated into Las Vegas's infrastructure is also contained in our amusements. The technologies and methods of surveillance, long the subject of dystopian nightmare, are now the tools for successful self-presentation. This is Planet Hollywood, and we are all celebrities. We smile for the camera. Actually, we're holding the camera, but it's a mirror. Today, the number one use of digital photography is selfies — those self-portraits that turn up in our online profiles in the telltale pose: arm outstretched to hold the phone. When *Poltergeist* premiered in 1982, the prospect of someone in the family being sucked into the television was presented as horror, the consequence of sacrificing morality for easy profits. Now, everyone can be his or her own TV station: "Please," writes Mr. Apple62 under his latest YouTube contribution, "like this video and subscribe to my channel."

Madame Tussauds knows the score: at her Interactive Wax Attraction, fame organizes the world, and local history is the history of entertainers, politicians, and gangsters. Celebrities are segregated into separate rooms where differences in historical era and context matter less than how they got famous: film and television stars here, sports heroes there, rooms each for music, crime, and politics. Gangsters fit easily into this mix, both from their ties to Las Vegas and their place in the history of popular movies. Unlike the Luxor's *Bodies . . . the Exhibition*, where you can't touch the dead, the celebrity bodies at Tussauds are interactive. Like Disney World's photo spots, however, the real point of the interactive exhibits at Tussauds is to be photographed in the sheets with Hugh Hefner or at the altar with George Clooney. This is what

interaction means now: to appear in the same image with someone else, even plastic people, preferably famous. What's different is the expectation that the pictures will be widely broadcast and publicized, shared, as we say, with anyone and everyone who will look at any of our several accounts on Facebook, Twitter, Tumblr, Flickr.

The omnipresence of cameras and social media turns everyone into a star, but what does celebrity mean in such a world? In her research on social media and Silicon Valley tech workers, Alice Marwick argues that celebrity is best understood now as a set of practices calculated to draw attention and make us "Facebook famous," that is, as the joke goes, famous not for fifteen minutes, but with fifteen people.[16] We follow ourselves the way we used to follow Hollywood stars, who now have to tweet in order to compete with each other and cats. Social media requires us always to see ourselves as others do, even though we can't actually control how they do that. Our profiles are versions of ourselves created for consumption by other people, many of whom don't know each other, some of whom we don't even know at all. We don't engage with other people so much as process their information. Friends are not necessarily the people we know but the ones we connect with publicly. We post pictures—over 300 million each day to Facebook alone, another 60 million on Instagram—planning how to present ourselves being clever, sensitive, informed, fun.[17] We use our online interactions and activity to constitute ourselves as a self, something to be consumed by others, especially in real time, because, after all, we're mobile too: all those overlapping Wi-Fi networks allow us to broadcast where we are, who we're with, when we've left one place and checked in at another, always connecting yet never quite with the people we're with except, like the men on the escalator, when the connection is mediated by our devices.

This begs the question of how much we actually engaged with each other before social media as well as the character and quality of those social interactions. Indeed, much of this sounds like a familiar social critique updated for new technologies, but the differences are telling: Erving Goffman turned to theatrical metaphors to explain face-to-face encounters, but his analysis of everyday social performance presumed a space offstage or backstage that is more difficult to find or imagine now.[18] Also, while my friends may ignore my social faux pas in the interest of maintaining everyone's collective illusion of who we are and what we're doing, my friends' friends, people I may not know and will likely never meet, may not be so accommodating. Public is always plural online: we interact with some people in the present, while others watch in silence from a distance in time and space. Every update, comment, or tweet plays for multiple audiences in different places at different times. Like Holzer's *Vegas*, it's a form of personal public address to everyone at once but no one in particular; it presumes an audience, but requires no response. After you're gone, people keep watching the traces you've left behind: photos, comments, links. This is the posture of the celebrity to her public, and we assume it with our "friends."

Though Facebook's Timeline was introduced as a tool for preserving one's personal history, it's really just a display case for this documented, consumable public self. Like Vegas, Timeline presumes a constant present tense, but it's a present projected as always having already happened—a kind of future past, as Nathan Jurgenson puts it.[19] Meanwhile, the past itself is either obliterated and replaced, like the Sands and Aladdin, first demolished then recreated as the Venetian and Planet Hollywood, or simply reorganized into minidisplays like the Neon Museum downtown ("saving signs since 1996"). Despite its newspeak name, Timeline is no line at all, not a narrative we tell of our past, but a profile we've constructed over time. Because most of us won't even bother to fill in other details and events from our lives that we had not already featured in a status update, there's a big blank hole between when we were born and when we joined Facebook and started posting. Most of us also lack the time or fortitude to systematically cull the years' worth of past updates automatically posted to Timeline, so we're stuck with a truncated biography of a self, either the one we want to be or have others believe us to be, or the one we think we should be if not the one we really are, which we know now since all those search engines base their recommendations for books, music, websites, even friends, on the data we've made available online and with our rewards cards. With its gestures at personalization negated by the standardizing template, Timeline literalizes the flattening of time and collapse of distinctions epitomized by the Las Vegas skyline with this one new addition: now our lives are more searchable than memorable.

Like Timeline, the old downtown trades in its past in a frantic effort to make itself relevant and attract attention to entice tourists off the Strip: several streets have been converted to a covered mall of casinos and gift shops, themed as "Real Vegas" and marketed unsuccessfully to outsiders as the Fremont Street Experience. When Jimi Hendrix used the term, *experience* implied shared knowledge of actual experiences, but in a postliterate society, where entertainment is culture, experiences are more likely branded "entertainment experiences." They occur overhead and around us, whether we participate or not. We collect them like souvenirs, and then post the pictures on Flickr for ourselves and strangers.

I'm at Chipotle Mexican Grill (Las Vegas, NV) Jodi Harris K@
    JodiHarris
I'm at MandalayBay Pool-The Beach Edwin Lee@EdwinKLee
I'm at Walmart Supercenter-Las Vegas heezus@hOllierOster
Pool side chillin at mandarin oriental L Vegas baby!! Telliswift@
    telliswift
Having steak and eggs at Bill's gambling hall and saloon Jane
    Kuenz@jkuenz
I'm naked in the Las Vegas airport glor@bbyglorr

"The reserve army of the bored zombie the earth," writes Wark, "fiddling with their cell phones, checking their watches."[20] They do that because they're anxious. If virtual reality gave us the sexy avatar, a digital stand-in capable of moving around freely in exciting virtual spaces, the networked city's new icon is this person tweeting in the Flamingo lobby and posting status updates under the false sky in the Forum Shops, standing alone in the middle of a mall, laughing at something no one in the room actually said. But at least we're laughing, sharing our whereabouts and following each other, though there's no actual invitation or expectation that anyone will join us at Bill's or poolside at the Mandarin.

The easiest response is to call this narcissism, but social networking sites and the personal portable technologies on which they depend encourage constant self-exposure, not just as commonplace and enjoyable but as a positive virtue, a form of creative individual expression, toward which any reluctance or hesitation renders one suspicious, thus justifying the surveillance in the first place. And the rewards of participation are clear, sometimes literally: Caesars Entertainment recently experimented with a program offering player's card points to people simply for showing up at any Caesars resort venue and checking in on a social network like Foursquare. But the real payoff is less tangible: immediate social and cultural capital, status linked directly to what and how much we reveal, a sense of intimacy and connection within the general flux and disconnect, and, perhaps most attractive, the belief that, unlike everywhere else in our lives, here we are recognized as unique individuals, and our work is seen as valuable and productive. It's called "status update" for a reason.

The brute truth of this existence is announced at Tussauds. Though it claims their resident porn star, Jenna Jameson, will whisper a personal message if you tickle the tattoo on her right ankle, the typical address from the wax celebrities is a slogan for each one's personal brand. Eventually, they start to sound alike and just as generic and disconnected as hotel signage and random tweets. Like the favorite quotations on our online profiles, most of these are paeans to individualism and advice for pursuing roads less traveled, the usual sops offered in lieu of actual opportunity: "I don't pretend to be captain weird," says Johnny Depp. "I just do what I do." Jodie Foster agrees, sort of, telling us, "I don't want to be a botoxed weirdo," while the real and rumored botoxed weirdoes resort to inane uplift advice that drives home the same point: "Your regrets aren't what you did, but what you didn't do. So I take every opportunity" (Cameron Diaz); "You'll never know what you're capable of until you try" (Sarah M. Gellar). The celebrity statements at Tussauds almost uniformly preserve the myth of the American Dream that effort, hard work, and just being yourself lead to success with the significant difference that now success is synonymous with fame.

For those of us unlikely to be immortalized by Madame Tussaud, online fame is the salve for the loss of opportunity and identity everywhere else. But it's a technical individuality, coded and aggregated into networks that track, measure, perform, and display the self as the sum of our data.[21] What's important is what's shared; hence the incessant fine-tuning of its algorithms and privacy protocols betrays the real concern in Facebook's business plan not just to create productive online relationships, but also to capture anything they produce: every quantifiable follower, friend, link, like, and share.[22] If the joke and fear in the 1990s was that you couldn't really know who you were interacting with online, now we are increasingly expected or required to access everything through one or two accounts, typically Facebook or Twitter, and not just other social media but online shopping too, such as Groupon and LivingSocial. Ostensibly for our convenience, the real point of signing in to Facebook for everything is to verify that we are who we say we are. Otherwise, how to judge the value of knowing who's at the Chipotle by Harrah's and who's eating steak and eggs at Bill's? As Zuckerberg famously remarked, "Having two identities for yourself is an example of a lack of integrity."[23]

As the celebrity quotes at Tussauds suggest, at bottom, much of this is finally about work: "Be yourself," they urge, "but not too different!" And, above all else, keep working. As Deleuze predicted, the thing about repressive forces isn't that they prevent us from expressing ourselves, but that they require us to.[24] The constant posting, commenting, friending, and liking of our own and each other's content is the very image of the incessant self-branding, networking, retraining, and flexibility required of workers in a global, post-Fordist economy hoping a steady display of ever more inventive self-actualization in the workplace will balance their actual economic vulnerability and invisi-

bility.[25] If a profile is our online body, then the status update and tweet signal a pulse: stop posting and people think you're dead. Blackberries and iPhones made it impossible ever to leave the office; now Facebook and Twitter extend this logic into the last remaining space: all free time must be dedicated to the creation and tweaking of the self and its network of friends and preferences, all doubling as labor or product or both. Either we're promoting someone else's for-profit content by linking to articles in magazines or to clips from films and TV shows, or we're creating the content for them, all those Grumpy Cat Tumblr memes eventually repackaged and sold back to us at the toy store. Our record of interactions, contacts, and clicks, every silly poll question and game, is salable product for the people with the machinery and money to move it.[26] Social media extend the transnational-but-really-nowhere city online, where it produces and manages the always-working neoliberal subject, mainly by cultivating and managing the self as a profile without a body, a collection of tastes, preferences, and likes, one piece in a larger network of connections that includes but does not recognize us. Some fame, this: soon, likes will be the only currency we have.

The Shipping Container Capital of the World

In Facebook's ideal city, all citizens are always working and all are connected. This ideal is now proposed for Las Vegas by Tony Hsieh, the CEO of Zappos. In 2013, the giant online retailer moved its offices into Las Vegas as part of a broader proposal to revitalize the downtown and turn Sin City into "the most community-focused large city in the world."[27] Described in the *New York Times* as an attempt "to retrofit downtown with, well, a downtown," Hsieh's ambitious plan of real estate investment and start-up grants seems designed to contrast pointedly with the vision of urban living imagined by CityCenter.[28] According to its website, the Downtown Project will "bring together communities of passion" in "a vibrant, connected urban core" with sufficient residential density and "ground level gathering places" to allow artists and entrepreneurs to meet and work together. Where CityCenter touts internationally acclaimed architects with big budgets for showcase constructions devoted to an exclusive clientele, the new downtown will emphasize flexible urbanism with repurposed spaces that can adapt to the community's evolving needs. Unlike CityCenter's focus on leisure and luxury consumption, the Downtown Project emphasizes sustainability and community building and promises investment in new businesses, education, and the arts.

The key trait required of participants in the Downtown Project is "passion." The word is used twenty times on the website, some variant appearing in almost every paragraph: the project is put forward by "a group of passionate people"; they are looking for other "passionate people" to come on board, if not entire "communities of passion"; they hope the changes downtown encourage others "to follow their personal passions," yet they also want to create public spaces where people can "gather around common passions," maybe even "develop new passions." In the list of criteria for successful applicants for startup funds, the first asks, "Are you passionate about the idea?" Passion about one's idea precedes the next criterion, which is being capable of actually executing it. Though it's the necessary element in the Downtown Project's inception and future success, "passion" is never defined. It's just something some people have and know they have. It also has no specific qualities: one person's passion is distinguished from another's not by its object but by its intensity.

The Downtown Project especially wants "passionate entrepreneurs." In the same way that social media makes us all entrepreneurs of the self, every update and share an investment in the personal brand, the new Las Vegas imagined by the Downtown Project is one where the entrepreneur is the model citizen, if not the only kind allowed.[29] This goes for the kids too, whose education will "focus on creativity and entrepreneurship."[30] Though the project's organizers insist "a community must remain accessible to people from all economic backgrounds," they announce up front which particular communities they really want: technology, fashion, photography, art, and music. The list invokes the ideal of economic diversity, but does so only by negating class. If passion is objectless, communities are defined by affinity and product. This is why the list is so narrowly conceived, since it's unlikely "art" includes poetry. Finally, each of these communities is a variation on the same theme. We're told, for example, that successful entrepreneurs are "passionate about their craft," as though entrepreneurs are really just artists or skilled labor, but the opposite also follows: all artists and laborers are really businesspeople in training, following their passions in a world where all human activity can be, and really should be, a form of entrepreneurial activity. Here, social rights and obligations manifest as private aspirations and interests—one's passion—the pursuit of which inevitably translates into public goods, such as, for example, using tax money to finance the purchase of the old city hall for your own vision of an urban core or treating your personal art collection like the city museum with the tax write-offs to match. It's announcing your commitment to public education but investing in a charter school just in case.[31]

In promoting community, the Downtown Project also emphasizes the importance of "connectivity." Like passion, connectivity is a catalyst for a

transformed urban center, where a "connectivity infrastructure" allows residents "to collide," like molecules in a physics experiment or friends on Foursquare. These serendipitous encounters among artists and techies will lead to "the sharing of knowledge [and] ideas and [improve] productivity." "Happiness," too, is geared to "economic output," as though the two were the same thing. That so much of this ends in the language of the bottom line suggests that these are less like chance encounters among people from different backgrounds and experiences and more like a Davos meeting, where anyone invited already agrees on the essential points.

On the one hand, connectivity is about bikes and the open and accessible public areas that will create a dense, but livable, urban center where people can get around without a car. Where they will be getting around to is the area's new Container Park, which will house cafés, boutiques, bars, and galleries. Combined with outdoor seating and playgrounds, the Container Park will "activate the center of our neighborhood" and, like Disney World, "make magic happen faster"—that is, help entrepreneurs prosper. It's called Container Park because shops will be operating out of repurposed shipping containers, which will allow the flexibility required of new businesses moving in and out of the park. The lynchpin of global capital's distribution system, the temporary home-in-transit of all those cheap souvenirs available in casino shops as well as much of the food in their buffets, shipping containers are emblematic of Las Vegas's future status as the Shipping Container Capital of the World.

Boutiques, bike paths, and playgrounds are attractive to most people, but the concept of connectivity is actually appropriated straight from the Internet and social media, where *connect* describes both the digital network and the form of social interaction it fosters. We are connected to it and we connect with each other on it. The Downtown Project is striking for the way it makes virtual spaces and online communities the models for urban neighborhoods and how people interact in them. Neighborhood itself is redefined in terms of interest and affinity, which is the point of targeting specific kinds of people—artists, musicians, designers, and techies. It's not that they're excluding others, only that the effect of the infrastructure is to bring similar people together and let the others recede to the background. Google does the same thing when it responds to a search by listing sites with which you probably already agree. Similarly, Facebook rewards participants who follow, comment, or like each other's posts by pushing these friends to the top of the newsfeed and gradually relegating others to the bottom where no one ever sees them again.

At the same time, the distinctions among these different people and their various passions disappear since a connected downtown erases old boundaries between artist and entrepreneur, work and play. These boundaries are especially permeable because specific places are no longer required in order to perform specific tasks, only a temporary container in the park or Wi-Fi on the playground. We don't need a room with a sofa and TV to watch the president, nor a dedicated office and desk to check e-mail, only a phone, preferably near a plug. We need the plug because, in a connectivity infrastructure, what matters most is access. Without access, there's no freedom to move around online and enjoy the sights. As William Mitchell observes, lose your rewards and credit cards, forget your login or password, or just let your phone die, and you're stuck outside, knowing what's available but unable to enjoy it, like a homeless person wandering alone in a city of plenty.[32]

As for access, the key question is always "access to what?" The best answer is to each other, but again only on networks owned and operated by someone else. This is, after all, a top-down model for bottom-up development led by a billionaire online retailer with definite ideas about how things work. Start-up grants, for example, will go to businesses that are "unique" or "the best" or just "story worthy," which means "worthy of a story in a major publication or national news outlet," something that will be talked about or talked up, shared and promoted, though the profits from the sharing again go one way. As with social media, the preferred model is lots of passionate people working for free, which is spelled out in the Terms of Use section of the Downtown Project's website:

> f. Submitting ideas. You also agree that we shall be free to use any ideas, concepts or techniques embodied in any communication you submit to us [whether] through an online forum, through e-mail or any other writing, transmission or communication ("Submission") for any purpose whatsoever, including, but not limited to, developing, manufacturing, and marketing products or services incorporating such ideas, concepts, or techniques without your approval or compensation to you. You waive any rights you may have in modifications or alterations to your Submissions or in the event that your Submission is changed in a manner not agreeable to you. In addition, you hereby waive all moral rights, copyrights and any other rights you may have in any materials uploaded to the Service or sent to us by you.[33]

In announcing his latest philanthropic venture, Facebook's Mark Zuckerberg identified "connectivity" as "a human right." His Internet.org hopes to

bring Internet service and presumably Facebook to 5 billion currently unconnected people. Its slogan is predictably, if obliviously, Orwellian: "Everyone of us. Everywhere. Connected."[34] He means via the web, but it's also looking likely that we will be connected in other ways. In 2008, more than 50 percent of the world's population was urbanized. The United Nations predicts that by 2050, 70 percent of us will live in cities. At this rate, the entire world will be urbanized by 2092. As Michael Batty asks, when that happens, will we be living in different cities or will it be one big urban spread, a kind of continuous non-place?[35] Will the difference even matter when all the cities are global and everyone everywhere is connected economically and socially to everyone else?

The fastest-growing cities in the world are in China, which now has forty with populations over a million and anticipates 220 such cities by 2030.[36] This didn't happen by accident; it's one effect of the country's rapid transition from planned to market economy in the last thirty years. The profound transformation in how China does business drew people from the countryside into urban areas and, in the process, produced one of the most unequal societies on the planet. The gap between China's rich and poor is greater now than before the 1949 revolution, and, in a complete reversal of the earlier trend, the poverty rate is now higher in the cities than in the country.[37] Impoverished by economic changes vastly out of their control, the rural poor have moved into China's burgeoning cities looking for work, only to find their labor is not needed or is redundant in a state increasingly entranced with the liberalizing policies of the West.

Some of them landed in places like the giant Foxconn factories in Taiyuan, where the iPhone 6 is made, or outside Shanghai in a place known locally as iPod City. Here, several hundred thousand people live and work inside a one-and-a-half-mile walled campus, a kind of gated community or "container park" for the working class, complete with its own factories and dorms, banks, restaurants, fire stations, hospitals, and, of course, security guards. Employees at Foxconn's Shanghai factory typically work twelve hours a day for the equivalent of $100 a month, half of which they must pay back to the company for housing and food. It's not much, but still enough to send something to those family members back home on the farm and considerably more than what their less fortunate peers get, those who also came to the city but never got through the gate. Some experts estimate that almost a third of China's urban inhabitants are undocumented migrants from the countryside, members of the "floating population" displaced by globalization. Many of these people end up unemployed, without health care or other social services, and

finally dead and unclaimed in city morgues.[38] Some of them end up in Las Vegas casinos.

Human Capital

There are bodies in the Luxor pyramid. When it opened, the resort's designers wanted to display a real Egyptian mummy to complete the Nile River Tour and replica of King Tut's tomb that were part of its original theme. That never happened, but now they've got the real deal: *Bodies . . . the Exhibition*. A knockoff of Gunther von Hagens's original *Body Worlds* shows of plastinated corpses, *Bodies* is promoted and run by Premier Exhibitions, "a major provider of museum-quality touring exhibitions throughout the world," as the company's promotional materials proclaim.[39] Premier Exhibitions makes a lot of money off the dead: besides *Bodies*, Premier also sponsors spinoff corpse shows internationally under different names — *Bodies Revealed* and *Our Body: The Universe Within* — along with other "museum-quality exhibits" like *Titanic: The Artifact Exhibition*, which Vegas tourists can also see in the Luxor. In fact, they're right next to each other, an unfortunate juxtaposition for the *Titanic's* lost passengers. Like many other companies in the tourist and entertainment industries, Premier Exhibitions was hit hard in the recent recession, but it still managed to salvage $1 million in quarterly profits in the middle of it. About a fifth of Premier's profits comes from the *Titanic* shows; the bulk, however, comes from people paying to see human bodies preserved in plastic and posed running with a football, shooting a basketball, skiing, or riding a bike, even performing a ballet or conducting a symphony for the edification and amusement of the living.[40]

For history buffs, *Titanic: The Artifact Exhibition* offers the usual rewards of detail and narrative, and, like Madame Tussauds and csi: *The Experience*, it's interactive. Upon entering, I'm given a boarding pass with the name of one of the ship's passengers, which would be disconcerting enough except that the point of the interaction is for me to figure out if I survived. The walkthrough is accompanied by sound effects — the ship's horn, snippets of conversation, and the music of the heroic string quartet — but the real focus here is on people and their things. Entire rooms are given over to passengers' belongings, usually very intimate, everyday items of personal care or private use. Most are identified by name, as a particular person's particular property — in other words, items that were already labeled or were recovered from staterooms. The exhibit is accompanied by the eerie, green underwater footage of salvagers poking through what's left of the sunken ship. Indeed, for all its debts to Jacques Cousteau and *Antiques Roadshow, Titanic: The Artifact Exhibition*, like the Holocaust Museum in Washington, DC, on which it's clearly based, is haunted by what's not there: each item of the passengers' effects substitutes for the body not recovered.

In *Bodies*, on the other hand, the corpses are very much present, both whole and in parts, kept intact and vivid through a process invented by von Hagens called plastination, in which water and fat are replaced with liquid silicone, thus enabling the bodies to be posed upright like life-sized Barbie dolls—though, actually, mainly Ken—or arranged in slices like Damien Hirst cows. The plastinates are often explicitly presented as art, arranged in ten "galleries" according to major organ system, and the spaces themselves are set up like museums, complete with prohibitions against photography and phones, as though it were the Ferrari dealership in the Wynn, though here the signs can be confusing, inviting us to see "real human bodies" but warning us not to "touch the cadavers." Some are whole body displays; in others, organs or organ systems are separated out and shown on their own: a skull and spinal cord, for example. Posed on pedestals and spotlighted for best effect, the various pieces can be strangely beautiful, like the blues and pinks of the heart. At other times, the result is simply macabre, such as when the entire alimentary system is mounted on the wall like a painting.

In a world that increasingly takes total visibility as given and has created and integrated the surveillance technologies and entertainment culture necessary to accomplish it, a world in which we are always, in some way, exposed and in the public eye, where, especially after 9/11, the inside must be as visible as the outside—in this world, the value of shows like *Bodies* is that they literalize the metaphors. "To See Is to Know" reads the sign greeting visitors entering *Bodies*, as though doubling for one of Holzer's *Truisms* or TSA instructions in the airport security line.[41] Elsewhere, the signs tell us "The Body Never Lies," implying that we do, that we may be in conflict with our bodies, betrayed by them, and that it is against such lies that the body must be examined and made visible, public, and known.

Promoted under the rubric of self-knowledge, visibility, and truth, *Bodies . . . the Exhibition* invites us to identify with the medical gaze and the technologies that extend it, often playing with tropes of introspection, seeing and being seen, such as when a single body is sliced in half and arranged so that each half regards the other. In others, we see what the MRI or airport scanner sees: the surveilled body, figured as a series of films or views. Indeed, like the Bellagio fountains, some of the poses in the von Hagens shows especially, such as a single body presented entirely as slices, are, as Barbara Maria

Stafford writes, "unimaginable without the backdrop of new electronic media and the concept of both science and art as disembodied information."[42] Though always recognizably human, the bodies suggest the lack of any interiority that cannot be rendered observable, while harnessing any lingering concerns about ever-greater levels of surveillance and visibility to our desire to be so obviously on display, sometimes literally inside out. This impulse is channeled into popular culture like *Bones*, one of several television shows based on forensic anthropology, and haute couture, such as Jean Paul Gaultier's Flayed Skin line, Lady Gaga's "meat dress," and Heidi Klum's 2011 Halloween costume, in which she appeared as a skinned corpse.

In her study of memory and museums, Uli Linke argues that "the very proximity of bodies in the museum satisfies an intense desire for realism and authenticity," particularly among a consumer public for whom pain, suffering, death, and even the past itself are grasped mainly through historical objects in museums and now shows like *Titanic: The Artifact Exhibition*.[43] As the name *plastination* suggests, however, the emphasis on the realness of the bodies and their availability to visual consumption and knowledge is contradicted by their obvious manipulation. Arranged and posed, sometimes to humorous effect, the bodies can be seen like any other bodies on the Vegas Strip: showgirls, most obviously, but also the living statues at the Venetian or any of their gaudy stone cousins at Caesars. Rather than the real located in the material, the manipulation of bodies for effect or to reproduce the poses and themes already known to us from art history and now advertising underscores instead the copy or the virtual body manipulated with Photoshop, altered with plastic surgery, or augmented with circle lenses for those who aspire to the "real" look of an anime heroine. In other words, corpse shows like *Bodies* direct our nostalgia for authenticity to a model that, while giving us a real body, already presents it as fake.

At the same time, the insistence on these bodies as evidence of the real heightens their value as objects for display. This is what *Bodies* shares with the *Titanic* show: both emphasize access to "real objects," including "real human bodies" conceived and portrayed as objects. The insistence on real human bodies both invites the criticism that follows the shows around and deflects it. It is at the root of objections to displays of the dead and lack of respect for the corpse, and it is the basis of the claims to science, education, and public health that, especially in the United States, are their primary justification. The website for the Luxor show includes extensive classroom materials for educators and information about school field trips. Like Steve Wynn's art collection, body shows can cite public service for what is actually private gain.

Bodies epitomizes the display of corpses for entertainment. Specifically, it enacts as entertainment the instrumentalization of the body in commodity culture. The displays showcasing organ systems, for example, illustrate nicely how the discourse of science and medicine constructs the body as parts. More importantly, as Hsu and Lincoln argue, the Premier shows impose a particular attitude toward the body, both the one on display and one's own. Not only are bodies and body parts commodified and exchanged—a logical extension of patented cell lines and an international black market in organs or, where legal, a market skewed toward those with more resources—but health itself is conceived as a personal production, something each person can control and is therefore responsible for.[44] Like our Facebook profiles, our body is something we need to work on, as good health becomes another arena for investing in and improving the self, like whitening your teeth as a form of career development. This attitude is implicit in books like *You: The Owner's Manual*, on sale in the attached gift shop, which popularizes the demand that we see our body as a thing like a car, requiring maintenance, for which we alone are responsible. The lesson of seeing diseased organ systems in a *Bodies* show is that you had best make good choices, and too bad if you're born with Dad's bad genes or next to a toxic waste dump. Next time, choose more wisely. Like insisting that entrepreneurial success is available to anyone with sufficient passion, construing health as the effect of our personal choices is the typical fable of self-making that takes no account of difference and confuses market logic with public and self-interest.

This bootstrap ethos is now required even of the dead, who can no longer merely be dead, but must be put to work creating value for someone else. Though the illusion of agency is asserted through the appearance of motion in how they're presented, these bodies are commodified in every way: as the raw material for the plastinates—practically a renewable resource—and as finished product: an apparatus posed and arranged like action figures into everyday postures and activities that, rather than individualizing them, transform them into types. Dry, hard, odorless, clean, they are parceled out in pieces, displayed for profit, then reproduced on souvenirs: T-shirts, postcards, mouse pads, coasters, and key chains. Not just objects, but commodities, plastinates occupy a legal limbo, neither dead nor alive, not persons nor even dead persons: one German court ruled them not corpses at all under the law and thus not subject to laws governing the handling of the dead.

The catalog on display at the Luxor includes the notice that "all of the anatomical specimens . . . are legally received and painstakingly prepared by medical experts for the purpose of study and education." Premier has included this because of numerous complaints that the company relies on extremely suspect sources for their corpses, many of which are the unclaimed remains of China's executed or indigent poor.[45] Their bodies are processed at places like the Dalian Hoffen Bio-Technique factory in Dalian, China, one of ten such body factories in the country, where medical students and other "experts," some on assembly lines, preserve and arrange them or their parts for private sale and show. Because plastination is a growing and profitable international business in China, exhibitions like the one at the Luxor have the added benefit of serving as trade shows. Though an attempt to deflect criticism, the recourse to law and credentials in Premier's catalog begs the question of what's not specified, such as whose laws were observed, how expert status was certified, or why having an unclaimed corpse prepared by someone with an MD rebuts questions about its origins.

The bodies in the Luxor are obviously Asian. There's no other way to say it. The losers in capitalism's uneven development, they are people finally more valuable dead than alive or those from whose living body no more value can be mined. Some of them do look real, almost alive, so much that we're tempted to think we know what they're thinking. But for all their apparent visibility—some of them literally inside out—what we see is inversely proportional to the knowledge we have about them. Most of them are male, and we are encouraged to see them as universal human bodies, but they're not. In the same way that they are posed to mimic familiar postures from Western sculpture, the bodies on display are treated as projections of a Western consciousness and experience, since it's unlikely any Chinese dissident ever played American football.[46] These were individual persons with specific histories, stripped like their skin of any identifying personal markers and explicitly presented and traded as commodities. Though in the comments people often ask who they are and where they came from, curious about them as persons, no such information is given or even acknowledged as necessary. They are identified not by the names of the people they once were, but by the disease, organ system, or activity they represent. If *Titanic: The Artifact Exhibition* features particular persons but no bodies, *Bodies* features particular bodies but no persons.

Actually, the most common responses in the visitor comment book at *Bodies* are, in this order, (1) "This proves the existence of God"; (2) "This proves Darwin was right"; and (3) "I can see myself." While much of this last is about seeing the body as the intricate and beautiful machine Renaissance anatomists imagined it to be, it also suggests something else. Both valuable and value producing, the plastinates circle the globe, exhibit to exhibit,

pausing long enough in shows like the Luxor's to hold a mirror up to us. We are connected to them by the shipping containers that brought them here and the iPhones we use to take their picture, posed like store mannequins with our friends. They aren't us, but they show us something about ourselves: how, in the end, not just our online identities but even our corpses can be branded and sold. These plastinated bodies are the obvious correlate to the social media profile, twin images of the self under global capital, the material body rendered into something else at once both exposed and anonymous, sorted, arranged, owned. It's a stark image to put next to CityCenter and Hsieh's Container Park, but the right one. Beneath it all is the common view of exploitable human capital in a world where everyone is connected, yet only some have access.

One visitor writes, "It's ironic to see this in a casino in Las Vegas," but that's not quite right. The irony is producing competing models of the social that are all iterations of the same logic of radical transparency and its array of false choices within a private realm of managed tastes and experiences. Culturally, Vegas serves this function for the United States as a whole: forcing us into an ever more privatized vision of community as commodity, refocusing desires for social connection into an opportunity to value only what we are sold. But what if, when we looked at the plastinates, we saw them not as ourselves, but as people connected to us and to whom we have a connection that serves our collective interests? If the dystopian potential of the connected city is represented by these plastinates and those digital bodies forever inhabiting the columns of the Cosmopolitan lobby, like gorgeous gargoyles set up to scare the living, what does the utopian look like?

One night in Vegas, it's 2:00 AM before I can get back to my hotel. Even in the middle of the night in the middle of January, there are people on the street. Everyone has a phone. They have them in their cars and on the bus, in the casinos, restaurants, shops, and clubs. They have them in their rooms. They carry them in bags and pockets, but often just in their hands, texting and Googling and updating and posting. Here's the joke about CityCenter: as "urban theater," it was dated before it even opened. The Cosmopolitan makes that clear, at least in terms of conceptualizing experience as a product. But it's more than that: as Goffman understood, the real theater is all around; it's not a place but a mode of interaction. Now, it's connected, and it moves. On any Vegas Friday night, as on any Friday night in any city, the streets and walkways fill up with people, especially young people, who use their phones and mobile devices to map connections and relations, communities of interest, across the overlapping and competing networked public and private spaces that constitute the contemporary world, a world that otherwise has few places for them. At some point you have to wonder: if enough of my friends check in at the same place at the same time, will that place be ours? Would we be a mob or a movement? As I walk with the crowd back to Paris, the Planet Hollywood Jumbotron above us flashes neon in the cold night. "Which celebrity will you see inside?" it asks me, and will I be its friend on Facebook?

NOTES

1. Mark Augé, *Non-places: Introduction to an Anthropology of Supermodernity*, trans. John Howe (London: Verso, 1995).

2. The term is from Saskia Sassen, *The Global City: New York, London, Tokyo* (Princeton, NJ: Princeton University Press, 2001).

3. "CityCenter, Las Vegas," HalcrowSea, http://halcrowsea.com/Projects/36.html (accessed January 28, 2015). "Desert arcade of capitalist desire" is Mike Davis's description of Dubai in "Sand, Fear, and Money in Dubai," in *Evil Paradises: Dreamworlds of Neoliberalism*, ed. Mike Davis and Daniel Bertrand Monk (New York: New Press, 2007), 50.

4. Fred Scharmen makes a similar critique in "'You Must Be Logged In to Do That!': Myspace and Control," May 2006, http://www.sevensixfive.net/myspace/myspacetwo pointoh.html.

5. Matt Richtel and Kevin Sack, "Facebook Is Urging Members to Add Organ Donor Status," *New York Times*, May 1, 2012.

6. See a video of the Occupy projections and interview with "bat-signal" organizer Mark Read at Xeni Jardin, "Interview with Creator of Occupy Wall Street 'Bat-Signal' Projections during Brooklyn Bridge #N17 March," *Boing Boing*, November 17, 2011, http://boingboing.net/2011/11/17/interview-with-the-occupy-wall.html. Images of the Tahrir laser show are at Team Palestina, "#Egypt—Laser Lights Show on the Government Building in Cairo," Facebook, July 2, 2013, https://www.facebook.com/media/set /?set=a.560205390688698.1073742349.198580813517826&type=1.

7. Mike Davis, introduction to *Evil Paradises: Dreamworlds of Neoliberalism*, ed. Mike Davis and Daniel Bertrand Monk (New York: New Press, 2007), 6.

8. Alexander Galloway examines the Internet as a regulated and bureaucratic system whose powers of control are rooted in the technical protocols that determine how our devices interact with each other online in *Protocol: How Control Exists after Decentralization* (Cambridge, MA: MIT Press, 2006).

9. According to Guy Standing, the term *precariat* combines "precarious" and "proletariat" to describe "a multitude of insecure people, living bits-and-pieces lives, in and out of short-term jobs, without a narrative of occupational development, including millions of frustrated educated youth who do not like what they see before them. . . . They are denizens; they have a more restricted range of social, cultural, political and economic rights than citizens around them." "The Precariat: The New Dangerous Class," *Policy Network*, May 24, 2011, http://www.policy-network.net/pno_detail.aspx

?ID=4004&title=+The+Precariat+–+The+new+dangerous+class. Standing has expanded this argument in *Precariat: The New Dangerous Class* (London: Bloomsbury Academic, 2014).

10. Lev Manovich defines augmented space as "physical space overlaid with dynamically changing information [that is] likely to be in multimedia form and . . . localized for each user" in "The Poetics of Augmented Space: Learning from Prada," *Visual Communication* 5, no. 2 (2006): 220. For an extended tour of our connected way of life in such spaces, see William J. Mitchell, *Me++: The Cyborg Self and the Networked City* (Cambridge, MA: MIT Press, 2004).

11. Though some of the rules are loosening in some casinos, cell phones have traditionally been banned in the sports betting areas and at the card tables, especially because the dealer can't distinguish between patrons making a call to a spouse and those making one to a bookie placing bets at another casino with a better spread. At the card tables, the fear is collusion.

12. See Manovich, "The Poetics of Augmented Space," 225, for further illustrations of the difference between virtual and augmented reality.

13. Anthony Vitagliano, executive creative director for Digital Kitchen, speaking in REVEAL: *Inspired Experiences from Cosmopolitan Las Vegas*, the fourth of six promotional videos shown on the Sundance Channel and released on YouTube in the months before the hotel opened (https://www.youtube.com/watch?v=8sqC4iePoAk#t=27; accessed January 4, 2015).

14. On the growing interrelationship between architectural and virtual and augmented spaces, see the essays in Friedrich von Borries, Steffen P. Walz, and Matthias Böttger, eds., *Space Time Play: Computer Games, Architecture and Urbanism: The Next Level* (Basel: Birkhäuser, 2007).

15. McKenzie Wark, *Gamer Theory* (Cambridge, MA: Harvard University Press, 2007).

16. Alice Marwick, "Status Update: Celebrity, Publicity and Self-Branding in Web 2.0" (PhD diss., New York University, 2010), especially chapter 4, "I Can Make You an Internet Celebrity Overnight: Performing Micro-celebrity."

17. Cooper Smith, "Facebook Users Are Uploading 350 Million New Photos Each Day," *Business Insider*, September 18, 2013.

18. Erving Goffman, *The Presentation of Self in Everyday Life* (New York: Anchor, 1959).

19. Nathan Jurgenson, "The Facebook Eye," *Atlantic*, January 13, 2012. See also Jurgenson's discussions of time and "documentary vision" in "The Faux-Vintage Photo: Full Essay, Parts I, II, and III," Cyborgology, *Society Pages*, May 14, 2011, http://the societypages.org/cyborgology/2011/05/14/the-faux-vintage-photo-full-essay-parts-i-ii -and-iii/.

20. Wark, *Gamer Theory*, no. 153.

21. And it can backfire: since 9/11, Homeland Security has relied on data mining technology that assumes access to vast amounts of information. As in Vegas casinos, this technology works mainly by identifying deviations from typical patterns of consumption, including patterns of Internet use. This is why the actual terrorists tried to

appear as indistinct and bland as possible: "They dressed and acted like Americans," said then-FBI director Robert Mueller, "shopping and eating at places like Walmart and Pizza Hut" (Robert S. Meuller III, Address to Commonwealth Club of California, San Francisco, April 19, 2002, "Speeches," The FBI, http://www.fbi.gov/news/speeches/part nership-and-prevention-the-fbis-role-in-homeland-security). In other words, the more genuine differences and individuality are made manifest through the data of our consumer tastes and preferences, the more likely they are to signal a problematic person. In the same way that Vegas winners are probable cheaters, real individuals are real terrorists. Thus, on the days between the Boston Marathon bombing and his dramatic arrest, terror suspect Dzhokhar Tsarnaev posted a series of innocuous updates and text messages, including the Instagram self-portrait with its faux vintage filter that later appeared on the front page of the *New York Times*. Nathan Jurgenson writes that an attractive selfie could be a "paradigmatic modern example" of what Erving Goffman called "identity 'face work,'" which demonstrates and maintains "a 'working' acceptance, not a 'real' one." According to Jurgenson, this is precisely what Tsarnaev attempts to pull off in his *New York Times* front-page selfie. See Jurgenson, "A Page One Selfie," Cyborgology, *Society Pages*, May 6, 2013, http://thesocietypages.org/cyborg ology/2013/05/06/a-bombers-page-one-selfie/.

22. While each of our likes and links provides useful information to advertisers by itself, what is as or more significant is the net of relationships our online interactions create. This is also the case for the NSA, which defended itself against revelations of domestic spying by distinguishing between capturing metadata and actually looking at individual people's personal e-mails and calls. By assuring us that no particular item was seen except in cases when a warrant had been obtained, the NSA tried to deflect attention away from the bigger issue: that the "3-hop" analysis enabled by metadata—in this case, who called whom, not what they said—effectively let them canvass millions of people.

23. Quoted in David Kirkpatrick, *The Facebook Effect: The Inside Story of the Company That Is Connecting the World* (New York: Simon and Schuster, 2010), 199.

24. Gilles Deleuze, *Negotiations*, trans. Martin Joughin (New York: Columbia University Press, 1995), 129.

25. "In the societies of control, one is never finished with anything," writes Deleuze. The boundaries of the school are replaced with the "perpetual training" and lifelong professional development of the worker. Gilles Deleuze, "Postscript on the Societies of Control," *October* 59 (1992): 5.

26. On social media as free or a form of immaterial labor, see Mark Andrejevic, *iSpy: Surveillance and Power in the Interactive Era* (Lawrence: University Press of Kansas, 2009); Mark Andrejevic, *Reality TV: The Work of Being Watched* (Lanham, MD: Rowman and Littlefield, 2003); Rob Horning, "Facebook and Living Labor," Marginal Utility, *New Inquiry*, May 17, 2012, http://thenewinquiry.com/blogs/marginal-utility /facebook-and-living-labor/; Tiziana Terranova, "Free Labor: Producing Culture for the Digital Economy," *Social Text* 18, no. 2 (2000): 33–58. See also Maurizio Lazzarato, "Immaterial Labor," in *Marxism beyond Marxism*, ed. Saree Makdisi, Cesare Casarino, and Rebecca E. Karl (London: Routledge, 1996).

27. Downtown Project, http://downtownproject.com (accessed August 15, 2013). All quotations are taken from the project's website. The Project cites Richard Florida's *The Rise of the Creative Class: And How It's Transforming Work, Leisure, Community, and Everyday Life* (New York: Basic Books, 2004) as an inspiration and Edward Glaeser, *Triumph of the City: How Our Greatest Invention Makes Us Richer, Smarter, Greener, Healthier, and Happier* (New York: Penguin, 2011).

28. Michael Kimmelman, "Latest Vision for Las Vegas: A Downtown Vibe," *New York Times*, July 4, 2013, http://www.nytimes.com/2013/07/05/arts/design/latest-vision -for-las-vegas-a-downtown-ambience.html.

29. "*Homo economicus* is an entrepreneur, an entrepreneur of himself." Michel Foucault, *The Birth of Biopolitics: Lectures at the Collège de France, 1978–79*, trans. G. Burchell (New York: Palgrave Macmillan, 2008), 226.

30. Identifying its students as "human capital," the 9th Bridge School, the Downtown Project's educational arm, describes its "unique approach for educating children based on neuroscience and social-emotional learning, with a focus on creativity and entrepreneurship." 9th Bridge School support staff–teacher assistant position posting, http://9thbridge.theresumator.com/apply/Lw65k9/Support-Staff-Teacher-Assistant. html (accessed January 28, 2015).

31. "For our city to thrive, families must not only aspire to live here but also to educate their children here. Investment in public and private education programs is critical to the community as a whole. For us, that means investing in the Clark County School District through our partnership with Teach for America, by exploring innovative ideas and techniques in teaching, and in our planned investment in a private or charter school in Downtown Las Vegas." Downtown Project, http://downtownproject .com.

32. Mitchell, *Me++*, 60–61. In his analysis of social media, Rob Horning argues that, because "we are what we share," what threatens our identity online is not inauthenticity or phoniness—such notions no longer make sense, especially as moral categories—but "lack of access" to networks and information. See Rob Horning, "The Rise of the Data Self," Marginal Utility, *Pop Matters*, January 25, 2012, http://www.popmatters.com/post /153721-/, and "Data Self Redux," Marginal Utility, *Pop Matters*, January 30, 2012, http://www.popmatters.com/post/153910-/.

33. "Site Terms of Use and Privacy," Downtown Project, http://downtownproject .com/site-terms-of-use-privacy/ (accessed August 20, 2013). On the site, "whether" is mistyped as "wither."

34. Vindu Goel, "Facebook Leads an Effort to Lower Barriers to Internet Access," *New York Times*, August 20, 2013, http://www.nytimes.com/2013/08/21/technology /facebook-leads-an-effort-to-lower-barriers-to-internet-access.html?_r=0. The slogan is on the website at http://Internet.org.

35. The UN figures are cited in Michael Batty, "When All the World's a City," *Environment and Planning A* 43 (2011): 768.

36. For Batty, "Chongqing is significant because it has reached this size seemingly without most people, even in China, knowing about it, and many never having heard about the very existence of the city." Batty, "When All the World's a City," 765.

37. Figures are cited in Anne-Marie Broudehoux, "Delirious Beijing: Euphoria and Despair in the Olympic Metropolis," in *Evil Paradises*, ed. Davis and Monk, 94. Broudehoux describes "Beijing's nouveaux riches" who "seek to escape the capital's downtown pollution, noise, high density, and visible social polarization" by hiding in "gated communities, guarded by video surveillance and patrolling security agents" (96).

38. For information on China's "floating people," see Dorothy J. Solinger, *Contesting Citizenship in Urban China: Peasants, Migrants, the State and the Logic of the Market* (Berkeley: University of California Press, 1999); Michael Dutton, "Street Scenes of Subalternity: China, Globalization, and Rights," *Social Text* 60, no. 17 (1999): 63–86; and Ann Anagnost, "The Corporeal Politics of Quality (Suzhi)," *Public Culture* 16, no. 2 (2004): 189–208.

39. "About Premier Exhibitions, Inc.," Premier Exhibitions, http://www.premier exhibitions.com/corporate/all/about-premier-exhibitions-inc (accessed November 10, 2014).

40. "Premier Exhibitions Salvages $1 M Q1 Profit," *Atlanta Business Chronicle*, July 12, 2011, http://www.bizjournals.com/atlanta/news/2011/07/12/premier-exhibitions-posts -1m-q1-profit.html.

41. The phrase plays on the more familiar "seeing is believing," with the significant difference that visibility is identified with truth rather than just faith. The terms also flirts with the much older "Know thyself," famously written on the walls of Delphi.

42. Barbara Maria Stafford, "The Creeping Illusionizing of Identity from Neurobiology to Newgenics," in *Controversial Bodies: Thoughts on the Public Display of Plastinated Corpses*, ed. John D. Lantos (Baltimore, MD: Johns Hopkins University Press, 2011), 106.

43. Uli Linke, "Touching the Corpse: The Unmaking of Memory in the Body Museum," *Anthropology Today* 21, no. 5 (2005): 13.

44. Hsuan L. Hsu and Martha Lincoln, "Biopower, *Bodies . . . the Exhibition*, and the Spectacle of Public Health," *Discourse* 29, no. 1 (2007): 26–27; see also Megan Stern, "Shiny, Happy People: 'Body Worlds' and the Commodification of Health," *Radical Philosophy* 118 (2003): 2–6.

45. Under the settlement reached with the state of New York in 2008, Premier must provide documentation for the origin and cause of death of each of the cadavers on display. Though not required to remove from the South Station exhibit in New York existing displays whose identity and fate cannot be determined, Premier was required by the settlement to post a warning to future visitors that the body parts they will see "may have come from Chinese prisoners who were tortured and executed." Premier never denied that the corpses were poor, unclaimed, or unidentified dead in China. Sewell Chan, "'Bodies' Show Must Put Up Warnings," *New York Times*, May 29, 2008, http://cityroom.blogs.nytimes.com/2008/05/29/bodies-exhibit-must-put-up-warn ings/?_r=0.

46. Hsu and Lincoln, "Biopower, *Bodies . . . the Exhibition*, and the Spectacle of Public Health," 17.

TEN

Ghosts of Weddings Past, Present, and Yet to Come

Past

I recently needed to renew my passport and had the unhappy luck of running afoul of the U.S. State Department.* There were problems with the name I gave on my renewal form. The fact that the name on the form matched the name on my driver's license had little merit with the State Department. To resolve the situation and establish a verifiable identity, I would have to supply the State Department with an unbroken paper trail of my names from birth, through school, and into marriages and dissolution of marriages. I discovered firsthand what many people — and most especially, women — will face in states where Republican-dominated legislatures, like my own in North Carolina, aim to implement laws requiring a photo ID in order to vote.

In the course of making myself right in the eyes of the government, I had to secure evidence of my first marriage, performed in the 1960s in Las Vegas and lasting only a few months. Needless to say, I would have to find documentation of its termination as well. This is not a period of my life that I try

---

* Susan Willis

to remember. I was pregnant and the marriage was something my parents desperately wanted in order to ensure that their first grandchild would not be illegitimate. The times were definitely different, and even though they were a-changing, they weren't changing fast enough to anoint my single mother-hood with respectability. So my parents set about arranging a shotgun marriage of convenience that involved getting the Marine Corps to relinquish my husband-to-be for a day and finding a place where a marriage could be performed quickly before I popped. That meant Las Vegas.

The arrival of an official copy of my Clark County marriage certificate jogged my memory and provoked as close a reconstruction of that day as I can summon. My father accompanied us, and I think he was there to vouch for my husband-to-be. I was nineteen at the time and needed only a photo ID to obtain a marriage license. But my husband-to-be was only eighteen and had to demonstrate parental consent. I'm not sure why my father represented the necessary consent, unless Clark County had a special clause for shotgun weddings wherein the bride's father calls the shots. Today, things are a bit different. No one over the age of seventeen need have a parent—and for those aged seventeen, a notarized statement will suffice. The definition of a shotgun wedding is also quite different today. Instead of the iconographic Daisy Mae, gun-toting dad, and begrudging groom, Las Vegas enables brides and grooms to fire submachine guns and pose with Uzis and ammo as part of their wedding package. In a contrarian twist on the nation's aghast sorrow over the school massacre in Newtown, Connecticut, members of Las Vegas gun shops and shooting ranges offer special wedding packages, including one dubbed "take a shot at love." One wonders if this is a feminist redefinition of misogyny or just patriarchy on steroids. In either case, the gun cements the union, just as in days of yore.

If in the 1960s *shotgun* meant bowing to parental pressure to marry, it also implied the social necessity to "do the right thing," "take responsibility for one's actions," and "suffer the consequences." But responsibility was a tricky question in the 1960s. Clearly, my intended and I were not very responsible in the area of pregnancy prevention, even though we both had access to birth control. (I had a diaphragm from a public health clinic and my husband-to-be could obtain condoms—although in those days you had to ask for them and suffer the pharmacist's comments.) Nevertheless, we were deemed responsible enough to marry, have a child, and, in the case of my husband-to-be, serve in the military, although with the war in Vietnam escalating by the day, responsibility may have had little to do with the necessity of the times. It seems truly odd, then, in hindsight and certainly also in terms of the gathering cultural momentum that would explode at the Democratic National Convention in 1968, that neither of us was deemed responsible enough to vote. But then, the Voting Rights Act had passed only two years before our Vegas wedding and even though neither of us is black, voting still smacked of privilege and social control. So it's not odd that I would recall the day shortly after I turned twenty-one when I went to the Registrar of Voters, toddler in tow. "Don't worry," said the nice woman helping me to register, "I had my first baby before I could vote, too."

What I remember less well is the day of the marriage. I know I boarded a plane with my father and husband-to-be. The flight was an extravagance given the fact that we could have easily driven to Las Vegas from Southern California where we lived. Indeed, the famous Las Vegas Strip is a testament to car culture. But that might have occasioned an overnight stay, and none of the three of us would have wanted that. Besides, my husband-to-be was on a limited leave from the Marines. So the flight was a necessity. The whole thing—travel and ceremony—could be done in a day. I would be transported out of a socially awkward state that had my parents fabricating explanations as to why I was not yet married. And I would land in a place where normal laws didn't pertain. Counterintuitively, I would then be made right—and with documents to prove it.

Coincidentally, Joan Didion also traveled to Las Vegas in the 1960s and focused her authorial wit on the city's wedding industry. Her essay "Marrying Absurd" casts the Strip, with its eighty-foot-high, illuminated billboards, as incongruous against the stark "moonscape" of the desert.[1] Musing, she wonders if this is a place where brides will feel comfortable in satin and lace. Not surprisingly, Didion encountered a "marriage of convenience" and conveyed the absurdity of a bride too young to drink the celebratory champagne but old enough to have gotten herself "in trouble." With a bit of irony, Didion concluded that besides convenience, Vegas markets "'niceness,' the facsimile of a proper ritual, to children who don't know how to find it, how to make the arrangements, how to do it 'right.'"[2] As I now see it, finding out how to do it right has a twofold meaning—a bride would become respectable and she'd have all the trappings of a proper ritual.

Looking back on the urgency of the time, I realize my parents were probably not aware of the numbers of mothers of girls in my high school graduating class who were already raising a daughter's out-of-wedlock child at the time of graduation. These mothers were passing the child off as their own, and they hadn't even resorted to the ruse of wearing an inflatable belly bump

under their clothes to prepare their neighbors for the new arrival. This was a strategy employed by one of the Desperate Housewives a few years back.

No, my parents wanted a legal solution to my dilemma, and legal it would be. The Strip—its brazen architecture, the boat-sized cars—all of it flashed by as we sped from the airport to the marriage license bureau. In the 1960s, between 30,000 and 40,000 licenses were issued per year in Clark County. Today, the number has tripled. But even at the time of my marriage, Las Vegas was known as "the marriage capital of the world." There's much to suggest that the city's rise to prominence as a mecca for marriage is linked to the state's relaxation of divorce laws. In 1931, the state legislature, looking for ways to stimulate the economy, legalized gambling and reduced the state's residency requirement to obtain a divorce from three months to six weeks. At that time, Nevada had little more than a railroad, speakeasies, and cowboys. Many of the ranches conveniently redefined themselves as dude ranches where prospective divorce seekers could establish their residency. Given the desirability of maintaining respectability during the process, divorce seekers may have seen the dude ranch as a western equivalent of the convent—in this case, a convent with cowboys. Women could wait out their residency in the healthful environment of sagebrush, horses, and men. Then, once the divorce was granted, they could immediately remarry, thanks to Nevada's other innovation in social management—no waiting period between the issuance of a marriage license and the enactment of a new marriage. The quick turnaround between divorce and marriage is, finally, what established Las Vegas as a marriage capital—all the better that newly minted couples could, then, celebrate their instant marriages with unlimited gambling, and, beginning in 1933, legal alcohol.

As for my own instant marriage, I suppose I was surprised by its perfunctory and bureaucratic nature. Not that I harbored romantic notions about weddings, unlike many of the Vegas brides today who parade the Strip in full bridal regalia and pose for photos by family members and strangers alike. Nevertheless, the six-minute giving and taking of vows was either so anticlimactic as to be unmemorable, or so horrifying as to have fallen into some deep well of forgetting beyond the reach of Sigmund Freud himself. What I do remember is the environment of normalization that set the stage for the actual ritual. The Clark County courthouse had an entire area devoted to marriages. Upon entering, couples took a number from a dispenser like the ones that determined order of service at the Baskin Robbins 31 Flavors Ice Cream stores. Here I was about to undergo the civil washing of my sins, and I was regarded as just another customer in for a quick sugar fix. The waiting area was one of those big, anonymous spaces only found in government social welfare offices—the places you go when you've lost your social security card or you're waiting to see if you'll be selected for jury duty. None of the other people trapped in the limbo of waiting gave the impression of being eager brides and grooms. There were no flowers or fancy dresses—not even a witness or two. Of the dozen or so couples with their numbered chits in hand, most appeared to have made their decision to marry the night before. Their clothes had that slept-in appearance and their faces betrayed fatigue mixed with expectation. I most remember the cowboys—boots, jeans, plaid cotton shirts, all of it held together with a big belt. Their brides-to-be were equally memorable—big hair, flashy jewelry, heavy makeup. They might have strolled off the set of *Gunsmoke*. Of the assembled candidates for marriage, we were the oddities—a man in a Marine uniform, a woman paying her price, and a dad doing his duty.

We might have been part of a crowd had we married in Las Vegas just two years earlier—August 26, 1965, to be exact. Lyndon Johnson had just announced that at the stroke of midnight on that very day, the draft exemption for married men would come to an end. On August 27, married or not, you could be one of the 35,000 men called up each month to fight in Vietnam. This is where the absence of a waiting period came in handy. If the president could issue a spontaneous summons, Las Vegas would respond with an instantaneous solution. It's impossible to know how many of the close to two hundred souls married in Las Vegas on August 26 were draft dodgers. Sadly, their victory was Pyrrhic because shortly thereafter, all marriage deferments were rescinded.

I understand why I was married in Las Vegas, but for the life of me I can't figure out why anyone famous would choose to marry there, although performers like Wayne Newton, Judy Garland, Betty White, and Old Blue Eyes himself (all married in Las Vegas in the 1960s) performed there so often that it might have felt like home. It's said that the silent film star Clara Bow set the trend when she married cowboy actor Rex Bell in 1931. Their marriage endured until death did them part. As did Paul Newman and Joanne Woodward's, also in Vegas. Perhaps the all-time famous wedding in Las Vegas occurred on May 1, 1967, just a few days before my own Vegas wedding, when Elvis married Priscilla at the Aladdin; and their ceremony lasted a full two minutes longer than mine.

I have to admit I scarcely thought I would run into a celebrity on that fate-

ful day in 1967. Instead, I was captivated by Vegas itself, although the overall look of the place was just an exaggeration of the familiar highway landscapes of Southern California—four lanes of blacktop, chock-a-block with motels and outsized signage. With the ceremony over and the atmosphere inside the rental car no less solemn on our return to the airport than it had been during our journey to the courthouse, I pressed my attention through the window glass. What I saw was an image of Las Vegas that can now be found only among an assortment of antique postcards at a flea market. Giant marquees crowded against the roadway. Their bold letters hawked two and three star attractions a night. Carnival statuary—a huge thunderbird, an imposing jinni, a pink flamingo—competed for attention to distinguish one motel from another. The Strip was a jumble of attractions, each one shouting for the visitor's attention. Some years later, a team of Yale architects led by Robert Venturi would call this an "architecture of communication." Indeed, the famous motels were all dwarfed by their emphatic signage, making the built environment all the more compelling by comparison to the surrounding void of the desert. Most of the motels would be truly splendid at night, when the neon signs turned tawdry into fantasy. I recall that I'd seen photos of Vegas at night and, because I could still be counted a teenager, most wanted to see the multicolored, animated neon figures. But we would be long gone before nightfall. So I contented myself with the oasis ambience of the lush lawns and forests of palms that girdled the motels and set them apart from the acres of asphalt parking. Back then, irrigation was a fact of life throughout the Southwest. No one would have questioned the normalcy of a verdant lawn in the midst of a desert. But then, no one would have thought it odd that I needed to get married. My day had been extraordinary—but it had not been unexpected.

Now, in the present, having successfully reconstructed my identity and supplied the State Department with a convincing trail of names, I can't help but ponder the curious connivance between our society's definition of morality and the uneven legal systems that uphold it. My Las Vegas marriage was a ritual that preserved more than my personal morality and my parents' desire for the family's morality. It also satisfied California of the morality of one of its residents. And it did so in a place known for its immorality. I can't help but wonder, though, why my Vegas marriage was accepted in California. After all, my marriage failed to meet my state's requirement for a blood test and a waiting period. Back then, no one believed a Tijuana marriage would pass muster in California. Was Tijuana truly beyond the pale while Las Vegas wasn't? I recall the hucksters who lined the sidewalks of Avenida Revolución much like the smutters in today's Las Vegas. They approached young couples with sly winks and half smiles, attempting to lure them into the wedding parlors crowded in among the curio shops. "Wanna get married?" Or better yet—"Want a divorce?"

Of course, there was another service that Tijuana supplied in the 1960s, one that no state in the union dared offer: abortion. Truth be told, I got married in Las Vegas because I didn't want an abortion in Tijuana. What's most difficult to fathom today are the prevailing social strictures that made Las Vegas and Tijuana the only options. Was that then? And this is now?

Present

Was it a warning or a plea? Before we left Connecticut for our trip to Las Vegas, my boyfriend's father gave him a bit of pocket money and said, "Don't spend it all in one place, don't get mugged, and don't get married!"*

We spent our first morning in Las Vegas walking down the Strip with no real destination in mind. The constructed serenity of the sidewalk along the Bellagio Hotel's version of Lake Como was fractured by salespeople who stepped into our path and tried to tempt us with the promise of free shows. These vendors, with their flip books of the city's performances, seemed to be everywhere on this particular visit to Las Vegas. Was there something different about this time of day or time of year, or was there something different about me on this trip that signaled that I was a target? Unlike my other research visits, I was accompanied on this trip by my boyfriend. So as not to get separated, I held his hand as we walked through the masses, the hustlers, the impersonators and street performers. There was even a bride in a white gown lifting her skirts with a bouquet in hand as she stepped onto the sidewalk. But the closer we got to one another in the face of the obstacles, the worse the assault. Vendors stepped in our path and asked about our evening plans and ticketing needs. The body language of the couple in Las Vegas seemed to signal consumer potential: a physical declaration, "open for business."

Chris and I got pretty good at pushing our way down the street as we declared, "No, thank you," and "Not interested." But inevitably, we got caught. Tempted by the opportunity to get free show tickets for Cirque du Soleil's *Mystère*—a show we planned to buy tickets for that very afternoon—we stopped to talk with a time-share street vendor. He waved his colorful flip book of free entertainment choices: comedians, burlesque, variety shows, mu-

---

* Stacy M. Jameson

sicians, magicians, and Cirque du Soleil. All we would have to do is sit through a forty-five-minute (once we were clearly hooked, the time changed to ninety minutes) time-share presentation and we could get the free tickets, "no purchase necessary." Subtly the conversation changed from what free shows we could see to personal questions about our relationship status and household income. Our not being hitched seemed to be a hitch.

"Ya know, you can get married down at one end of the street and then later go get divorced at the other!" the vendor suggested with a smile. His words brought home the paradox of the institution of marriage as a bedrock of economic exchange but one that is simultaneously treated as superficial, flexible, and temporary. It quickly became clear that being a married couple (or at least a cohabiting couple with documentation, such as driver's licenses with the same address) was the gatekeeping distinction that would open the doors to multiple consumer opportunities: for free shows or slot play, but, more importantly, for time-share properties. Our eligibility to participate required special approval—after all, what sort of consumer commitment can you expect from the uncommitted? Interpellation, the "hailing" of Chris and me into a buying unit, was not enough. Phone calls had to be made: "I have a really nice young couple here: they're cohabitants" (the street salesman lied into the phone). Our relationship got labeled, considered, and finally approved by the faceless powers that be on the other end of the phone. If we returned in an hour and a half, an escort would accompany us to the presentation, an authority figure as witness and voice to make us official, to thus ensure our admittance. Thinking perhaps we were working the system, we continued our walk down the Strip with plans to return at the appointed time.

The you're-in-Vegas-why-not-just-get-married attitude voiced by the street salesman echoed a general assumption made by family and colleagues back home in Connecticut. For more than just Chris's father, "We're going to Vegas" over the holidays meant "We're getting hitched." The social anxiety this engendered was not the same as it might have been in the mid-twentieth century. As Cele Otnes and Elizabeth Pleck argue in their book *Cinderella Dreams: The Allure of the Lavish Wedding*, Las Vegas weddings have, to some extent, shed the air of garishness and unacceptability that tainted them in the 1940s and 1950s. The Las Vegas wedding today instead presents couples with a "celebrity patina" grown out of a history of famous (though often short-lived) weddings, including those in recent years of stars such as Britney Spears and Kim Kardashian.[3] The possibly tainted view of the Las Vegas wedding—given its associations with less-than-wholesome things, including gambling and strippers—has further been displaced by the excitement of the "destination wedding" and the pursuit of American consumerism, which has become a moral responsibility.[4] Indeed, it's even a patriotic duty, as President George Bush reminded American citizens in speeches following the September 11 attacks: we should "fly and support American destination spots" and shop to show our "participation and confidence in the American economy!"[5]

Any lingering social unease about Vegas weddings—such as that voiced in the warning "Don't get married"—seems instead to reflect the ways in which a wedding in Sin City is divorced from traditionally grounding social structures, namely religious institutions and the family unit. Indeed, Vegas chapels are more often connected to themes or gimmicks than to particular religious affiliations. Chapel options abound, from Graceland and Princess to the re-creation of destinations like Tuscany or the completely mobile Wedding Wagon; there is even a Chap-Hell in the Goretorium haunted house where couples can get married flanked by zombies. Additionally, ceremonies are notably small and may leave the extended family out of the picture entirely. Indeed, many chapels provide couples with a witness—complementary with the package—so that they need not bring their own from home. Instead of religion or family (or even the law in some cases), the wedding that Vegas leaves us with—for better or for worse—is the pure packaged consumer experience.

Just steps beyond the street time-share hustler, Chris and I encountered our first opportunity to make both our relationship and the time-share-show ticket transaction legal. The Pop-Up Wedding Chapel fills the prime real estate along the sidewalk of the Cosmopolitan Hotel and Casino, offering everything from the real ceremony to a faux performance of one. Floor-to-ceiling glass windows allow passersby to wedding window shop. As the signage declares alongside happy stick figures of a bride and groom, this is a space to commit and to consume. Here "I Do" is placed, quite literally, on equal footing with "Shop" and "Celebrate." Visiting couples can get hitched or renew their vows while walking down an aisle lined with merchandise and souvenirs. There is a refreshing transparency in this contemporary design, where storefront and chapel merge. Indeed, many wedding chapels offer opportunities for wedding souvenirs, as if the wedding itself is a tourist experience: temporary, perhaps exotic, and fun. The Graceland Wedding Chapel, for example, offers a gift shop with candles, chapel license plates, Elvis memorabilia such as sideburn sunglasses or Elvis scarves, and of course "Just Married," "Tied the Knot," and "Did It Again" T-shirts. But the street-side Cosmopolitan wedding

chapel takes the connections to consumer spectacle a step further, offering commitment to the institution of marriage as a commodity itself for the window shopping of fellow tourists.

The Pop-Up Chapel combines the fast-paced instant digital experience with the wedding ceremony. The design of the chapel specifically mimics an Apple Store, and, appropriately, the wedding officiator reads the vows from an iPad. And like an avatar, here you can experience the world of weddings without that binding legal or real-world hassle. The Pop-Up iDo wedding chapel offers complete "On a Whim" or "Faux Wedding" packages. You are provided with souvenir eraser wedding rings so that you can wipe your names from your pretend certificate the next day. Las Vegas weddings have a notable temporality; they are both quick to arrange and feature brief ceremonies. Indeed, chapel time is one of the things you pay for when you purchase a wedding package. Certainly, there are many quickie wedding options in the city, from drive-up ceremonies to the Wedding Wagon, which meets you at a specified location and does the job on the spot. But the pop-up wedding is unique in the ways that it folds the brevity of the wedding into the mystique of digital culture. If, as writer Rebecca Mead suggests, Las Vegas is the one place where there exists a sense of marriage as more of a "provisional engagement" than an enduring commitment, then the aura of new media further lends credence to the institution as potentially innovative, changeable, and temporary.[6] In a city known for both quickie divorces and no-hassle elopements, now we can live out the ideal Vegas wedding: all the spectacle and consumer satisfaction without the lasting imprint. It's the Twitter marriage: a brief blurb that pops up and quickly gets replaced in the posting stream. Maybe Chris's dad wouldn't mind this sort of wedding; in fact maybe I wouldn't either, but then what's the point of it?

Such a quickie digital wedding experience corresponds with the popular culture mystique most recently reified by films such as *What Happens in Vegas* (2008), in which a couple wakes up from a wild night with a hangover and wedding rings on their fingers. In reality, it is not so simple to get legally married in the city. Even your impromptu, on-a-whim ceremony demands an in-person visit to the Clark County Marriage License Bureau, where you are required to pay a fee of $60 and present photo identification as proof of your age, name, and even your sex — as only a biological male and a biological female may marry in the state of Nevada. I wondered about a friend of mine who, by accident or visual misrecognition, got her gender misidentified on her driver's license. While she was unconcerned about the label and viewed it as a social protest of such limited gender distinctions, the incident speaks to the complexity of the disconnect between documentation, regulations, and individual life choices. In light of these checks and balances for legal marriage, the commodity that is the Vegas wedding is a false package of instantaneousness that only pretends the state does not exist. The mystique is the wedding that is spatially and temporally removed from legal as well as social institutions, leaving the couple instead with the experience of pure shopping.

Passing up the experience of the pop-up wedding, Chris and I—still hoping to reap the consumer rewards that the wedding would have guaranteed—showed up at our allotted appointment for the time-share presentation. Like going to the DMV (or indeed the Marriage License Bureau), we had to traverse several desks, waiting rooms, and ID checks. Our names and addresses still didn't match—would we be viewed as unacceptable interlopers, "Others"? Indeed, only two things seemed to matter in this liminal space that opened into our meeting with the time-share agent: a credit card and a secure relationship, signified by government-issued ID cards. The two went hand in hand.

In this way, business shows itself to be as bureaucratic as the legal system, though more egalitarian in at least one aspect: gay relationships. A female friend of mine, waylaid by a similar street time-share salesman, was asked about her husband, to which she responded, "I'm not here with my husband. I'm here with my girlfriend." To participate in the offer—in this case, the perks of viewing the time-share sales pitch included both hotel and airfare—she would have to produce both said girlfriend and proof of cohabitation in the form of government-issued IDs. Again, what matters is dual income, backed by documentation and accessed with a credit card.

When Chris and I finally met with an actual GeoHoliday agent, what we experienced was not a typical advertising campaign or sales pitch. Rather than a smiling salesperson wooing us into a purchase, our agent was openly hostile. She did not offer us a show of goods for purchase. Rather, we sat at a round table in a large conference room, where we were grilled on our income, vacation habits, past hotel rooms, and so on. Repeatedly, she asked us, "Do you own the hotel room you are staying in? The car you rent? The airplane? Do you own it?" Her comments and questions emphasized the power and authority of possession—an association not inappropriate to the subject of weddings as an organizational event for the exchange and inheritance of property—even while the time-share marks possession as partial and temporary. Originally, time-shares, which began in Europe in the 1960s alongside the growth of commercial jets, enabled the partial purchase of an actual property; a flat rate, plus a lifetime of maintenance fees, guaranteed the use

of a specific unit for a set time frame, often at the same time each year. Today, more time-share businesses are vacation clubs that operate on a points program that is flexible about when and where you travel. With this model, what you end up owning is time itself—a certain number of hours in a condo, almost anywhere. Further, the share seems to suggest some level of ownership in the reverse direction as well. The contemporary marriage is not just between you and your spouse, it seems, but rather also opens the door to all those other interests (commercial, political, social) that can benefit from your years of joint buying power.

Thus, the structures and meanings of marriage are now something different from what they symbolized to the baby boomers. Midcentury American weddings offered women—with fewer opportunities for economic independence—a chance to unite themselves to a breadwinner. The post–World War II development of the suburbs joined the companionate marriage with the ideal of the single-family home with picket fence, TV set, and an automobile. By contrast, the contemporary wedding promises a different lifestyle. Instead of investing in a mortgage, the time-share model allows couples to invest in a future of family vacations. This was made clear to us when we entered the viewing room to watch a video of GeoHoliday time-share client testimonials. I looked around the small room before the lights went out. The audience appeared to be a picture of racial, ethnic, and generational diversity. Yet we all sat in heterosexual pairs with the occasional nuclear family group. Like the Disney theme park ride, this space doesn't know what to do with the individual.[7] We see the nuclear family reflected back at us in the video. Shares are presented as an investment in the longevity of the marital relationship and the future connectivity and happiness of the family unit. The moving images of smiling couples poolside and three generations relaxing in a luxurious condominium reify the vacation as a means of domestication, an experience in renewal of the home, not—despite the often exotic locales—a taste of new experiences or values.[8]

We never actually saw a condo representative of the values and lifestyles the GeoHoliday workers hoped we would buy—though we did get our free show tickets. Nevertheless, some days later, we unknowingly got the chance to inhabit a time-share resort without actually buying into it. As it happens, Chris and I were in Las Vegas during the week of Christmas and New Year's, a time of family holidays, parties, and resolutions. In comparison to my other visits to Sin City, the entertainment capital was bustling with strollers and kids, which seemed at odds with my typical vision of the space and its pleasures. Vegas may be the wedding capital of the world, but it is distinctly not a place for families. No matter what hotels do to try to present themselves as kid friendly (Circus Circus offers games and shows for teens and children in the Midway, for example), laws bar anyone under twenty-one from even accompanying their parents to the casino floors or bars. Rules of morality might further restrict even teens access to a number of shows with nudity. As one blogger advises a twenty-year-old vacationer, "You may want to go to Mexico, instead of Vegas." The city wants to celebrate the wedding without those pesky things that marriage valorizes: kids, home, and so on. The time-share, however, purports to bridge this incongruity between Las Vegas and the family.

Our last night in the city was New Year's Eve, and hotel prices and street parties drove us a little way off the Strip to a time-share complex—where price and atmosphere were seemingly unaffected by social turmoil or holiday bustle. In contrast to the description of our generic hotel room voiced by our GeoHoliday agent, "a box with a toilet," the time-share offered us a condo with living room space and all the technological trimmings, a complete kitchen, a washing machine, and a bathtub the size of a hot tub. In a place that banishes the everyday, such living seemed strange in Las Vegas. Nevertheless, just behind the Flamingo, the time-share offered a so-called home space in a literal gated community with security guards to keep Sin City and its New Year's Eve revelers at bay. In the end, we didn't buy a Las Vegas wedding, but we got to experience firsthand the life of a couple in a time-share marriage.

Yet to Come

Vegas earned its title as wedding capital of the world not only because it offered quick and easy weddings, but also because these impulsive marriages and shotgun weddings, like cheaply made products that break after a few years and need to be replaced, often ended in divorces that provided repeat customers.* Relying on a clientele that expects cheap prices, nostalgia, and kitsch in any combination, Vegas chapels have thrived on prepackaged weddings with predictable Vegas-only themes. But when the recession hit in 2008 and the price of gasoline soared, the number of visitors to Vegas fell sharply. Las Vegas still offered bargain weddings, such as the basic package at Mon Bel Ami Chapel for $79, which included a loaner bouquet, boutonniere, and witness. Yet many people just couldn't afford to get there. Indeed, marriage licenses in Clark County dropped 28 percent in the six years following 2004.[9] The recession meant a loss of revenue not only for the hundred-plus wedding

---

* Karen Klugman

chapels in the city but also for the Clark County government, which collects a fee for each marriage license. The languishing wedding business in Vegas was looking for a way to rejuvenate its livelihood when along came a fresh opportunity: vow renewals. Americans' growing love affair with vow renewals figuratively stamped expiration dates on marriage certificates and created a new base of return customers among the city's already married tourists.

In the words of writer Rebecca Mead, "If Ford's cars or Maytag's washing machines had the same record of success as do American marriages, both companies would be out of business."[10] While a wedding might be a gateway to other areas of consumption, its market value as an enduring product poses a problem. Soon after the Industrial Revolution expanded the supply of mass-produced commodities, manufacturers and advertisers alike learned the value of planned obsolescence.[11] Since that time, even products that are not physically stamped with expiration dates grow stale if they are not replaced or at least upgraded to meet new uses, improved applications, or latest technologies (anyone with an iPhone knows this), and the demands of fashion. Instead of using a purchased product until or beyond a natural time for replacement, what Roland Barthes refers to as a "rhythm of dilapidation," fashion creates more occasions to consume simply out of the desire for new forms, styles, or colors.[12] While America might not be ready for an attack on the institution of marriage itself—proven by the fears espoused in right-wing public dialogue over how gay marriage might alter the meaning of marriage—the ceremony itself offers a product that could be refashioned with a potential shelf life.

When vow renewals came into vogue, it was a piece of cake for Vegas wedding enterprises to add yet another layer to the tiered structure of wedding packages. Since virtually any wedding ceremony could be repackaged as a renewal event just by replacing the word *wedding* with *vow renewal*, the growing social practice of renewing vows opened up a low-overhead growth opportunity for the well-established marriage industry. Like couples making original pledges, couples renewing their vows could choose from the same potpourri of Vegas signature packages: Elvis packages, Grand Canyon helicopter weddings, drive-throughs, ceremonies with photos at the Welcome to Las Vegas sign (or a reproduction of the sign), or destination packages such as the nearby Valley of Fire or Red Rock Canyon National Conservation Area. Vegas wedding chapels simply reinvented their wedding packages as vow renewals by revising their titles. In place of the active verbs that identify levels of service and prices of wedding selections, such as *cherish*, *ignite*, and *enamor*, the chapel Vegas Weddings repackaged its offerings with titles suggesting a love redux, such as *rekindle*, *re-create*, and *relive*. With price tiers for renewals that match wedding options, couples restating vows can choose to "renew" for $199 or "reinvigorate" for $2,099.

The vow renewal package at the Mandarin Oriental exemplifies this broader Vegas postrecession turn to the upscale. Rising from the ashes of the old Boardwalk Hotel, the Mandarin Oriental defines the new Vegas—a competitor with modern style in the global marketplace. One of a chain of forty-four hotels in twenty-seven countries aimed to attract an international clientele (and those able to afford international travel), the Mandarin Oriental has an ambience that couldn't be more different from the homespun nostalgia that the Boardwalk promoted. No Elvises here. For its deluxe wedding package, it "[teams] up with an unprecedented array of the world's elite couture" to offer a celebration for two hundred guests and provide the couple with luxury brands of perfume, shoes, jewelry, and toasting glasses with a starting price of $100,000 (music and flowers not included).[13] Orders of magnitude above the cost of reinvigorating one's marriage, a Mandarin Deluxe renewal would require most couples to reevaluate their lives. There is not even the hope that one might hit it rich at the casino, since there is no casino on the property. While there are still many bargain weddings on the Strip, the stratospheric prices of wedding packages at the new upscale hotels mirror the increasingly skewed income inequality worldwide.

The government of Nevada is quick to keep up with changes in the city's wedding industries to ensure its piece of these profits. Indeed, to make up for recession-era lost profits on the dwindling numbers of wedding certificates, Clark County officials attempted to charge a fee for official vow renewal certificates that would have the original marriage date printed on them as well as the Las Vegas stamp (considered a collectible for international tourists). While Las Vegas chapels liked the idea of a certificate, they objected to sharing the fee with the county and feared that even an optional advance trip to the Marriage License Bureau and the fee would discourage customers.[14] Vegas chapels instead decided to include their own free version of the certificates as part of their vow renewal packages. In addition to being Vegas souvenirs, the vow renewal certificates, like windshield stickers posting the mileage of an oil change, function to remind customers of when it might be time to recharge their relationship.

In the 1970s, when the divorce rate in the United States skyrocketed, various public rituals developed to bolster the institution of marriage. The Catholic Church held group ceremonies for couples celebrating their golden anniversary, a practice that grew into regularly scheduled events in many parishes. By

2010, couples celebrating fifty years of marriage often numbered in the hundreds. Some churches loosened the requirements for these mass anniversary Masses to allow participation by couples married twenty-five years or even any year divisible by five. In spite of the traditional Catholic belief that vows originally made before God should hold up forever, some parishes started to refer to the ceremonies as vow renewals. Then, in 1990, Bill McCartney, who was the football coach at University of Colorado at Boulder, organized the group Promise Keepers, Christian men who called themselves warriors and made seven promises. Promise number 4 was to build strong marriages and families through love, protection, and biblical values. The Promise Keepers gathered in sports stadiums to hug and pray and to publicly renew their vows to spend more time with their families. Additionally, the religion-based group Let's Strengthen Marriage brought together various organizations to promote marriage and to lobby the U.S. Congress, which in 2012 declared the week preceding Valentine's Day to be National Marriage Week USA.[15]

It is unclear, then, when vow renewal ceremonies became mainstream in the United States, but a case could be made for 2001, the year that Hallmark issued a vow renewal card. Although the vow renewal card remained in Hallmark's niche market, available only in a few well-stocked stores, the Internet card market answered America's desire to customize every possible milestone with choices of colors, images (raindrops or elderly hands crossed over a wedding gown), specific anniversary number (only those divisible by five), and relationship status ("Congratulations, Son and Daughter-in-Law on Your Wedding Vow Renewal"). A sure sign that vow renewals had branched out from their serious, if not religious, origins was the introduction of humorous greeting cards, such as one by PaperCards that depicts middle-aged friends at a backyard gathering tearing up as the bespectacled and slightly overweight Ed and Erma exchange vows, indicated by one word in their respective thought balloons: "Whatever."

By 2002, vow renewals had become popular enough for Vegas chapels to include them in their packages, but there were few highly publicized renewal ceremonies until the Harley-Davidson dealership in Orlando, Florida, made it into the Guinness Book of Records when 325 biker couples renewed their vows simultaneously during Biker Week. Realizing the marketing and client-building potential in mass vow renewals, other civic and commercial enterprises held highly publicized record-breaking vow renewal attempts, but none surpassed the world record set by Miami University in 2009, when 1,087 couples simultaneously renewed their commitment to one another and, by their attendance at the Miami Merger reunion, to the university.[16]

As vow renewals increased in popularity and became normalized, they also shifted somewhat from their original intent to mark major anniversaries. Indeed, people began to ask, "How often should couples renew vows?" One online etiquette adviser suggests that vow renewals are valid whether people are "'formalizing' [an] elopement, commemorating an anniversary, or marking the end of a difficult time in [their] lives together."[17] Some couples decide to renew their vows to finally have the big wedding celebration they couldn't afford when they first got married. The boxer Mike Tyson certainly could have afforded a lavish wedding at La Bella Wedding Chapel in Vegas, but because a few days earlier his four-year-old daughter from a previous marriage had died in an accident, he opted to have a private ceremony with no guests present. Two years later, Tyson and his third wife renewed their vows in a Muslim ceremony at the M Resort in Vegas, surprising hundreds of friends, who had thought they were attending a birthday celebration. For many, vow renewals have become a way to redo the original celebration with an extravagance they may not have been able to enjoy or afford the first time around, using luxury and pageantry to signal not only a recommitment to a spouse but a new status in life.

There is no one-size-fits-all renewal ceremony. Indeed, in Las Vegas, where changing identities are offered up as a game, the chapels expect and even encourage customers to bend the rules. "Just come as you are" or "We trust you" were the answers I received from Vegas chapel coordinators when I asked if I needed to show proof of marriage to have a vow renewal. In this regard, renewals open up spaces for variety and creativity not wholly possible in a legal wedding ceremony. Even alternative weddings officiated by a friend ordained on the Internet that include personal vows must adhere to specific rules of content in order for the ceremony to be legal. In contrast, *Renewing Your Wedding Vows: A Complete Planning Guide to Saying I Still Do*, by Sharon Naylor, encourages couples to invent their own celebrations and create new vows to make up for impersonal, formulaic rituals that might not have expressed how they actually felt when they originally married. As Naylor puts it, "There was no negotiation, no customizing, no taking out the word 'obey.' You were young or you hadn't found your assertiveness yet, so you agreed to repeat those traditional vows."[18] When Matt Damon renewed his vows after seven years of marriage, he promised to always give his wife the side of the bed closer to the bathroom. The Graceland Wedding Chapel suggests that, since vow renewals have no legal status, couples might want to have Elvis act as minister or exchange Elvis and Priscilla's vows instead of their own. In this way, the Elvis factor can't be ignored. In the Vegas wedding business, Elvis

has given people license to make a game of their celebrations, thus turning skeptics into serious-minded party poopers.

Nevertheless, some might question whether vow renewals should happen at all. An article in the *New York Times* style section maintains that "restating vows is not a panacea for the evils of divorce, and may even bring into question the sturdiness of the original utterances. The first time, you mean it, but if there's the chance that down the line you'll really, really mean it, then does that change the way you might have felt the first time?"[19] The *Huffington Post* even suggested that vow renewals (by five celebrity couples at least) might correlate positively with divorce.[20] After all, the German model Heidi Klum and the musician Seal famously renewed their vows annually until after seven years they divorced. Their fifth vow renewal, themed as a white trash wedding with Heidi's hair done up in cornrows and her gown revealing her pregnant belly, was held in Malibu, although, significantly, the official Vegas celebrant Elvis officiated. In an online Catholic forum discussing the validity of vow renewals, a priest quoted from ancient religious documents to prove that a vow renewal ceremony would be sacrilegious, since it implies that the original promise before God did not count. In the midst of an intellectual debate about the validity of vow renewals, one woman wondered why she couldn't just make a party of it: "I think it would be fun to stand up in front of Elvis and testify your love."[21]

The vow renewal as a potential sign of the impermanence of the wedding ceremony is further appropriate to Las Vegas as a city of constant evolution, change, implosion, and construction. When David and Lauren Blair set a Guinness record for number of vow renewals for a single couple, it was their eighty-third time and it took place in 2004 at the Boardwalk Hotel and Casino in Las Vegas. A commemorative photo of the couple shows them standing in front of four Elvis-themed slot machines. This budget, Coney Island–themed establishment with a fake roller coaster and a fake Ferris wheel, located between the Bellagio and the Monte Carlo, was also fondly remembered by a couple who reported on the website Yelp that they eloped there from San Francisco in a car without air conditioning. After the demise of the Boardwalk Hotel in 2006 (memorialized online along with a slew of other videos of Vegas hotel implosions), the nostalgic couple from San Francisco declared a kind of online vow renewal to the hotel, pledging to return to the site for future anniversaries, no matter what was constructed in its place. Could they or the Blairs ever have imagined that the new hotel built on the same site, right there in the middle of the Strip across from the old Aladdin (now Planet Hollywood), would have no casino and offer not even one Elvis wedding package?

Vow renewals are only one of several ways in which the Vegas wedding industry has achieved a financial boost. Perhaps more than the renewal of a continuing marriage, the encore wedding has escaped the shroud of the tawdry to be flaunted and commemorated with splendor. It is not that second weddings are at all novel—indeed, as Otnes and Pleck describe, "by the 1980s, divorce in the United States had become mundane and ordinary, but weddings for the divorced were still excessively bound by rules of etiquette formulated in an age when divorce proceedings were regarded as shameful."[22] What is significant, then, is extravagance and spectacle. Rather than quiet, private affairs, the repeat wedding is now a space for the reappearance of many of the signs once avoided or downplayed, such as the princess white wedding dress. In doing so, the meaning of the wedding as a testament to the bride's purity, virginity, and fertility instead becomes a celebration of luxury, romance, and magic.[23] Speaking to the often more mature (and thus already economically and domestically established) status of the encore wedding couple, these ceremonies typically lack showers and have embargoes on gifts. What better place than Vegas, less troubled by taboo or etiquette and already a popular destination for older Americans, to realize the untapped potential this niche market offers for the lavish and the upscale?

Another change for the Vegas marriage industry has been prompted by the decline in couples opting for commitment ceremonies as more states legalize same-sex marriage. At the same time that religious and conservative political groups were planting the seeds that would nurture vow renewal ceremonies, commitment ceremonies—civil celebrations to publicly (though not legally) recognize the relationships of gays and lesbians—were sprouting up like weeds to make up for the lack of legal options for same-sex couples. For all but the religious-based chapels such as Little Church of the West and the Little White Wedding Chapel, commitment ceremonies became yet another set of relabeled wedding packages with minor tweaks, such as possibly two bouquets or two boutonnieres. Now that more states have legalized same-sex marriages, commitment ceremonies have begun to lose their appeal and, once again, Vegas is losing an important revenue stream. However, if and when Nevada makes gay marriage legal, Vegas stands to gain enormously from out-of-state couples choosing to hold their special event in this gay-friendly city. As Dianne Schiller, of Renta-Dress and Tux Shop in Las Vegas, said, "If we really want to sell ourselves as the Wedding Capital of the World, we need to open the doors and embrace everyone."[24]

When TV star Shanna Moakler held a high-profile divorce party at the Bellagio, she signaled another evolution for the Vegas wedding industry: the ritu-

alization of the act of dissolving a wedding. The Vegas divorce rite mimics and rethinks some of the traditions of the wedding ceremony, in this case the cake topped with a blonde figurine, from which blood-colored icing drips decoratively down the tiers, leading to a floppy supine plastic figure at the bottom that is clearly recognizable as a dead groom. Party suppliers that cater to other Vegas flings, such as bachelor and bachelorette parties, have easily incorporated new party favors such as toilet paper imprinted with a spouse's name or a veteran's parade of lifeless, beheaded, knife- or gun-toting bride and groom cake toppers. Divorce parties became trendy in Japan in 2010, with couples smashing their rings with frog-shaped mallets that symbolized the positive aspects of change. In the United States, the ritual sometimes has a similar cooperative tone, such as that espoused by *The Joy of Ritual*, by Barbara Biziou, who encourages couples to acknowledge what's been positive in a marriage and let go of the negatives.[25] However, this cooperative celebration is not the divorce ceremony that has caught on in Vegas. Instead, divorce Vegas-style gives women full rein to symbolically destroy things. They may opt to burn their wedding gowns, hit a pecker piñata, or prick husband-like voodoo dolls. The Divorce Party Planner, a Vegas-based enterprise run by Glynda Rhodes, touts a thriving business in what she calls upscale divorces. In 2012, Rhodes told the *Las Vegas Sun*, "I think this will become big business for Las Vegas; after all, there are bachelorette parties and wedding receptions galore here. We have more to offer than most cities, so divorce events can be a whole new thing to celebrate."[26] Indeed, if Vegas has been at the forefront of the wedding industry, ever ready to expand into new niche markets, it's only logical for the city to begin offering tailor-made divorce rituals complete with documentation. If a Vegas wedding package is labeled "cherish," and a vow renewal "rekindle," will a packaged divorce be sold as "liberate" or "commiserate"? Only time will tell.

We might compare the Sin City wedding to another Vegas ritual: the striptease. Roland Barthes has said of the Parisian striptease that the act embodies a contradiction in that the woman is desexualized at the same moment that she is completely stripped, her shed disguise of eroticism leaving "nakedness as a natural vestiture of woman, which amounts in the end to regaining a perfectly chaste state of flesh." Further, the French striptease has attained a middle-class and potentially nationalistic patina that functions in part to tame its eroticism through the many ways in which the act is brought into the public sphere (as a specialized vocation and the focus of social clubs).[27] In Las Vegas, it is the bride, not the stripper, who is a disruptive force, though one that is ultimately normalized. The Vegas bride is not a contradiction in and of herself (like the stripper), but rather marks a paradox in relation to the space of the city. The bridal figure is a frequent vision around the city, a moving billboard for the wedding who poses for pictures around town and saunters through casinos and hotels on the way to and from a chapel. The white gown is an unmistakable sign inserting private life into the public parade, the image of chastity an out-of-place inversion of the visual terrain of glitzy lights, burlesque advertisements, and call girl billboards.

Like the bride in white in the city, marriage ceremonies in Las Vegas suggest acts of contradiction. At once known as both Sin City and the international wedding capital, the city celebrates the formalized ritual of the wedding but not the domesticity or the family that might follow. As a popular destination for elopements, Vegas challenges the popular idiom that what happens in the city stays there; indeed, the city serves as a way station for couples, a legitimating and necessary stopover to accessing a myriad of benefits (legal, social, and economic) back home. Similarly, despite the landscape of diversions where the Strip forswears necessary things like schools and supermarkets in favor of sites of leisure, gambling, and play, the wedding by definition solidifies connections to traditional institutions governing kinship and inheritance. The Vegas wedding can vary between legally binding commitment, a rite of entertainment alone (as in the faux wedding), or tradition without permanence (as in the vow renewal or encore wedding). Indeed, the staging and celebration of the Vegas wedding has even become comparable to its opposite: the ritualized divorce. If the Vegas wedding is a liminal sphere where meanings can be ambiguous and at times paradoxical, then it is also a temporary transitional space through which contradictions become laundered and disciplined—a rite of passage through which the couple is transitioned into the civic order.

In the popular imaginary, Las Vegas seems a city apart from the nation: temporally, geographically, and socially. Vegas is often marked as dichotomous to the structures of everyday life and work and at odds with normative social values about such things as drinking, sex, and gambling. Yet the omnipresence of weddings in the city—an architectural fixture, an economic bulwark, the emphasis of much county government work, and of course a system of interconnected rituals of celebration and play, from bachelor(ette) parties to honeymoons—tell of a concurrent reality where Las Vegas is not so much aberration, but rather an umbilical cord that nourishes the American civic body. Indeed, the carnivalesque ambience of the so-called wedding capital undergoes, with every ceremony, an inversion that reinforces or restores traditional social values.

1. Joan Didion, "Marrying Absurd," in *Fifty Great Essays*, ed. Robert Diyanni (New York: Longman, 2004).

2. Didion, "Marrying Absurd."

3. Cele Otnes and Elizabeth Pleck, *Cinderella Dreams: The Allure of the Lavish Wedding* (Berkeley: University of California Press, 2003), 238.

4. Otnes and Pleck, *Cinderella Dreams*, 237.

5. Frank Pellegrini, "The Bush Speech: How to Rally a Nation," *Time*, September 21, 2001. Also Tom Murse, "Did President Bush Really Tell Americans to 'Go Shopping' after 9/11?," About.com, September 14, 2010, http://usgovinfo.about.com.

6. Rebecca Mead, *One Perfect Day: The Selling of the American Wedding* (New York: Penguin, 2007), 166.

7. Susan Willis, "Public Use / Private Space," in The Project on Disney, *Inside the Mouse: Work and Play at Disney World* (Durham, NC: Duke University Press, 1995).

8. As American studies scholar Amy Kaplan explains, exploration and travel abroad have anachronistically provided fertile ground for self-discovery. Indeed, the origins of the field of American studies, she explains, and the conceptual practice of considering the meaning of America are connected to exotic exploits, where trips abroad have historically functioned as a means of visualizing a coherent identity back home. See Kaplan's critique of the exploits of Perry Miller into Congo and how such a visit functions as a means to be "left at home with America." Amy Kaplan, " 'Left Alone with America': The Absence of Empire in the Study of American Culture," in *Cultures of United States Imperialism*, ed. Amy Kaplan and Donald Pease (Durham, NC: Duke University Press, 1993), 3–21.

9. Alison Vekshin, "Las Vegas Woos Wedding-Vow Renewals as Quickie Marriages Decline," Bloomberg, July 21, 2011, http://www.bloomberg.com/news/2011-07-21/las -vegas-woos-wedding-vow-renewals.html.

10. Mead, *One Perfect Day*, 164.

11. Susan Strasser, "The Alien Past: Consumer Culture in Historical Perspective," in *The Advertising and Consumer Culture Reader*, ed. Joseph Turow and Mathew McAllister (New York: Routledge, 2009), 25–37.

12. Roland Barthes, *The Fashion System*, trans. M. Ward and R. Howard (New York: Hill and Wang, 1983), 297–98.

13. Mandarin Oriental Las Vegas, http://www.mandarinoriental.com/lasvegas/hotel -venues/weddings/packages/ (accessed March 2013).

14. Tim O'Reiley, "County Abandons Wedding Vow Renewal Plan," *Las Vegas Review-Journal*, July 29, 2011.

15. "Photos of U.S. Congressional Representatives and U.S. Senators at the 2012 Inaugural U.S. Congressional Launch of National Marriage Week USA in the U.S. Capitol," National Marriage Week USA, 2012, http://www.nationalmarriageweekusa .org/news-room/photos-of-congressional-meeting (accessed March 2013).

16. "Miami Breaks World Record for Wedding Vow Renewals," *Dayton Daily News*, February 4, 2010, http://www.daytondailynews.com/news/news/local/miami-breaks -world-record-for-wedding-vow-renewals/nM8pM/.

17. Tracy Guth, "Vows: How to Renew Yours," *The Knot*, http://wedding.theknot .com/wedding-planning/wedding-ceremony/articles/how-to-renew-your-wedding -vows.aspx (accessed March 2013).

18. Sharon Naylor, *Renewing Your Wedding Vows: A Complete Planning Guide to Saying I Still Do* (New York: Broadway Books, 2008).

19. Anna Jane Grossman, "Vow Renewals: When One 'I Do' Is Not Enough," *New York Times*, Fashion and Style Section, September 17, 2010.

20. "Heidi Klum, Seal Divorce: Five Other Couples Who Renewed Their Vows, Then Divorced," *Huffington Post*, February 1, 2012, http://www.huffingtonpost.com /2012/02/01/heidi-klum-seal-divorce-f__1248205.html#slide=656804.

21. Catholic Answers Forum, post dated April 5, 2011, http://www.forums.catholic .com (search for "Vow Renewal Vegas").

22. Otnes and Pleck, *Cinderella Dreams*, 251.

23. Otnes and Pleck, *Cinderella Dreams*, 251.

24. Andrea Domanick, "Las Vegas Wedding Businesses: We'd Love to See Gay Marriage Legalized," *Las Vegas Sun*, March 25, 2013, http://www.lasvegassun.com/news /2013/mar/25/vegas-wedding-businesses-wed-love-see-gay-marriage/#ixzz2UdEx6igi.

25. Barbara Biziou, *The Joy of Ritual* (New York: St. Martin's Press, 1999).

26. Robin Leach, "Las Vegas Divorce Parties: Burn the Dress, Photos and Marriage Certificate," *Las Vegas Sun*, September 19, 2012, http://www.lasvegassun.com/news /2012/sep/19/las-vegas-divorce-parties-burn-dress-photos-and-ma/#ixzz2UdTbA4nw.

27. Roland Barthes, "Striptease," in *Mythologies*, trans. Annette Lavers (New York: Farrar, Straus and Giroux, 1972), 84–87.

ELEVEN

Memories: Made in China

It's the third day of your four-day Las Vegas vacation.* You've trudged up and down the Strip, exceeded your limit at the slots and tables, stuffed yourself at the all-you-can-eat buffets, and become so accustomed to the lights and incessant ring tones of the gaming areas that now your hotel room seems uncomfortably quiet. As the journey home looms on the horizon, you decide that this is the day to shop for souvenirs—if not for yourself, then for the kids left at home with the sitter, or your friends and coworkers stuck in their routines and eating their hearts out over your good fortune.

So step off the Strip and enter any one of the casino hotels. Now, instead of allowing yourself to follow the sounds and activity to the gaming floor, take a detour into the casino gift shop. Here you'll find the mother lode of trinket souvenirs. It hardly matters which casino gift shop you choose because all the shops carry the same sorts of items—paperweights, key rings, shot glasses, T-shirts, refrigerator magnets. Each is distinguishable only by design. For instance, the Flamingo Hotel stuffs its souvenir shot glass with a pink golf ball,

---

* Susan Willis

while the Venetian drapes its shot glass with a mini–bridal veil. The Paris Casino offers a full range of Eiffel Tower paraphernalia, including key chains inscribed with the words "Paris, Las Vegas" so as not to be confused with the Eiffel Tower key chain on offer at Disney's EPCOT, or possibly the Boulevard St. Michel in Paris, France. Thematic branding is enforced and recapitulated from one gift shop to the next. Excalibur's key chains feature a sword in a stone; the Venetian gives you gondolas; and the Flamingo contends with Jimmy Buffet's Margaritaville for the rights to colorful birds and palm trees.

Not wanting to sacrifice valuable floor space to trinket sales, the casinos cram boatloads of souvenirs into tiny shops that double as convenience stores where the necessities—TUMS, Advil, and Crest—are tucked behind the counter. Before attempting to negotiate the cramped aisles, tourists would do well to linger in the doorway and cast an appraising eye from bins to shelves to kiosks. It's hard to imagine a category of trinket that's not available. There are bottle openers and flasks, sunglasses and visors, panties and socks, coloring books and mouse pads, chocolate poker chips and gummy candy dice. There are even snow globes, none of whose miniature scenes depicts Las Vegas, where it does occasionally snow, but rather the medieval castles, white tigers, pink flamingos, and Egyptian sphinxes associated with the Strip's branded properties.

In her book *On Longing*, Susan Stewart maintains that our fascination with souvenirs has to do with their being miniatures.[1] All the sights, sounds, and aromas of a place, as well as the moods and desires that we attach to that place, are somehow compressed into a token whose function is to preserve our memories and activate our remembering. As Stewart puts it, "The souvenir contracts the world in order to expand the personal."[2] Stewart's thoughts about souvenirs derive from her extended meditation on disproportionate human bodies—giants and dwarfs—where the interior space of the subject fancies itself in miniature by comparison to the outsized notion of the state or the world. With the body as the gauge for knowing and calculating distance and scale, desire seizes upon the small as something the body's imaginary might conceivably attain. Stewart alludes to the word *fetish* with respect to souvenirs. I see this aspect as particularly appropriate. The ceramic ashtray painted with flowers and the word *Benidorm* encapsulates the seaside resort in token form. If ours were a more spiritual or animistic society, we might say that the spirit of Benidorm infuses the ashtray, so that when I hold it and contemplate its artistry, that spirit of place touches my psyche and enables me to journey there again.

Sadly, I have never been to Benidorm. The ashtray was a gift from a class-

mate who did, indeed, travel to Benidorm, where she bought me a token of her vacation in exchange for minding her cat. So for me the ashtray provides connection to a place that I know only as a dot on a map—and the recollection that her cat, locked up for three weeks, infested her entire apartment with fleas.

My ashtray from Benidorm underscores a meaning of the fetish that is especially appropriate for our society: the nature of the commodity as embodiment of the invisible living labor necessary for its production. As tourists, we travel the world and purchase our commodity remembrances from vendors. Rarely do we come in contact with the people who make ceramic ashtrays. What's more, very few of us find our souvenirs by happenstance. How many of us comb beaches for seashells and driftwood? Do we glean our pasts for images and objects, as does France's great filmmaker Agnès Varda? Her films *The Gleaners and I* and *The Beaches of Agnès* practice the art of documentary as a form of gleaning. In Las Vegas, only children can pass as gleaners. They dawdle behind their parents and harvest the call girl cards that litter the Strip.

Something of a gleaner myself, I've gathered call girl cards off the street and even accepted them from the smutters who hand them out. I tell myself that everything in Vegas is potentially important for research—especially a marketing ploy that produces 90 percent of the litter on the Strip. Remarkably, of the thirty or more cards that I've gleaned, none is a duplicate. Nor do any of the women shown on the cards have the same name—although most have the same phone number. Here's Vanessa wearing only nipple pasties and a pink thong. Then there's Sandy stretched across the card like a gazelle on a bed. And there's Tony, bent over and peering between her stiletto-enhanced legs. Is she trying to see the star-shaped pastie on her ass?

Parents who catch their kids putting together a deck of pornographic trading cards display various levels of anger. Some make a magnificent show of throwing the cards back into the litter after struggling to wrest them from their baffled children's hands. A few take the more progressive parenting approach and try to explain what's wrong about the cards. Others pretend to ignore their child's pastime, hoping some new interest will present itself. Most atypical was the Brazilian mother I observed, who leaned over her young son's shoulder and appraised his cards one by one while offering comments about each of the women on view.

Kept as souvenirs, the call girl cards underscore another meaning of fetish: its association with sexual arousal. While some parents who bring their children to Las Vegas try to guard their kids from the culture of sex, others throw

their children into it as if enacting a perverse rite of passage. Such apparently was the aim of one mother who thrust her two young daughters into the embrace of a Chippendale. With aplomb born of practice, he straddled the eight-year-old across his thigh and hugged the older girl to his naked chest. The ecstatic mom bought the keepsake photo of her daughters' initiation into the joys of man worship.

Because sex in Las Vegas is both literal and explicit, it's not hard to discern which souvenirs function as a sexual fetish. To paraphrase Freud, "In Las Vegas a cigar is always more than a cigar." Not so outside Vegas, where an innocuous object among a general clutter of commodity souvenirs may or may not harbor powerful, even disturbing, sexual meanings. With the deepest abhorrence, I recall the Kewpie dolls that I consistently won at my elementary school's carnival fund-raiser. These were given as booby prizes to the children who failed to throw the softball into the clown's mouth or hook the wooden fish in the wading pool or toss the rings over the Coke bottle. I hated those dolls. After all, they were for losers—a fact made abundantly clear by the words stamped into the doll's body, "Made in Japan." As every child in the 1950s knew, Japan lost the war. But my real antipathy for the Kewpies derived from a visceral revulsion that at the age of seven I couldn't articulate, even though I knew it had to do with the doll itself. Made of plastic, the Kewpie was naked but for a tuft of baby bird feathers attached to its bottom. Stubby arms and legs emerged from its otherwise featureless body. Without a neck, the Kewpie's head seemed an extension of its body, much like a banana-shaped balloon that's twisted in the middle so as to make two balloons. And, like a balloon, a tiny stem grew out of the Kewpie's head. The overall effect was imbecilic. As I think back I realize that the Kewpie conveyed a sense of deviance that I now see as comparable to that quality that Diane Arbus captured in her black-and-white photographs of dwarfs, giants, and circus performers. Indeed, with its bodily deformity, the Kewpie fits Susan Stewart's definition of the miniature to a T. But I knew that the Kewpie was a great deal more. A sexually charged object, the Kewpie represented everything tantalizing and disturbing about sex—all of it masquerading under my parents' watchful eyes as no more than infantile and folkloric.

Nothing in Vegas is obscenely innocent, like the Kewpie. Rather, everything is bathed in blatant, commodified sexuality that beckons the would-be shopper to partake with abandon. Stalking the tourists through the Strip's gift shops, I witnessed a number out to acquire a piece of the action for friends and family at home. Typical were two men, possibly a father and his son having some man time together. They were pondering a pink French-cut

T-shirt clearly intended for a woman. A more obvious memento for some-one left at home is the Excalibur teddy bear, whose bright red shirt offers the message, "Someone who loves me very much went to Las Vegas and bought me this Teddy Bear." You can imagine the craft of miniaturization that enables this many words to fit on the chest of a teddy bear. Less typical were the four middle-aged women who were obviously shopping together but who had fanned out to the shop's four corners, from where they broadcast their finds. So caught up in their girl time, they let everyone know that they were shopping for an entire family tree of nieces and nephews. Noticing a brightly colored stuffed parrot on a perch, one of the women pulled its cord. To the flapping of mechanical wings, the bird squawked, "Show us your tits!" Oops! The parrot was one of those inappropriate Vegas souvenirs, but definitely worth a chuckle.

The fetish object bought for the loved one not loved enough to be included on the trip assuages the feeling of abandonment by displacing exclusion with a longing to one day be the one who makes the journey and thereby experience the other's presumed pleasure (possibly consummating that pleasure with the purchase of a parrot or a teddy bear for someone else left at home). Thus the souvenir fetish is always a token of a lack. What's more, the glut of souvenirs in Las Vegas can't help but signify the one thing that everyone wants to take home but only few actually do—money. The only souvenir not on offer in any of the shops is a big win. Passed from hand to hand as the medium of ex-change, money can't be turned into a souvenir except by those proud owners of a mom-and-pop store who hang a dollar bill on the wall to memorialize their first sale. Because money is the only real object of desire in Las Vegas, every souvenir for sale is relegated to junk status at the outset. The shot glass left to accumulate dust, the key chain tossed in a drawer—the Las Vegas sou-venir is an object so meaningless that it hardly attains the quality of fetish attached to any other commodity.

But maybe I just haven't been looking in the right place. Somewhere in this mecca of desire there must be a memorable object. Best turn my attention away from the casino gift shops and take a peek in one of those stand-alone emporia. They tend to offer more generic Las Vegas memorabilia like poster-sized nightscape photos of the Strip, fuzzy dice to hang in a car, playing cards guaranteed to have been used in one of the casinos, and enough csi gear to dress the tv show's entire cast. One such shop greets its visitors with a store-front sculpted out of faux sandstone in a style reminiscent of Fred Flintstone's cave. Oh, pardon my mistake. The dim lights and dense racks of T-shirts ob-scured the shop's sign. This was no cartoon cave but the Grand Canyon. On

a streetscape that includes mock-ups of far-flung destinations such as Paris, Egypt, Rome, and Venice, it seems odd to find a reference to a place so close at hand. Indeed, the real Grand Canyon is less than a day's drive away. Wishing to capitalize on the proximity, tourist agencies on the Strip hawk excursions to the national park as part of a vacation package, sometimes kicking in an extra night on the Strip for those who sign up for the Grand Canyon bus tour. Indeed, the Strip and the Canyon are wonders worthy of each other. On the one hand, you have a colossal built environment that rises abruptly on both sides of eight lanes of blacktop, and on the other, a deeply gouged canyon carved by the Colorado River through the strata of geologic time. The Strip and the park are dramatic antithetical mirror images: the one, an over-the-top monument to the hollow spectacle of capitalism, the other, the hollowed-out, but concrete, manifestation of nature as a material force.

Clearly, the Grand Canyon gift shop is no natural wonder. Once past the T-shirts and hucksters who offer trips to the real Grand Canyon, I encountered a labyrinthine system of branching caves and canyons so dimly lit and stuffed with merchandise that the shop's egress abruptly vanished. With no exit sign in sight, I pushed deeper and deeper into the cavern's embrace. There I found an array of souvenir objects that I hadn't seen anywhere else on the Strip. Yes, the Grand Canyon is a wonderland of the pornographic, home to all those items that shun the bright lights of the casino gift shops. Here, key rings feature naughty teddy bears that shit piles of poop, wind-up action dolls that mechanically fornicate until their springs unwind, and racks of thong panties that offer risqué messages like, "Sorry boys, I eat pussy."

Overcome by claustrophobia, I cast about once more for an exit. An escalator to the second floor seemed the only option. Dreading more of the same, I began my ascent. Luckily, the second floor offered relief. Once out of the schlock, I found myself in a pristine shrine to Native American art. Rather than shoppers giggling over tacky merchandise, I beheld a menagerie of carved wooden animals—bears, moose, horses, elk, raccoons, and ravens. Feathered dream catchers hung suspended like Calder mobiles, while figurines dressed in beaded leather stared stoically from the shelves. Like artifacts in a museum, these objects exuded a patina of authenticity. Fingering a turtle displayed in a group of tiny baby turtles, I turned the carving in my hand and noticed its tiny tag. "Made in China." Crestfallen, I inspected the other items. Dream catchers: also made in China. Colorful woven baskets: made in Pakistan. Strands of beads (some of them made of colored corn kernels): strung in India. What a stunning gallery of knockoffs.

But then, I shouldn't be amazed that our souvenirs come from every place but home. The production of curio mementos was leap-frogging around the world long before any of us started hearing about globalization. If Japan furnished the Kewpies of my childhood, Taiwan was the supplier of souvenir curios for my eldest son, born in the 1960s, while subsequent children born in the 1970s and 1980s could expect the now-familiar "Made in China" mementos. Thus, the souvenirs that embody our memories derive from ever more disparate and economically desperate parts of the world that few of us will ever see.

Not seeing where and how goods are made distinguishes the mass-produced commodity from objects we recognize as handicrafts. Today, many localities host an annual craft fair, perhaps as an antidote to the things for sale in the big box stores that the same communities wooed with tax incentives. Before the recent recession put a damper on unnecessary spending, many shoppers looked to the craft fair as a place to find unusual and unique holiday gifts. As a child, I can't recall ever having been to a craft fair. But no matter—we did our Christmas shopping in Tijuana. Back in the bygone, folkloric pre–drug gang days, Tijuana was an epicenter of handicraft production. A drive from the border into the downtown where the glassware, leather goods, and pottery were sold traversed miles of ramshackle sprawl where many of the goods were made. I remember peering through the window of our sedan into the backyards where people—men, women, and children—painted flowers and birds on the crockery that my mother favored. Other backyards were stacked with tires. This is where the rubber sandals were made. Some backyards were hung with brightly colored woven blankets. Others reeked of freshly cured leather. The more substantial buildings housed glass factories where we would stop to watch muscled, shirtless men fashion goblets and pitchers at the end of long metal pipes that they blew into. But the most magical thing in all of Tijuana—the one thing that I truly would have called a souvenir—didn't appear to come from any of the backyards: jumping beans. They were sold in little slide-open matchboxes. I couldn't wait to take them home and then to school. Jumping beans were the universally accepted proof of a trip to Tijuana. By comparison, a trip to Las Vegas is apt to yield no more than a tall tale and a credit card bill best left forgotten.

Pondering the glut of commodity souvenirs and the varying degrees of distance that separate us from their producers, I now understand the meaning of the locked glass display cases that lined the walls in the upstairs gallery of the Grand Canyon gift shop. This is where the real treasures were kept. The ceramic bowls, stone pipes, turquois necklaces, and animal figurines— these had to be authentic, if only for their inaccessibility. How odd to stare

into the locked cases and know that I beheld the work of Native artists, all the while surrounded by a host of replicas fabricated in the world's far-flung sweat shops.

I wonder, though, if it matters whether the lightning bolt patterns painted on a particular terra-cotta bowl were painted by a Chinese factory worker rather than a Navajo artist. Louise Erdrich offers an answer when she tells the tale of a misguided attempt at economic self-improvement on the Ojibwe Reservation in her novel *Love Medicine*.[3] The book depicts the intersecting lives of extended family members, one of whom, determined to modernize and combat chronic unemployment, opens a factory dedicated to the manufacture of cheap curios. Thus, real Indians work on assembly lines cranking out tiny tomahawks, toy bows and arrows, and a variety of beaded necklaces, belts, and bracelets. Everything they make is indistinguishable from containers full of curios shipped from China. Imagine the irony of Native American workers in a race-to-the-bottom competition with cheap imports. Luckily for the Ojibwe, production comes to an explosive halt when love rivalries among the workers spark a melee. The assembly line crashes, beads fly everywhere, and the orders for tomahawks, bracelets, and belts will never be filled.

But what about the Chinese workers who continue to fashion those tiny tomahawks and dream catchers? How do they perceive us when they fill our orders for totem animals and beaded belts? And what do they think of the dolls they sell us that don't look at all like Barbie but instead have brown skin, long braided hair, and clothing made of fringed leather? Does someone tell them of our indigenous tribes and the lore that surrounds their culture? Do the Chinese who oppress their non-Han others wonder why we shop for mementos of our non-Anglo others? And finally, while China fashions the stuff that fixes our desire to the commodity, should we find it odd or just the reality of globalization that China holds our debt and cycles it back to us in the trinkets we buy to guard our memories?

I encountered yet another fetish souvenir on my trip to Las Vegas: a tiny bear, no bigger than the first joint of my thumb. It was carved out of stone, its midsection girdled with a thread that bound a sliver of pointed bone to its side. This truly was a fetish object. I came upon it unexpectedly. After four days of research in Las Vegas, I was driving to the real Grand Canyon, indeed, the remote North Rim. The route traverses the desolate high desert of Navajo country that Tony Hillerman captures so well in his mystery novels that depict the exploits of tribal police Joe Leaphorn and Jim Chee. Here, the endless miles of chaparral give way to piñon pine as the elevation rises to the rim of the canyon. With very few cars on the road, the journey seemed an endless

quest for the horizon. Then, looming and growing in the distance, the bulge of a roadside pullout beckoned. There a man had set up a table of wares. Of course, I stopped.

Among the silver belt buckles, tie clasps, and necklaces, I spotted the fetish animals. I've seen other such animals offered for sale on the blankets that Native craftspeople spread out to showcase their merchandise in Albuquerque's Old Town Plaza. And I remember them from one of Hillerman's novels, *Dance Hall of the Dead*.[4] Hillerman maintained a lifelong friendship with the Navajo, an association that enabled him to write from a Navajo point of view. Thus, the crimes that his tribal police investigate entail as many spiritual considerations as jurisdictional or legal ones. *Dance Hall of the Dead* is unique among Hillerman's novels as it brings together both Navajo and Zuni characters. The fetish animals are Zuni and represent a symbolic relationship with the Zunis' complex cosmology. Neither Hillerman the author nor Leaphorn the detective presumes to understand the significance of the little "mole carved from a piece of antler" that the detective finds among the keepsakes that Cecil Bowlegs stores in his school lunchbox. By comparison to the boy's other treasures—a spark plug, a magnet, a ball of copper wire, the wheel off a toy car—the little mole evinces a special aura. Tied with a buckskin thong that "secured a tiny chipped-flint arrowhead to its top," the mole, Leaphorn recognizes, is a fetish, and he conveys his sense of wonderment by not attempting to elaborate its meaning.[5] So, too, did I immediately apprehend the little carved animals as special. Indeed, they spoke to me out of the singularity of the moment and the setting.

I didn't keep the bear I bought that day. Rather, I gave it to a friend, and not as a souvenir of my trip (she didn't know I'd been to the Southwest, much less Las Vegas), but as a compellingly curious object in its own right. As for me, the brief possession of the bear seems to have left me with an enduring and magical affect. I recall the bear, the man, the roadside stand, the crisp air, the lowering sun, and the sweep of the gray-green landscape, even its aroma—all of it, an indelible sensory memory. Can this be a souvenir?

In answer, I offer an anecdote. Some time ago, when I was a graduate student in San Diego, two visiting professors came from France to offer their seminars: Françoise Gaillard and Jacques Leenhardt. Like others who came before them, they were fascinated with the university, which was at the height of its countercultural moment. But what captivated them the most was the ethos of the west, and particularly its landscape. Of course, they went to the Grand Canyon. As Jacques told it, Françoise would lay awake at night during their stay at the canyon and then for nights after their return—telling in ever more detail what she had seen and inviting Jacques to add to the account until between the two of them they created a verbal souvenir. As Jacques put it, "She wanted to remember it all."

Is it possible to imagine a verbal souvenir of Las Vegas—one that captures it all? Only Funes the Memorious might achieve such a task.[6] Invented by the great Argentine fabulist Jorge Luis Borges, Funes was a tragic figure blessed with the curse of too much memory. Capable of storing everything in his dispassionate brain, Funes could recall every word on every page in every book he ever read. He could see and remember "all the leaves and tendrils and fruit that make up a grape vine." Could he not, then, view the Strip from atop one of the pedestrian bridges and record its glorious compendium of trivialities—every garish billboard juxtaposed discordantly against each and every façade, every traffic-choked vehicle and every footsore tourist, and more lights than can be counted in a lifetime, more goods than can be housed in all our nation's Walmarts?

I suspect that poor Funes would have died of memory overload. But even if he were to succeed, his Google-sized data bank would not constitute a souvenir. This is because the essence of the souvenir (and what makes it a fetish) is its necessary relationship to all that we forget.

NOTES

1. Susan Stewart, *On Longing* (Durham, NC: Duke University Press, 2005).

2. Stewart, *On Longing*, xii.

3. Louise Erdrich, *Love Medicine* (New York: Harper Collins, 2001), 298–324.

4. Tony Hillerman, *Dance Hall of the Dead* (New York: Harper Collins, 1990).

5. Hillerman, *Dance Hall of the Dead*, 92–93.

6. Jorge Luis Borges, *Labyrinths* (New York: New Directions, 2007), 59–66.

EPILOGUE

Sucker Bet

My career in gambling began in childhood when my father taught my siblings and me to play poker.* Gathered around the kitchen table, we would bet with anything, usually pennies or matches, though the clearest evidence of who among the six of us had inherited his gambling instinct and who had not was the degree to which we cared what we won or lost. The nongamblers by nature always tended their piles of pennies protectively; my dad and I, not so much. For us, the focus was always the cards, the rhythm of play, hand to hand, as my father's steady chatter called the game. "Pair of Jacks," he would say as he dealt seven-card stud, "six and eight, possible straight," or, worse, "ten and two, nothing happening." I can't remember if I was any good, only that I could have played forever. Actually, that's not true. I can remember.

Yet in my first three research trips to Las Vegas, I never gambled more than $20 at any one time and that only on slots, and even those little adventures could not have added up to more than $100 total. In fact, in the research for this book, none of us spent any significant time actually gambling, as op-

* Jane Kuenz

posed to watching other people gamble, watching what was going on around the other people gambling, or, like me, dropping an occasional $20 on slots. This would not do, so I took a final trip back to Las Vegas just to gamble; and gamble I did, for three full days and four nights, which, as it turns out, is a really long time to gamble in Las Vegas. I played blackjack, craps, and roulette, though by the end my preference for cards won out. I gambled on the Strip and downtown at Fremont, with the locals up Nevada Route 599 at Fiesta Rancho and with the quality among the palms at the Wynn. I drank coffee at the blackjack table with electric wheelchaired retirees at 7 AM in the Flamingo and gin that night at the craps tables among the miniskirted flocks that inhabit Planet Hollywood. It helped that I was staked enough to keep me going that long, though probably not the way it might have encouraged some: I was too cautious and methodical ever to bet it all and just lucky and good enough not to lose it all. It was, by any nonprofessional's accounting, a serious stint of determined and steady wagering. Now, looking back, beyond the obvious insight that you should quit while you're ahead, something everyone already knows to do without actually knowing how to do it, I can express my accumulated wisdom thusly: be cool to the craps dealers and don't play blackjack on the Strip.

The second is easy, since it is a general rule in Las Vegas that the fancier the casino, the worse the odds for players. For example, if you don't pay attention and sit down at the wrong table, you may get a 6-to-5 payout on a natural blackjack rather than the more generous 3-to-2 elsewhere. This means that a $10 bet will return $12 instead of $15. The swankier spots also usually have more decks in the shoe; the minimum bets are higher, and they increase as the night advances. At one table, I was the only one betting $15 because the others were grandfathered in with their earlier $10 bets. On the upside, the drinks get stronger as the minimums go up, though one sees how this might be counterproductive in the long run. It is also in the long run that one feels the accumulated effects of a 6-to-5 payout over a 3-to-2.

It pays to be cool to the craps dealers, because anyone who is not completely familiar or comfortable with the game has to depend on them a lot, such as when they know my betting system better than I do and remind me when I haven't followed my usual pattern or when they hand over a payout I didn't realize I had won. One dealer estimates that at any given time a quarter of the people at the craps table have no idea what they're doing. I had some idea what I was doing, but only because a friend trained as a craps dealer had coached me in both craps and roulette at his house two weeks before. With the felt spread across the dining table and miscellaneous kids and spouses

playing for fun, Cam explained pass-line bets and come-out rolls, odds and points. He spends a day and a half with me in Vegas before heading on to California, but even with his help, my first time out is a series of rookie mistakes: the dice careen off the table at one point and into the dealer's stack of chips at another; when I cup them in both hands before shooting, the stickman asks me to stop; later, she motions for me to take my drink off the rim of the table, where it threatens to fall into the play area.

Similarly, at blackjack, I have to be told not to touch the cards and where to place my bet, even though there's a circle marked on the table just to tell people like me what to do. At other times, I simply miss the social cues. While I'm playing single-hand blackjack at the Four Queens, one of the two men beside me becomes increasingly agitated and exasperated. He cocks his head at the pit boss walking by and, as the dealer shuffles the deck again—too often, apparently, for his liking—jokes to me about how this always happens to him just because he changes the amount of his bet. I have no idea what he's talking about but nod politely and say something I hope sounds innocuous, a bad habit not shared by the man on my other side, who never looks up from his cards and certainly never offers an opinion about an unspoken accusation of card counting. Finally, the first throws his cards down (you get to hold them in single-hand; it's part of the charm), saying to the pit boss, "Fine, I'm leaving" as he walks out.

As with the etiquette of the various games, players might also need to draw on the higher criticism just to master the slang, though, as with any new language, total immersion is still the best way to pass as a native: when I prepare to leave my first craps table, the dealer points to my chips and asks me to "color up"; as I linger tentatively behind one blackjack table, a player invites me to join the game if I'm not just "wonging." Some of it seems vaguely suggestive. As I settle in to the dealer's right in the Bellagio, a man two seats down announces to the table, "Well, here comes third base," and I have to think hard, briefly, whether or not this is a come-on. At the craps table in Planet Hollywood, a new player winks at the stickman and asks if he's "short sticking" tonight, and I unconsciously look down at my blouse. There are "Georges" who leave good "tokes" for dealers, and "pigeons" and "gorillas" who amuse or irritate them. Context is all: as I stand at a blackjack table in the Four Queens on Fremont fishing for cash in my wallet, the pit boss appears at my side, gently touching my elbow and whispering in my ear like an unctuous usher at the Mother's Day buffet. "Did we bring our Players?" he coos, and, truly, I look for the corsage and want to slap him.

And then there's the language of betting itself. In blackjack, it seems simple

enough: you make a bet, maybe you double. All the fancy stuff is on the side: lucky ladies and lucky pairs, high-low and match the dealer. At roulette, however, you can bet inside or outside, "straight up" on a specific number or "split," either between two, on a "street" of three, or a "corner" among four (the cartographic metaphors predominate). Outside, the bets are broader, with whole columns of numbers or categories of possible number combinations: red or black; even or odd; the first eighteen numbers on the layout or the second eighteen; the first, second, or third dozen numbers; and, for the adventurous, the mysterious "snake bet," with chips on numbers snaking across the whole range of possibilities. In craps, betting is everything, and much of the fun for a lot of people is simply getting to yell weird things down the table: "craps," obviously, but also "naturals" (winning seven or nine), "yo eleven," "box car," "Big John" (ten) and "Little Joe" (four), "anything the hard way," "the horn." There are frontline or pass bets for when a player first shoots the dice, and come-out bets on the pass line for subsequent throws. There are place bets and field bets, the ever-elusive "hop bet," and the obviously fantastical "fire bet," for that rare occasion when the same shooter makes four different points on the same turn.

Almost all of the dealers at any game will answer questions or offer advice, like the blackjack dealer at Caesars who explained to our table the finer points of strategy and the wisdom of not buying insurance against his ace. Another at the Wynn advised me flatly to bet more if I wanted to make any money. But it is the craps dealers more than the others who really earn their tokes because they have to keep up with so many players' bets, the points made (usually multiple bets for each shooter), the different odds for each bet, and, consequently, the different payouts. That doesn't include the various sucker bets in the field and down the middle. Though my math skills are pretty good, particularly the in-your-head, on-the-spot-calculating kind, I simply stopped bothering trying to keep track of how much any one of my bets should be paying out on any one roll. Indeed, because of the speed of the game, part of the experience of winning for the casual gambler is losing track of precisely how much you are winning and exactly how. The stack of chips grows according to a process not entirely clear. At any given time, I had bets on multiple numbers, usually two in addition to the point, and sometimes when the table was crowded and the play fast, I would lose track of where my bets even were, though I had the sense not to say so and quickly learned that when the dealer pushed a stack of chips toward me, I should take it. In fact, if the dealer ever asks, "Whose chip?" the correct answer is always, "Mine."

The problem of keeping track continues once you leave the gaming tables.

While walking through the casino or pausing outside the bathroom, I would try to count my chips or cash to see where I stood, but this was difficult with chips in a crowded place and somewhat tacky or dangerous with cash. You can't fit a lot of chips in your pocket, so if you forget to color up to larger denominations or the dealer doesn't make you, you're stuck carrying them around like tokens at Chuck E. Cheese's. Occasional players like me have to trust the dealers and cashiers at the cage. More than once I did a double take after I colored up or cashed in, having either overestimated or underestimated what I thought I had. This was particularly the case at roulette, where the special chips specific to roulette keep players twice removed from their cash. At no time, however, did I ever question a cashier's or dealer's calculation when it contradicted my own. This is not how I am in real life, yet the atmosphere of the place and the rhythm of the play encouraged an overly casual attention to actual money, as though it were already gone when we bought in at the beginning—a sort of theme park entrance fee—and the rest of it just a kind of entertainment to pass the time in an alternate universe where one nonchalantly pulls out $100 bills and tosses them around. It is in this environment that one understands the logic of the free drink: on our first night in town, when Cam and I lost $240 in the first two hours after stepping off the plane, we joked about how the same two $75 vodka tonics at the craps table were only $45 at roulette. We reasoned that the drinks would be cheaper if we bet less, though someone pointed out helpfully that we could also just drink more. It is a measure of my innocence that I thought this was original.

The unreality of the chips is heightened not just by the fact that you can use them to tip the server or housekeeper like scrip in a company town, but by the way they seem to fluctuate wildly or circulate in completely different economies within any one place. Like housing prices that rise and fall without any changes in the actual house, value is variable. Cam and I plow through $200 in ten minutes just betting the $10 minimum at craps, while the same $200 might keep us in the game longer in blackjack and longer still in roulette. At the Bellagio, however, I lose $100 at blackjack in minutes. When I tell the dealer I'm not feeling the love, the young Asian man across from me catches my eye and nods. He mouths to me, "Don't play here," as the dealer takes my last $15. Yet at the Wynn the next day, I play blackjack for over an hour and leave with the same $300 I started with even after toking the dealer.

While playing with a larger roll makes it easier to get back to where you started, the seeming randomness of my successes and losses belied all of my attempts to claim skill over luck. I understand now the stories about a hot or cold table: on the first full day, I won all day on every game; on the second, I lost at everything. I was tired on the second day, but I didn't do anything differently. I played craps the same way, with the same strategy: betting on the pass line and then coming out two more points beyond that, playing odds each time. I played the same basic strategy with blackjack, the same square bet in roulette (four numbers that make a square on the board), and even on the same numbers. No difference. It's just that eventually you will lose, and once you start losing, you sense you may always lose, though you keep playing until, in fact, you do. At the Flamingo, after I've already put $300 into blackjack, I draw eleven against the dealer's five. Because this combination of hands is very good odds for the player, all blackjack gurus would advise doubling my $25 bet, but instead of pulling out only the $25 I need to double, I buy in for another $100, win that hand, and then proceed to lose it all. Perhaps it goes without saying that the heady feeling of having more money than you can keep up with and the disorientation of not entirely understanding how you ended up with the amount you did is entirely a feature of winning. No one loses track while the stack of chips becomes progressively smaller and easier to count. By the end, one feels humbled, as though some moral failing has been exposed, and it's not the gambling.

Thus, one takes refuge in superstition. All across town, players seem to be banking, if not on a coherent or recognizable strategy, then on their own private system of gestures and magical incantations. This is especially true in craps and roulette, which also have the most visible paraphernalia and machinery to pray over, though even blackjack has its moments, such as when players ignore what they know to be the best play because of some feeling emanating from the gut. One man hits on twelve against the dealer's four, announcing his departure from basic strategy by saying, "I always hit on twelve," as though it were on principle. Unfortunately, one's gut is likely to be wrong, and, in any case, one can always check with any of the various online guides to blackjack, as Cam did, at one point Googling an answer after we debated, in the middle of a hand, the advisability of standing on sixteen against the dealer's seven (no).

In craps, every move is a potential harbinger of bad luck, so much so that the various superstitions threaten to cancel each other out: throw the dice off the table and everyone sucks in a collective breath of horror, but reach for the new dice offered by the stickman and they yell "Same dice!" in unison as though switching now would only compound the error. At Fiesta Rancho, "The Royal Flush Capital of the World," the dealer next to me, Jake, who is less than half my age but calls me "honey" and "sweetheart" repeatedly, confides what at this point is obvious: for some people, he says, sticking with the same dice when they're on a good roll "really matters." Another thing that really matters in craps is how the shooter picks up the dice when they're first put in front of him. From the six dice the stickman offers him, Cam carefully selects two showing a six and a one, and then, as if to prove the virtue of this strategy, throws a seven, followed by an eleven, two winning come-out rolls. Some shooters will rub their hands on the felt before handling the dice; others will roll the dice along the table, sometimes several times, before finally tossing them to the end, like batters unable to take a swing without first going through their usual home plate routine. One man repeatedly stacked and restacked the six dice in some kind of obscure process of elimination lasting three or four minutes until he finally settled on the two he would throw. While some of these contortions may be rooted in cultural memory of house cheating—Are the dice loaded? Do they have all the right numbers in all the right places?—prayer seems the most likely explanation for the orisons that begin once the shooter actually has the dice in hand and calls out the desired number while the assembled congregation responds in kind.

Of course, much of the mystique of craps is that it has never lost its macho, back-alley allure. Though the life of the Vegas tourist is basically nomadic, with players regularly moving from table to table, casino to casino, in search of greener grass, craps highlights the culture of the social group in one place at one time, and that group is overwhelmingly male. The game is loud and physical; yelling generates more yelling, and victory is often a group effort: when the dice land akimbo against the boxman's chips, one man beats the stickman to the call, shouting out "ten," a winning point, to the cheers of the table. There's no way at this moment for the dealers to walk that back, so everyone gets paid. While in the service of the house, the famed sociability of craps is real for many of the players. We are largely strangers, but as we play through one shooter's very long roll, the men around the table start giving each other familiar nicknames, referring to Cam repeatedly as Hat Guy. I am not so honored.

Still, it's no secret why people of both genders demur when faced with craps. The game looks complicated, with its playing area carefully marked off into spaces and rows, each meticulously labeled, though none of it especially helpful to the neophyte: come, field, the pass line, the don't pass line, points versus place bets. It helps once you realize each half simply mirrors the other, so that, rather than doubling the betting options, the table merely accommodates more players, but there's not much to let new players know, for example, that "big six" means the shooter has to roll a six before a seven. There's even less information forthcoming about how unlikely that is. The cocky, "if you have to ask," insiders-only atmosphere is heightened by the height of the table, which alone encourages a certain aggressive posture in men and, as "short-sticking" suggests, renders shorter women vulnerable to clothing malfunctions either in front or behind. On the other hand, women can hide behind gender stereotypes in a way men cannot; thus, when my dice fly off the table, I immediately and unconsciously fall into my Scarlett O'Hara routine. But masculine gender anxiety crops up in blackjack too: under the dripping crystal chandelier at the Cosmopolitan, I play with three very young men who don't seem to know what they are doing. Betting very badly but finding safety in their numbers, they join and leave the game as one, each seemingly afraid to make any move without the cover of the other two, like teenage boys sitting a seat apart in the movie theater: they'll neither go alone nor sit together.

While the superstition in craps centers on the dice, in roulette it's all about the numbers. With some players, apparent mathematical precision eventually reveals itself as random nonsense. At the Golden Nugget, for example, a man stands beside the roulette table, refusing to sit, as though standing somehow provided a better perspective on the workings of a game board that actually never changes and where other people's bets have no effect on anyone else's play. For every spin, he places six chips on each of five different numbers, pausing after each number ostensibly to calculate where the next stack of six should go. When I finally ask him how he chooses his numbers, and why five, he never looks up but says something about how he goes to where his hand feels drawn, as though the table were a sort of Ouija board drawing us to our fates. Two spins later, he leaves. (Perhaps I should note at this point that it's generally not a good idea to query players about their methods while engaged in play.)

For others, the choice of numbers appears to be governed by the same principles deployed in lotteries. Another man announces without my asking that his system is to play on the birthdays of each of his immediate family members. I wonder briefly if, as with electronic passwords, it might be safer to go with something less obvious, but such concerns ignore the reality that, like its unchanging layout, roulette is not exactly a bluffing game. More to the point, the great truth of roulette is that at no time does any one number have any greater chance of winning than any other, and no amount of strategy will ever change what is, after all, the very first, and ultimately governing, rule of probability. It simply does not matter how many times the flipped coin is heads, the next flip still has the same fifty-fifty chance of being heads again. Herein is revealed the wisdom of Einstein's dictum that the only way to win at roulette is to steal the money right off the table.

Hence, I was at a complete loss to understand Cam's devotion to 32 red. He professed his faith in it at our first roulette table and played it religiously thereafter. In fact, I also picked a number and played it consistently, because, as with craps and blackjack, I wanted to be able to stay in the games, but in such a way that I would also be able to pay attention to what was going on around me. In other words, I didn't want to have to think about any of it too much. At no point, however, as we walked through a casino on a completely unrelated mission, did I feel the need to know whether or not 17 black had won, such as, for example, at tables where I had not actually placed a bet. With Cam, however, whenever we passed a roulette table, any roulette table in any casino at any time, he would check the board showing recent winning numbers and note on which tables 32 red had hit, how many times it had hit, and in what order, pointing all of this out to me as further evidence of the essential rightness of 32 red. "See?" he says, pointing to the flashing 32 above one table. "I would have won there."

This makes no sense, and he knows it. As he had already explained to me in great detail, there is always only the same 1 in 38 chance of hitting 32 red on any spin, regardless of whether or not it has been hit before or how many times it has come up or how many times any other number has come up before or after it. Any difference in those odds suggests something is not right, probably the wheel. Cam has a head for numbers: where I would lose track in craps, he never did, even arguing at one point with a dealer about the odds, which, again, is not really a good idea, especially when, as in this case, the dealer turns out to be wrong. He would return to a particular play a day later to explain how a slightly different result on this or that roll of the dice would have affected the final outcome. He could calculate and recalculate our winnings, real and imagined, in his head, through various permutations and scenarios, yet he persisted in the belief, the classic gambler's fallacy, that a series of losses must eventually produce a win. Even so, he got the last word: after losing everything on 32 red one day, so badly that the dealer actually apologized when the number finally hit as he was leaving the table, Cam won it all back and then some the next day, all on 32 red.

That is not the moral to this story. As the fund managers like to remind us—always, alas, in the fine print—past performance is no guarantee of future results. Still, we cherish our systems, indeed, any path through the minefield, guided by the dealers, who, unlike fund managers, are as vulnerable here as the players. In fact, the entire etiquette of tipping actually turns them into players. While in some places I could tip a dealer directly, the more common practice, sometimes required by the casino, is not to hand over the tip, but to place it as

a bet. In this case, the dealer gets it only if the bet wins; otherwise, it goes to the house. While the immediate effect of this rule is to pit the players with the dealers against the house, which is more fun and allows the dealer to parlay that camaraderie into higher tokes, the upshot is to make the job into one big gamble. Occasionally, the strain of it seeps through: at one point, a craps dealer tells Cam testily that it's not his job to remind players when to place odds bets, though, in fact, a number of dealers had. At another table, in the midst of betting, the dealers and pit boss engage in workplace griping about the job, as though we aren't even there, even joking about escaping this table and us for some rest with the rubes at the roulette wheel. The game continues right along, though it is like trying to place an order at a fast-food counter while the cashier yaks to the fry cook about something that happened yesterday morning.

Elsewhere, the signals are mixed. At Fiesta Rancho, when I realize the player next to me at the craps table is playing a strategy different from my own, with bets on numbers across the top, I ask the nearest dealer about the two approaches. Almost everyone at the table, especially the four dealers, had addressed this player by name, so he is obviously a regular. Jake says my strategy is also a good one. "Actually," he says, lowering his voice, "your odds are probably better." Others, however, do not share his concern for players' feelings. In response to my query about a side bet on pairs, a blackjack dealer in the same place dismisses it with a wave of his hand. "It's just a sucker bet," he says, even though every player at his table except me has bet on it. Almost immediately, the woman to my left gets up in a huff and leaves.

Perhaps its location well off the Strip suggests the service at Fiesta Rancho is correspondingly remote, or perhaps something else is at work. Unlike on the Strip, where differences in class and race are demarcated spatially—immigrants on the streets with the girly cards, middle-class folks on the private sidewalks above—the crowd at Fiesta Rancho was heterogeneous and absolutely local, with a white, Hispanic, African American, and Native American middle- and working-class clientele playing in the shadows of the Denny's and Subway while their kids amused themselves in the attached ice skating rink and arcade. The first thing I saw walking into Fiesta Rancho was the flashing arches of McDonald's. The second was a poster advertising what looks like a new game but is actually just a payday program allowing patrons with an Amigo (player's) card to cash their paychecks in the casino. The stakes were low—$3 minimums at craps, $1 at blackjack, only 50¢ at roulette—and there was none of the theatrical yelling at the craps table that seems a feature of the game everywhere else. Where the typical opening buy-in on the Strip is made in $100 bills, here it was not unusual for someone to begin with $20.

Yet, for all of that, there was something depressingly and reassuringly similar about the gambling everywhere I went.

When I mention this to Maria at the considerably more upscale Wynn later that day, the full measure of the dealer's emotional labor becomes evident. As I sit down alone to her empty blackjack table, Maria asks me if I am having a good time in Las Vegas. I tell her that I'm doing research for a book. In fact, I've selected this table specifically to be alone with a dealer with the hope of having a conversation I couldn't have with other players around. But it was not to be: instead of taking the bait, her face gels into a plastic smile. When she asks politely what I have learned, I tell her that people seem to win and lose the same regardless of the quality of the place. Isn't that interesting? As though conscious of the cameras above watching and recording us, cameras that do not distinguish between us, equally curious about us both, Maria responds with the canned response of the trained Disney cast member: "Here at the Wynn," she recites, "we provide a unique guest experience."

My last unique guest experience took place at my last blackjack table, on my last night of betting in Las Vegas. As in the earlier dumb show about card counting, I had no idea what was going on until it was well under way and the dealer stopped, in the middle of a hand, to accuse the woman beside me of cheating, specifically of withdrawing part of her bet after seeing her own and the dealer's first card. In a truly impressive display of bravado, the accused rose half out of her seat, leaned in toward the dealer, and pointed to the ceiling, shouting in the dealer's face repeatedly, "Ask the cameras!" She turned to me and to the two men on her other side for confirmation of her honesty. One of the men left the table; the other stared at his cards; I started to mumble something, but the dealer moved on, leaving the bet as is and playing out the hand. Two hands later, the woman left and the man who departed returned to his chips. "I won't play with a cheater," he said, though he had no trouble playing with the house.

Last summer, my daughter wanted to get into the *Guinness Book of World Records* by playing the longest game of Monopoly. It required all of a day and a half for certain truths about the game to make themselves apparent, most especially the fact that, if played by the rules, Monopoly is not a long game. As soon as one person gets ahead and starts to buy properties, houses, and hotels, the downward trajectory of everyone else's fate is clear. Just as in real life, those who have more get more, while those who fall behind early end up staying behind.

Yet most of us think of Monopoly as a long game because, of course, we've changed the rules. Chloe and I sustained our game for two weeks by institut-

ing a number of adaptations designed specifically to keep all of the players viable when the normal workings of monopoly capital should have bankrupted them. Besides personal loans and gifts, the bank issued land development grants to help some players buy the houses and hotels that bring in revenue, and, of course, there was the Free Parking lottery. As anyone who's ever played Monopoly knows, one of the first things that have to happen in a game is settling the issue of Free Parking. Do you get that money in the center of the board when you land on Free Parking or not? In fact, there should not be anything to settle about Free Parking, because, according to the published rules, it awards nothing to anyone and was designed merely as a breather from the otherwise constant strain of rents and taxes and fees.

How then to explain the persistent belief that the rules of the game include the possibility of free money? That the game itself cannot be played as it is designed? In the end, we did not get into the record book, but Chloe learned a few valuable lessons about economics: that exacerbating inequality is a feature of capital, not a bug; that equal opportunity is the illusory effect of a false belief that everyone has a chance at a windfall; and that the only way to sustain capitalism for very long is to turn it into socialism. Otherwise, you might as well be in a casino where everyone can win something in the short run, but play long enough, and they will take your very last dime even if it means breaking their own rules: when I'm down to eight chips at roulette, the croupier lets me keep betting under the $10 minimum until every chip is gone.

The game produces losers. This is the point. In both craps and roulette, the superstition highlights what the players believe they can control: the dice or the choice of numbers. The same is true of blackjack, though I flatter myself that it is not a game of chance, that my skill can correct for the odds. But the deficits are built in. At one point, Cam quizzes me by proposing that he and I bet opposite colors in roulette—he on black and me on red or, alternately, he on even numbers and me on odd. Wouldn't we then win on every spin? But it doesn't take long to find the green 0 and 00 at the top of the field that tilt the advantage to the house.

What people who don't gamble don't understand about gambling, however, is that the fun of it is distinct from winning and losing. It's the betting itself, the action, as they call it. This is what my dad and I played for around our kitchen table; it's why we were less concerned with keeping track of how much we won. Action is not something you do; it's something you have or try to get and retain, though it's never clear why you have it or how it comes and why it goes, much less what will happen next. Gambling is all about what happens next—the next card, the next spin of the wheel, the next roll of the

dice. When you gamble, you're always leaning into a future that is not a real future but instead a series of isolated moments or instants, each its own new opportunity to lose it all, because, as the real gamblers know, no one ever gets a chance to win it all.

Here's a tip: the best single wager in Las Vegas for the casual gambler is the pass-line bet on a come-out roll in craps. Actually the no-pass/no-come bet is slightly better, but it forces you to bet against everyone else at the table, so it's no fun. It's a sad fact of playing in an unfair game that the best chance of winning is to bet against everyone else. The pass-line bet has a 49.29 percent chance of winning, which is another way of saying it is a losing bet. These odds worsen with every subsequent roll. They're all sucker bets, but, as the story goes, it's pretty to think otherwise. At a Planet Hollywood craps table, I'm pretty much cleaned out, when I take my last two red $5 chips and ask the stickman where she would like me to place them as a toke. She defers to the judgment of the dealer opposite me, which suggests that she may not know what he knew, which is to put it on the pass line. The shooter rolls an eleven, and the money immediately doubles. At that point, they had the option of picking up their sure $20 or letting it remain in play for the chance to win more. I didn't hang around to see.

ON THE 201 BUS coming down Tropicana toward the Strip, a visibly distressed young woman sitting across from me cries for much of the way before falling into the aisle in an apparent seizure. When the paramedics arrive, they address her by name, Maggie, casually mentioning to the rest of us, mainly locals except for me, that they had already picked her up once that day and taken her to the emergency room, where doctors had done what little they could for someone without insurance in a state with few safety nets. We watch them help her off the bus and onto a gurney waiting on the sidewalk. She seems so small and alone from where we sit, almost disappearing in the green glare of the MGM Grand rising above her like the Emerald City of its earlier incarnation, now looking merely sleek and corporate. We can still hear her as the paramedics load her into the ambulance, a forgotten Dorothy: "I just want to go home," she cries. "I want to go home."

NOTE

I want to thank Justin Tussing and, especially, Cameron Trotter for their conversations about and lessons in casino gambling.

Bibliography

Adorno, Theodor. *Minima Moralia*. London: Verso, 1984.

Anagnost, Ann. "The Corporeal Politics of Quality (Suzhi)." *Public Culture* 16, no. 2 (2004): 189–208.

Andrejevic, Mark. *iSpy: Surveillance and Power in the Interactive Era*. Lawrence: University Press of Kansas, 2009.

———. *Reality TV: The Work of Being Watched*. Lanham, MD: Rowman and Littlefield, 2003.

Appadurai, Arjun. "Consumption, Duration, and History." In *Modernity at Large: Cultural Dimensions of Globalization*. Minneapolis: University of Minnesota Press, 1996.

Augé, Mark. *Non-places: Introduction to an Anthropology of Supermodernity*. Translated by John Howe. London: Verso, 1995.

Auslander, Philip. *Liveness: Performance in a Mediatized Culture*. New York: Routledge, 2008.

Ayanian, Stephanie, and Mark Cooper, dirs. *Liquid Assets: The Story of Our Water Infrastructure*. University Park: Penn State Public Broadcasting, 2008.

Banash, David. "Selling Surveillance, Anonymity and VTV." *Postmodern Culture* 11, no. 1 (2000): n.p.

Barthelme, Donald. "The Balloon." In *Sixty Stories*. New York: E. P. Dutton, 1982.

Barthes, Roland. *The Fashion System*. Translated by M. Ward and R. Howard. New York: Hill and Wang, 1983.

———. *Mythologies*. New York: Farrar, Straus and Giroux, 2001.

Bateson, Gregory. "A Theory of Play and Fantasy." In *The Games Design Reader: A Rules of Play Anthology*. Edited by Katie Salen and Eric Zimmerman, 314–28. Cambridge, MA: MIT Press, 2006.

Batty, Michael. "When All the World's a City." *Environment and Planning A* 43 (2011): 765–72.

Baudrillard, Jean. *America*. London: Verso, 1989.

———. *Selected Writings*. Cambridge, MA: Polity, 1988.

Benjamin, Walter. "The *Flâneur*." In *Charles Baudelaire: A Lyric Poet in the Era of High Capitalism*. Translated by Henry Zohn, 34–66. London: Verso, 1997.

———. "The Work of Art in the Age of Mechanical Reproduction." In *Illuminations*. Edited by Hannah Arendt, translated by Harry Zohn, 217–51. New York: Schocken, 1968.

Bennett, Susan. "Theater/Tourism." *Theatre Journal* 57 (2005): 407–28.

Berger, John. *Ways of Seeing*. New York: Penguin, 1990.

Biziou, Barbara. *The Joy of Ritual*. New York: St. Martin's Press, 1999.

Bordo, Susan. "Beauty (Re)Discovers the Male Body." In *The Male Body: A Look at Men in Public and Private*, 168–226. New York: Farrar, Straus and Giroux, 1999.

Borges, Jorge Luis. *Labyrinths*. New York: New Directions, 2007.

Borries, Friedrich von, Steffen P. Walz, and Matthias Böttger, eds. *Space Time Play: Computer Games, Architecture and Urbanism: The Next Level*. Basel: Birkhäuser, 2007.

Bourdieu, Pierre. *Distinction: A Social Critique of the Judgement of Taste*. Translated by Richard Nice. Cambridge, MA: Harvard University Press, 1984.

Brandt, Allan M. "The Cigarette, Risk, and American Culture." *Daedalus* 119, no. 4 (fall 1990): 155–76.

Brecht on Theater. Edited and translated by John Willett. New York: Hill and Wang, 1992.

Brents, Barbara G., Crystal Jackson, and Kathryn Hausbeck. *The State of Sex: Tourism, Sex, and Sin in the American Heartland*. New York: Routledge, 2010.

Callenbach, Ernest. *Ecotopia*. New York: Bantam, 1981.

Clarke, Alison. "Sweet Dreams™ Security: Aesthetics for the Paranoid Home." *Home Cultures* 3, no. 2 (2006): 191–93.

Clover, Joshua. *The Matrix*. BFI Modern Classics. London: BFI, 2004.

Cooper, Marc. *The Last Honest Place in America: Paradise and Perdition in the New Las Vegas*. New York: Avalon, 2004.

Cortázar, Julio. *Rayuela*. New York: Random House, 1966.

Dann, Gram, and Jens Kristian Steen Jacobson. "Tourism Smellscapes." *Tourism Geographies* 5, no. 1 (2003): 3–25.

Davis, Mike. *City of Quartz: Excavating the Future in Las Vagas*. New York: Vintage, [1990] 2006.

———. *Ecology of Fear: Los Angeles and the Imagination of Disaster*. New York: Vintage, 1999.

Davis, Mike, and Daniel Bertrand Monk, eds. *Evil Paradises: Dreamworlds of Neoliberalism*. New York: New Press, 2007.

Dawkins, Richard. *The Greatest Show on Earth: The Evidence for Evolution*. London: Bantam, 2009.

Debord, Guy. *Panegeric*, vol. 1. Translated by James Brook. London: Verso, 1991.

———. *Society of the Spectacle*. Detroit: Red and Black, 1977.

de Certeau, Michel. *The Practice of Everyday Life*. Berkeley: University of California Press, 1988.

Deleuze, Gilles. *Negotiations*. Translated by Martin Joughin. New York: Columbia University Press, 1995.

———. "Postscript on the Societies of Control." *October* 59 (1992): 3–7.

Denton, Sally, and Roger Morris. *The Money and the Power: The Making of Las Vegas and Its Hold on America*. New York: Vintage, 2002.

Desmond, Jane C. *Staging Tourism: Bodies on Display from Waikiki to Sea World*. Chicago: University of Chicago Press, 1999.

Didion, Joan. "Marrying Absurd." In *Fifty Great Essays*. Edited by Robert Diyanni. New York: Longman, 2004.

Dutton, Michael. "Street Scenes of Subalternity: China, Globalization, and Rights." *Social Text* 60, no. 17 (1999): 63–86.

Dyer, Geoff. *The Ongoing Moment*. New York: Vintage, 2007.

Emerson, Ralph Waldo. *Nature* (1836). In *The Annotated Emerson*. Edited by David Mikics. Cambridge, MA: Belknap Press, 2012.

Erdrich, Louise. *Love Medicine*. New York: Harper Collins, 2001.

Findlay, John M. *Magic Lands: Western Cityscapes and American Culture after 1940*. Berkeley: University of California Press, 1993.

Florida, Richard. *The Rise of the Creative Class: And How It's Transforming Work, Leisure, Community, and Everyday Life*. New York: Basic Books, 2004.

Foucault, Michel. *The Birth of Biopolitics: Lectures at the Collège de France, 1978–79*. Translated by G. Burchell. New York: Palgrave Macmillan, 2008.

———. *L'herméneutique du sujet, Cours au Collège de France, 1981–1982*. Paris: Gallimard Seuil, 2001.

Fox, William L. *In the Desert of Desire: Las Vegas and the Culture of Spectacle*. Reno: University of Nevada Press, 2005.

Galloway, Alexander. *Gaming: Essays on Algorithmic Culture*. Minneapolis: University of Minnesota Press, 2006.

———. *Protocol: How Control Exists after Decentralization*. Cambridge, MA: MIT Press, 2006.

Glaeser, Edward. *Triumph of the City: How Our Greatest Invention Makes Us Richer, Smarter, Greener, Healthier, and Happier*. New York: Penguin, 2011.

Glennon, Robert. *Unquenchable: America's Water Crisis and What to Do about It*. Washington, DC: Island Press, 2009.

Goffman, Erving. *The Presentation of Self in Everyday Life*. New York: Anchor, 1959.

Gombrich, E. H. *Art and Illusion: A Study in the Psychology of Pictorial Representation*. Princeton, NJ: Princeton University Press, 1956.

Goodwin, Joanne L. *Changing the Game: Women at Work in Las Vegas, 1940–1990*. Las Vegas: University of Las Vegas Press, 2014.

Gottdiener, Mark, Claudia C. Collins, and David R. Dickens. *Las Vegas: The Social Production of an All-American City*. Oxford: Blackwell, 1999.

Hall, Stuart. "Notes on Deconstructing 'the Popular.'" In *Cultural Theory: An Anthology*. Edited by Imre Szeman and Timothy Kaposy, 72–80. New York: Wiley-Blackwell, 2010.

Harvie, Jennifer, and Erin Hurley. "States of Play: Locating Québec in the Performances of Robert Lepage, Ex Machina, and the Cirque du Soleil." *Theatre Journal* 51 (1999): 299–315.

Hillerman, Tony. *Dance Hall of the Dead*. New York: Harper Collins, 1990.

Horning, Rob. "Data Self Redux." Marginal Utility. *Pop Matters*, January 30, 2012. http://www.popmatters.com/post/153910-/.

———. "Facebook and Living Labor." Marginal Utility. *New Inquiry*, May 17, 2012. http://thenewinquiry.com/blogs/marginal-utility/facebook-and-living-labor/.

———. "The Rise of the Data Self." Marginal Utility. *Pop Matters*, January 25, 2012. http://www.popmatters.com/post/153721-/.

Hsu, Hsuan L., and Martha Lincoln. "Biopower, *Bodies . . . the Exhibition*, and the Spectacle of Public Health." *Discourse* 29, no. 1 (2007): 15–34.

Humphreys, Lee. "Mobile Social Networks and Urban Public Space." *New Media Society* (2010): 763–78.

Hurston, Zora Neale. *Mules and Men*. New York: Harper Collins, Perennial, 1990.

Ignatieff, Michael. *Magnum Degrees*. Hong Kong: Phaidon, 2000.

Jameson, Fredric. "The Cultural Logic of Late Capitalism." In *Postmodernism*, 38–54. Durham, NC: Duke University Press, 1991.

———. *Signatures of the Visible*. New York: Routledge, Chapman and Hall, 1992.

Jameson, Stacy M. "Gagging on the Other: Television's Gross Food Challenge." In *Food and Everyday Life*. Edited by Thomas Conroy, 11–40. Lanham, MD: Lexington, 2014.

Jurgenson, Nathan. "The Facebook Eye." *Atlantic*, January 13, 2012. http://www.theatlantic.com/technology/archive/2012/01/the-facebook-eye/251377/.

———. "The Faux-Vintage Photo: Full Essay, Parts I, II, and III." Cyborgology. *Society Pages*, May 14, 2011. http://thesocietypages.org/cyborgology/2011/05/14/the-faux-vintage-photo-full-essay-parts-i-ii-and-iii/.

———. "A Page One Selfie." Cyborgology. *Society Pages*, May 6, 2013. http://thesocietypages.org/cyborgology/2013/05/06/a-bombers-page-one-selfie/.

Kaplan, Amy. "'Left Alone with America': The Absence of Empire in the Study of American Culture." In *Cultures of United States Imperialism*. Edited by Amy Kaplan and Donald Pease, 3–21. Durham, NC: Duke University Press, 1993.

Kirkpatrick, David. *The Facebook Effect: The Inside Story of the Company That Is Connecting the World*. New York: Simon and Schuster, 2010.

Kirshenblatt-Gimblett, Barbara. *Destination Culture: Tourism, Museums, and Heritage*. Berkeley: University of California Press, 1998.

Klugman, Karen. "The Alternative Ride." In The Project on Disney, *Inside the Mouse: Work and Play at Disney World*, 163–79. Durham, NC: Duke University Press, 1995.

Kolbert, Elizabeth. *Field Notes from a Catastrophe: Man, Nature, and Climate Change*. New York: Bloomsbury USA, 2006.

———. *The Sixth Extinction: An Unnatural History*. New York: Henry Holt, 2014.

Kraft, James P. *Vegas at Odds: Labor Conflict in a Leisure Economy, 1960–1985*. Baltimore, MD: Johns Hopkins University Press, 2010.

Land, Barbara, and Myrick Land. *A Short History of Las Vegas*. Reno: University of Nevada Press, 2004.

Lazzarato, Maurizio. "Immaterial Labor." In *Marxism beyond Marxism*. Edited by Saree Makdisi, Cesare Casarino, and Rebecca E. Karl. London: Routledge, 1996. *Generation Online*. http://www.generation-online.org/c/fcimmateriallabour3.htm.

Levin, Thomas Y., Ursula Frohne, and Peter Weibel, eds. CTRL[SPACE]: *Rhetorics of Surveillance from Bentham to 9/11*. Cambridge, MA: MIT Press, 2002.

Linke, Uli. "Touching the Corpse: The Unmaking of Memory in the Body Museum." *Anthropology Today* 21, no. 5 (2005): 13–19.

Long, Lucy M. "Culinary Tourism: A Folklorist Perspective on Eating and Otherness." In *Culinary Tourism*. Edited by Lucy M. Long, 20–50. Lexington: University Press of Kentucky, 2010.

Manovich, Lev. "The Poetics of Augmented Space: Learning from Prada." *Visual Communication* 5, no. 2 (2006): 219–40.

Marks, Laura. "The Logic of Smell." In *Touch: Sensuous Theory and Multisensory Medium*, 113–26. Minneapolis: University of Minnesota Press, 2002.

Marwick, Alice. "Status Update: Celebrity, Publicity and Self-Branding in Web 2.0." PhD diss., New York University, 2010.

Mauss, Marcel. *The Gift*. New York: Norton, 1967.

McKibben, Bill. *The Bill McKibben Reader*. New York: Henry Holt, 2010.

———. *Eaarth: Making a Life on a Tough New Planet*. New York: Henry Holt, 2010.

———. *The End of Nature*. 2nd ed. New York: Random House, 2006.

Mead, Rebecca. *One Perfect Day: The Selling of the American Wedding*. New York: Penguin, 2007.

Mitchell, Don. "The SUV Model of Citizenship: Floating Bubbles, Buffer Zones, and the Rise of the 'Purely Atomic' Individual." *Political Geography* 24 (2005): 77–100.

Mitchell, William J. *Me++: The Cyborg Self and the Networked City*. Cambridge, MA: MIT Press, 2004.

———. *The Reconfigured Eye: Visual Truth in the Post-photographic Era*. Cambridge, MA: MIT Press, 1992.

Morris, Errol. *Believing Is Seeing (Observations on the Mysteries of Photography)*. New York: Penguin, 2011.

Naylor, Sharon. *Renewing Your Wedding Vows: A Complete Planning Guide to Saying I Still Do*. New York: Broadway Books, 2008.

O'Brian, Matthew. *Beneath the Neon: Life and Death in the Tunnels of Las Vegas*. Las Vegas: Huntington Press, 2007.

Otnes, Cele, and Elizabeth Pleck. *Cinderella Dreams: The Allure of the Lavish Wedding*. Berkeley: University of California Press, 2003.

Parenti, Chris. *The Soft Cage: Surveillance in America from Slavery to the War on Terror*. New York: Basic Books, 2003.

Pine, B. Joseph, and James H. Gilmore. *The Experience Economy*. Boston: Harvard Business School Press, 1999.

Porteous, J. Douglas. "Smellscape." *Progress in Physical Geography* 9 (1985): 356–78.

Rosenblum, Lawrence. *See What I'm Saying: The Extraordinary Powers of Our Five Senses*. New York: Norton, 2010.

Rothman, Hal. *Devil's Bargains: Tourism in the Twentieth-Century West*. Lawrence: University Press of Kansas, 2000.

————. *Neon Metropolis: How Las Vegas Started the Twenty-First Century*. New York: Routledge, 2003.

Sassen, Saskia. *The Global City: New York, London, Tokyo*. Princeton, NJ: Princeton University Press, 2001.

Scharmen, Fred. "'You Must Be Logged In to Do That!': Myspace and Control." May 2006. http://www.sevensixfive.net/myspace/myspacetwopointoh.html.

Schlosser, Eric. "Why the Fries Taste Good." In *Fast Food Nation: The Dark Side of the All-American Meal*, 111–32. New York: Houghton Mifflin, 2001.

Smith, Alisa, and James MacKinnon. *Plenty*. New York: Random House, 2007.

Smith, Cooper. "Facebook Users Are Uploading 350 Million New Photos Each Day." *Business Insider*, September 18, 2013.

Smith, Susan J. "Soundscape." *Area* 26, no. 3 (1994): 232–40.

Solinger, Dorothy J. *Contesting Citizenship in Urban China: Peasants, Migrants, the State and the Logic of the Market*. Berkeley: University of California Press, 1999.

Solnit, Rebecca. *Wanderlust: A History of Walking*. New York: Viking, 2000.

Solomon, Steven. *Water: The Epic Struggle for Wealth, Power, and Civilization*. New York: Harper Perennial, 2010.

Sontag, Susan. *On Photography*. New York: Farrar, Straus and Giroux, 1977.

Spence, Charles. "Visual Display of Food: Historical Reflections." Paper presented at Thinking about Dinner seminar, Jackman Humanities Institute, University of Toronto, Toronto, March 1, 2013.

Stafford, Barbara Maria. "The Creeping Illusionizing of Identity from Neurobiology to Newgenics." In *Controversial Bodies: Thoughts on the Public Display of Plastinated Corpses*. Edited by John D. Lantos, 105–14. Baltimore, MD: Johns Hopkins University Press, 2011.

Standing, Guy. *Precariat: The New Dangerous Class*. London: Bloomsbury Academic, 2014.

————. "The Precariat: The New Dangerous Class." *Policy Network*, May 24, 2011. http://www.policy-network.net/pno_detail.aspx?ID=4004&title=+The+Precariat +-+The+new+dangerous+class.

Stern, Megan. "Shiny, Happy People: 'Body Worlds' and the Commodification of Health." *Radical Philosophy* 118 (2003): 2–6.

Stewart, Susan. *On Longing*. Durham, NC: Duke University Press, 2005.

Strasser, Susan. "The Alien Past: Consumer Culture in Historical Perspective." In *The Advertising and Consumer Culture Reader*. Edited by Joseph Turow and Mathew McAllister, 25–37. New York: Routledge, 2009.

Terborgh, John. *Requiem for Nature*. Washington, DC: Island Press, 1999.

Terranova, Tiziana. "Free Labor: Producing Culture for the Digital Economy." *Social Text* 18, no. 2 (2000): 33–58. Reprinted in *Digital Labor: The Internet as Playground and Factory*. Edited by Trebor Scholz, 33–57. New York: Routledge, 2013.

Veblen, Thorstein. *The Theory of the Leisure Class*. New York: Macmillan, 1899.

Venturi, Robert, Denise Scott Brown, and Steven Izenour. *Learning from Las Vegas*. Cambridge, MA: MIT Press, 1972.

Vinegar, Aron, and Michael J. Golec, eds. *Relearning from Las Vegas*. Minneapolis: University of Minnesota Press, 2009.

Ward, Evan. "Two Rivers, Two Nations, One History: The Transformation of the Colorado River Delta since 1940." *Frontera Norte* 11, no. 22 (July–December 1999): 113–40.

Wark, McKenzie. *Gamer Theory.* Cambridge, MA: Harvard University Press, 2007.

Wickstrom, Maurya. *Performing Consumers: Global Capital and Its Theatrical Seductions.* New York: Routledge, 2006.

Willis, Susan. "Public Use / Private Space." In The Project on Disney, *Inside the Mouse: Work and Play at Disney World*, 178–96. Durham, NC: Duke University Press, 1995.

Wilson, Edward O. *Biophilia.* Cambridge, MA: Harvard University Press, 1984.

Index

Adorno, Theodor W., 13, 15

advertising, advertisements, 45, 80, 74, 97, 190, 215, 229, 232, 250, 287n22; of Downtown Project, 270, 272; of shows and exhibits, 84, 184, 254

agency, de Certeau and, 12–13

air conditioning, 187, 195, 215, 218, 315. *See also* climate control

Aladdin, 2, 118–19, 264, 295, 315

alcohol, alcoholic beverages, 8, 26, 47, 294, 319; free, 60, 98, 345; ubiquity of, 114, 130, 184

America and American Dream, 10, 20, 267; patriotism and, 2. *See also* United States

animals, 121, 237, 240

anthropology, ethnography, 7, 8, 67–68

Apple: iPads, 275, 304; iPhones, 275, 284; obsolescence and, 310; stores, 304

aquariums, 187, 203, 215

architecture, 13, 51–52, 71, 176, 188, 193, 201, 245, 258, 297. *See also* façade; hotel-casinos

Aria, 185; art in, 147, 230, 250; Deuce Lounge, 149; Gold Lounge at, 139, 142

Arizona, 120, 132

aroma, 199–200; branding of, 195, 197. *See also* smell

art, 134, 158; in hotel-casinos, 135, 144–47, 149, 151, 229–30, 250; in Las Vegas, 144–53; Native American, 330–31, 334, 336

artificiality, 27; artificial plants and, 218, 220, 223, 224–26, 229

Art of Richard MacDonald Presented by Cirque du Soleil®, The, 144, 146

Art of the Motorcycle, The, 145

Asia, Asians, 162, 175. *See also names of Asian countries*

authenticity, 44, 47, 142, 280; souvenirs and, 330, 331, 334

avant-garde, 135

Bally's, 62, 104, 130

Bally Technology, iTable of, 73–74, 107n1

Barbie, 15, 67, 149, 278, 334

Barthes, Roland, 12, 310, 318

Baudrillard, Jean, 12, 61, 177

Beatles, 137, 139, 142

Bellagio, 93, 110, 193, 197, 245, 257, 298, 315; art in, 86, 135, 144–45, 146, 151, 158–59n7, 199, 229; belltower of, 121, 190; blackjack at, 341, 345; buffet at, 177; Cirque du Soleil's *O* at, 126, 130, 137, 144, 184–85; Conservatory and Botanical Gardens at, 223–24; employees of, 226; façade of, 176; fountains at, 2, 54, 114–

ecology, of Las Vegas region, 237, 240
Eiffel Tower: in Paris, France, 177; at Paris Las
	Vegas, 18, 44, 45, 176, 187, 190–91, 254; sou-
	venirs of, 145, 323
electricity, Hoover Dam and, 128
electronic transfers, 65, 66–67, 77
Elvis impersonators, 14, 27, 29; as ministers,
	313, 315
Elvis packages, 310
encumbrance, success as, 66
entertainment: branding of, 249; burlesque,
	298; cabaret, 139; of Cirque du Soleil, 137;
	commodity and, 145; display of corpses for,
	281; industry of, 277; Las Vegas as capital
	of, 47, 187, 191; privileging of, 120; products
	of, 155; public, 115; surveillance as, 76; tech-
	nology of, 124, 125; vaudeville, 139; water
	and, 111, 113, 244
environmental politics, 113, 235, 244
Epcot Center (Disney World), 44, 124, 176,
	323
escort cards, 7, 26, 31, 34, 66, 87, 325. See also
	smutters
escorts: services of, 12; as shamans, 5; on Strip,
	7. See also call girls
ethnicity, 173; ethnic food and, 175, 176
etiquette, on casino floor, 341, 349
everyday life, 3, 7, 113, 319; culture and, 12;
	frame of, 209; surveillance of, 76–78
Excalibur, 27, 192, 245; buffet at, 161, 181; sou-
	venirs of, 323, 328
exotic, 176, 204, 240
experience, 264; business of, 213–14n14
exteriority, built environment and, 18
extravagance, 113, 313, 316

façade, 187, 201. See also architecture
Facebook, 144, 249–50, 252, 261, 269, 272;
	algorithms of, 267; Mark Zuckerberg and,
	273, 275; photographs on, 263; profiles on,
	281; surveillance of, 78; Timeline, 264
facial recognition, 100
families, 27, 31, 34, 60, 307–8
fashion, 310, 232, 270, 310
Fashion Show Mall, 104, 177
fear, culture of, 81
Federal Bureau of Investigation (FBI), 78, 102,
	287n21

female body, 280, 318, 325; of dancers, 105; of
	Jenna Jameson, 42, 209, 266; stereotypi-
	cal, 34, 36
feminist scholars, 10
fetishes, fetishism, 15, 18; of commodity, 12, 67;
	sexuality and, 325, 327; souvenirs and, 323,
	328, 334, 336, 337
Fiesta Rancho, 339, 346, 351, 353
first-time experiences, 3, 5, 7
First World, 174, 180
Flamingo, 126, 150, 191, 215, 308, 339; black-
	jack at, 346; buffet at, 191–92; lobby of, 266;
	souvenirs of, 322, 323; swimming pool at,
	184–85; water and, 118; waterfalls at, 235
Flickr, 263, 264
Folies Bergère showgirls, 27, 29, 30, 36
food, 175; abundance of, 160; Coca-Cola Store
	and, 2, 113, 201–5; culture of, 160–82; ethnic,
	47, 176; foodies and, 134; Jell-O, 165; M&M's
	World and, 201–5; meaning and, 206; re-
	cycling waste of, 181; seasonality of, 161;
	Tastes of the World and, 203–5; vegetarian-
	ism and, 167; foodways, 173. See also buffets;
	restaurants and clubs; taste (sense)
Foucault, Michel, 13
fountains, 111, 113, 235; at Bellagio, 114–15, 120–
	21, 124, 129, 130, 132, 257, 258, 278; at Caesars
	Palace, 145; in CityCenter mall, 208; in
	Miracle Mile Shops, 119
Foxconn: factories in China, 275; smartphones
	and, 15
framing, frames: photography and, 24, 47;
	play, 209; of reality, 23–69; selective, 45
France, 176, 177
free speech rights, 89–90
Fremont Street, 29, 89, 90; Deuce and, 1, 102,
	104
Fremont Street Experience, 2, 89, 264
Freud, Sigmund, 8, 294, 327

gambling, 7, 54, 150, 300, 319, 339, 341; card
	games, 338; children and, 338; fun of, 355;
	legalization of, 294; privileging of, 120;
	revenue from, 71; state laws on, 96; super-
	stition and, 346. See also casino floor; slot
	machines; and names of specific games
gamespace, 254–60
gay relationships, 305, 316

331; Mexican food and, 47, 172, 175; Tijuana, 297–98, 331

MGM CityCenter, 74, 102, 125–26, 144, 244, 249

MGM Grand, 87, 89, 102, 104, 135, 146, 150, 176, 203, 245, 358; CSI: The Experience at, 78, 81, 84

MGM-Mirage Resorts and Casinos, 104, 197, 217

miniatures, 323, 327

Miracle Mile Shops (Planet Hollywood), 74, 118–19, 228, 249, 254

Mirage, 102, 142, 199, 240; Cirque du Soleil's Beatles Love at, 137, 142; volcano at, 124–25, 190, 228; water and, 118, 129

mob, 65, 166, 245

money, 345, 328. See also cash and coins

Monopoly, 353, 355

monorail, along Strip, 54, 87, 89

Monte Carlo, 245, 315

motto of Las Vegas ("What happens in Vegas stays in Vegas"), 26, 30, 71, 191, 209, 249

movement: super-modernity and, 244–45; without progress, 260

museums, 280; Holocaust Museum, 278; Indian Center, 245; King's Ransom, 84, 153–54; Liberace Museum, 105, 153–56; Mob Museum, 245; National Atomic Testing Museum, 245; Neon Museum, 264; personal, 146; touch and, 206; in Washington, 278. See also Madame Tussauds Wax Museum; and names of individual exhibits

music, musicians, 121, 124–25, 135, 139, 155, 190–91, 193, 195, 210, 264, 323; Beyonce, 208, 210; Britney Spears, 135, 300; Cher, 14, 139, 155; Celine Dion, 139, 193; Donny and Marie Osmond, 14, 185; Frank Sinatra, 14, 295; Jessica Simpson, 209, 210; Lady Gaga, 154, 156, 280; Michael Jackson, 121, 139, 193; Tupac Shakur, 42, 210; Wayne Newton, 14, 295. See also Beatles; Liberace; Presley, Elvis

Native Americans, 120, 330, 331, 334, 336, 351. See also names of individual tribes

nature, 199, 217–18, 232; branding of, 226; commodification of, 233; construction of, 228; culture vs., 121; as escape, 8, 10, 192, 233; Las Vegas and, 215–41; unpredictability of, 228

neoliberalism, 269; Las Vegas and, 86–87, 254

networks, 249; digital, 256; for surveillance, 71, 73

Nevada, 56, 84, 86, 96, 235, 311; Colorado River and, 120; divorce in, 294; driver's license of, 80; Lake Tahoe and, 65; prisons in, 86, 105, 108n13; same-sex marriage and, 304, 316

New York City, 141, 181, 190, 245

New York–New York, 44, 57, 62, 150, 245

New York Times, 269, 287n21, 315

9/11 attacks, 71, 73, 76, 86, 119

non-places, 87, 244, 258, 275

nostalgia, 199, 280, 308

oasis, Las Vegas as, 113, 115, 297

Orwell, George, 76, 275

O'Sheas Casino, 26, 190

oxygen bars, 44

Palms, 258

Paris Las Vegas, 49, 87, 104–5, 150, 233, 245, 285, 323; buffet at, 167, 170, 172; Eiffel Tower at, 45, 176, 190–91; fountains at, 235; Harlequin exhibit at, 149; L'Art de Paris in, 145, 149

penny slots, 7, 50–69; egalitarianism of, 50; jackpots on, 54, 56, 68–69; minimum wage jobs and, 60; players of, 57–61, 68–69; time and temporality and, 51, 54, 57, 61

performance studies, 187

phallic symbols, 8

photographers: points of view of, 74; as security risk, 90; signature stamps of, 230–31

photography, photographs, 44–47, 151; Cashman's Photo Magic and, 34, 36, 38; by Diane Arbus, 327; digital, 261; framing of, 24, 45, 47; galleries of, 230; at Madame Tussauds, 40–42, 261, 263–62; as mechanical reproduction, 121, 124; photo spots and, 26, 261; reality and, 24, 26; on social media, 263; as souvenirs, 240; surveillance cameras and, 70–71, 73; third dimension and, 38, 40; tourists and, 34, 36, 38, 40, 47; unspoken code of, 29–30

pit bosses, 100, 101, 341, 351

Planet Hollywood, 47, 135, 229, 240, 245, 264, 315; Aladdin and, 2, 118–19; gambling at,

streets, 87, 89, 90, 110–11, 153, 190, 256, 298.
See also names of individual streets
Strip, the, 2, 12, 18, 34, 89, 104, 110, 111, 249, 294, 358; architecture of, 15, 18, 176; black-jack and, 339; constructed nature of, 228; construction on, 52; cultures of, 7, 292; Deuce and, 1, 2, 14, 102, 114; gaze and, 10; global identity of, 245; Grand Canyon and, 330; hotel-casinos on, 2, 5, 118, 245; infra-structure of, 124; intensity of, 10, 71; litter on, 325; manmade ecosystems of, 233; as mobile stage, 3; as Möbius strip, 54; nature and, 215; pedestrians on, 115, 187, 298; pho-tography and, 47; security on, 74, 76, 86; sensory overload on, 172; sounds of, 190; souvenir shops on, 27; as spectacle, 62, 177; streetscape of, 74; water and, 129, 235
stripping, strippers, 3, 12, 301, 318. *See also* Chippendales; female body
super-modernity, geography of, 244
superstition, 346, 348, 355
surfaces, reality and, 18. *See also* façade
surveillance, 7, 81, 76, 249, 261; of everyday life, 76–78; technology of, 100, 278
surveillance cameras, 90, 104, 105, 249; Big Brother style of, 76; card counters and, 100, 87, 98, 353; photography and, 70–71; ubiq-uity of, 73
Surveillance Information Network (S.I.N.), 71, 73, 98, 100, 105
sustainability, 113, 182, 217, 235, 269–70
swimming pools, 111, 113, 125, 130, 135, 145, 184–85, 266

tarot, 139
taste (sense), 187; conditioning and, 188; equated with expense, 170; Las Vegas ex-perience of, 200–206; perceptions of, 204–5; subsumed by other senses, 201
taste (style), 134–35, 151; classification by, 149; stratification of, 135–36
taxation, taxes, 86
taxi drivers, 232, 240
technology: aroma systems and, 199; camou-flaging of, 229; crime scene analysis and, 81, 84; digital networks and, 256; enter-tainment, 124, 125; obsolescence and, 310;

stealth, 93; of surveillance, 100, 278; water spectacles and, 228–29
television shows: *American Idol*, 81; *America's Most Wanted*, 78; *Antiques Roadshow*, 278; *Bones*, 280; *CSI: Crime Scene Investiga-tion*, 81; *Entourage*, 150; *Gunsmoke*, 295; Liberace's, 153; mass consumers and, 212; *No Reservations*, 173; *Parts Unknown*, 173; reality TV and, 76; *The Real World*, 76; *Supermarket Sweep*, 170; *Survivor*, 81, 107n5, 174; *The Wire*, 76
terrorism, terrorists, 76, 90, 92, 98, 287n21
theater: aquatic, 184–85; Brecht and, 3
themes: of hotel-casinos, 118–19, 245, 297; of slot machines, 191, 192, 193, 315
time and temporality, 52, 137, 154, 192, 195, 264, 304, 307; penny slots and, 51, 54, 57
time-share industry, 5, 57; GeoHoliday and, 305, 307, 308; origins of, 305, 307; street vendors of, 298, 300
tipping, 349, 351
Titanic: The Artifact Exhibition (Luxor), 277–78, 280, 282
touch, 187, 188, 208; Las Vegas experience of, 206–13; in Madame Tussauds, 208–10
tourism, 110, 120, 121, 208, 277; culinary, 172, 175, 204
tourists, 1, 7–8, 57, 60–61, 80, 89, 98, 162, 195, 209, 212; bodies of, 192, 206; children as, 31, 34; culinary, 172, 175, 204; families as, 27, 31, 34; identity of, 191; metaphors for, 184; older, 5; photography and, 34, 45, 47; souve-nirs and, 45, 47, 325; vendors and, 110–11
Transportation Security Administration (TSA), 70, 278; posters of, 71, 78, 90, 92
Treasure Island, 87, 118, 130, 192, 195, 245; Cirque du Soleil at, 104, 137; water and, 129
Tropicana, 45, 125, 193, 358
Tropicana Avenue, 89, 153
Trotter, Cameron, 341, 345, 346, 347, 349, 351, 355, 358
Tumblr, 263, 269
Twitter, 251, 263, 267, 269, 304; tweets about Las Vegas and, 257, 260, 261, 266

unions, labor, 87, 89, 102. *See also names of individual labor unions*